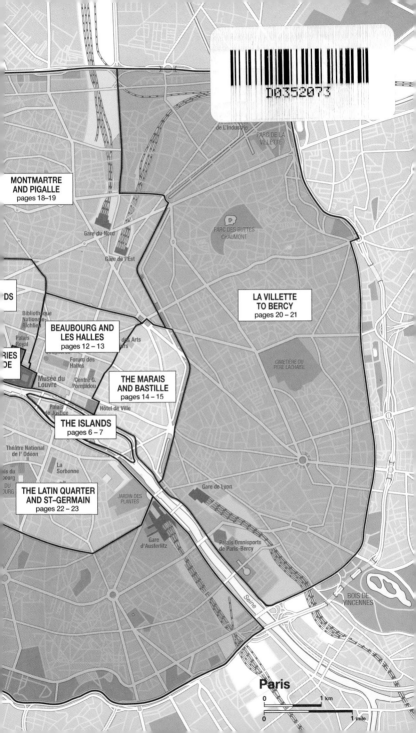

**MONTMARTRE
AND PIGALLE**
pages 18–19

Gare du Nord

Gare de l'Est

DS

Bibliothèque
Nationale
Richlieu

Palais
Royal

**BEAUBOURG AND
LES HALLES**
pages 12 – 13

des Arts

RIES
DE

Forum des
Halles

Musée du
Louvre

Centre G.
Pompidou

**THE MARAIS
AND BASTILLE**
pages 14 – 15

Palais
de Justice

Hôtel de Ville

THE ISLANDS
pages 6 – 7

Théâtre National
de l' Odéon

La
Sorbonne

ais du
bourg

DU
URG

**THE LATIN QUARTER
AND ST-GERMAIN**
pages 22 – 23

JARDIN DES
PLANTES

Gare de Lyon

Gare
d'Austerlitz

Palais Omnisports
de Paris-Bercy

de L'Industrie

PARC DE LA
VILLETTE

PARC DES BUTTES
CHAUMONT

**LA VILLETTE
TO BERCY**
pages 20 – 21

CIMETIÈRE DU
PÈRE LACHAISE

Seine

BOIS DE
VINCENNES

Paris

0   1 km

0   1 mile

SMART GUIDE

PARIS

smart guide

Contents

Areas

A–Z

Below: the *tricolore.*

Left: one of Guimard's signs for the Paris metro.

Atlas

Below: a gilded statue of Athena crowns the Palais Garnier.

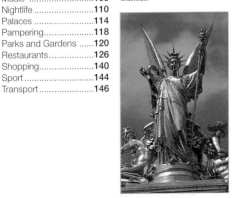

Paris

L argely undamaged by two world wars, Paris – the 'city of cities', as Victor Hugo put it – is the harmonious result of centuries of grandiose urban planning. According to writer Jean Giraudoux (1882–1944), the Parisian is more than a little proud to be part of a city where 'the most thinking, talking and writing in the world have been accomplished'.

Paris Facts and Figures

Population: **2.2 million** (3.6 per cent of the total French population)
Area: **87 sq km**
Population density: **24,783 inhabitants per sq km**
Visitors staying overnight in central Paris:
28 million per year
No. of World Heritage Sites: **2** (Banks of the Seine and Versailles)
No. of museums: **136**
No. of parks and gardens: **over 450**
No. of churches/temples: **171**
No. of restaurants with three Michelin stars: **10**
No. of cinema screens: **over 400**

Geography

Paris is a comparatively compact city and more suited to walking than many. The city runs for 13km east to west, and 9km north to south. On the map, 20 *arrondissements* (administrative districts, *see Addresses, p.54*) spiral out like a snail's shell, a pattern reflecting the city's historical development and successive enlargements.

The city is contained by the Périphérique, a ring road stretching 35km around it. Built in 1973 in an attempt to reduce traffic jams, the Périphérique is invariably congested itself, particularly during the rush hours, when approximately 150,000 cars storm its 35 exits.

Forming two concentric rings wrapped tightly around Paris, the suburbs (*la banlieue*) are divided up into *départements* or counties.

The River

'She is buffeted by the waves but sinks not', reads the Latin inscription on the city's coat-of-arms, symbolising a Paris born on the flanks of the River Seine. Lutetia (as the city founded by the Romans was called) was established in the first century BC on the site of a Gallic Parisii settlement on the largest island in the river. Today, however, the Seine cuts a swathe through the middle of the city, and, as the capital's widest avenue, is spanned by a total of 37 bridges, which provide some of the best views of Paris.

East–West Divide

In addition to this clear divide between the so-called Left (south) and Right (north) banks of the Seine, there's an important unofficial division between the traditionally working-class eastern end of the city and the mostly bourgeois west. In general, the further east you go, the further left you will find yourself on the political spectrum. Rents are exorbitant in the western *arrondissements*, while there is a substantial reservoir of more affordable property in the east. City planners have

Below: Rodin's *The Kiss*.

been struggling for decades to improve the balance, culminating in massive urban renewal projects in several parts of the east, notably at Bercy *(see p.21)* and around the Bastille *(see p.15)*.

Population

Paris is more densely populated than Tokyo, London or New York, and the Parisians' high stress levels can partly be put down to the fact that they live in such close proximity to one another, squeezed into small apartments, packed into the city's 87 sq km. A house and garden is an almost unheard-of luxury in the French capital. There is intense competition for desirable living space, with an average of 150,000 people looking for a home at any one time. It is an oft-cited paradox that this battle for a place to live occurs in a city where 16 per cent of apartments lie vacant. High rents also contribute to the fact that many Parisians have neither the time nor the money to appreciate the city they live in, being trapped in a monotonous routine they describe as *métro-boulot-dodo* (commuting, working, sleeping).

Nonetheless, for anyone fortunate enough to live in the city centre the rewards far out-weigh the demands. Human in scale, clean, comparatively safe, cosmopolitan and lively, Paris lives up to its reputation as one of the best cities on earth for living the good life.

Highlights

▲ **Musée d'Orsay** Fine art from 1848 to 1919, including an outstanding collection of Impressionist paintings.

▼ **Notre-Dame** Located in the heart of Paris, on the historic Ile de la Cité, the cathedral is a monument to Catholicism and the great Gothic architects.

▲ **The Louvre** From the home of kings to a showcase for one of the world's best collections of fine and decorative arts.

▲ **Centre Pompidou** This inside-out behemoth showcases art from 1905 to the present.

▶ **Arc de Triomphe** Dominating the eastern Champs Elysées, this arch honours Napoleon's victories.

▶ **Eiffel Tower** Built for the 1889 World Fair, Gustave Eiffel's mighty iron monolith is still one of the most enduring symbols of Paris.

The Islands

The Ile de la Cité in the middle of the Seine is the birthplace and topographical centre of Paris and has been its spiritual and legislative heart for more than 2,000 years. Invading the Parisii settlement already established there in 53BC, the Romans built a prefect's palace, law court and temple to Jupiter on the island. The island's importance continued through the centuries and the great cathedral of Notre-Dame de Paris still makes it the focal point for tourism in the city. Adjacent is a second, smaller island, the Ile St-Louis, known for its elegant mansions, many of which form the homes of Paris's élite.

See Atlas Pages 154 – 155

Ile de la Cité

The Ile de la Cité is dominated by the vast Gothic **Notre-Dame de Paris** ①, which occupies the eastern end of the island. Gazing up at the cathedral's ornate façade, it is difficult to imagine the building's poor condition when Victor Hugo wrote his novel *The Hunchback of Notre-Dame* in 1831. He and his followers were appalled at its dreadful state and, in 1841, succeeded in triggering a massive restoration programme, headed by architect Viollet-le-Duc. For the next 23 years, the architect overhauled the cathedral's entire structure. SEE ALSO CHURCHES, MOSQUES AND SYNAGOGUES, P.44; LITERATURE AND THEATRE, P.80

Palais de la Cité

West from Notre-Dame is the **Palais de la Cité** ②, the name for the complex including the **Conciergerie** (most famous as the antechamber of the

Above: the west front of Notre-Dame de Paris.

scaffold in the Revolution), the Gothic **Sainte-Chapelle**, a magnificent royal chapel built for Louis IX, and the Palais de Justice, headquarters of the French supreme court. SEE ALSO ARCHITECTURE, P.30; CHURCHES, MOSQUES AND SYNAGOGUES, P.45

Around the Pont Neuf

Having had your fill of the big sights, escape the shadows of the Revolution on the

Pont Neuf ③. Bisected by the island's western tip, it is the oldest surviving bridge in Paris. It was constructed of stone, rather than wood, and was the first bridge in Paris to be built without houses on it.

Look out for a flight of stairs behind an impressive equestrian statue of Henri IV, which stands on a small square platform between the two arms of the bridge. The statue, erected in 1818, is a copy of an earlier one that had stood on this site since 1635 but was destroyed during the Revolution. The stairs lead to **place du Vert-Galant**, a tiny, leafy square with excellent views across to the Louvre.

Place Dauphine ④

From place du Vert-Galant, it is easy to access the tranquil **place Dauphine**. Created in 1607 by Henri IV to offer a market place for traders near the **Palais de la Cité**, this

Left: elegant mansions line the banks of the islands.

On the same road, at No. 2, is the **Hôtel de Lambert** ⑤, designed by Louis Le Vau (one of the architects of Versailles) and constructed in 1640–52 for Lambert de Thorigny, then president of the parliament. This is probably the most important mansion on the island, though its simple exterior gives no indication of the wealth of decoration inside. The writer and philosopher Voltaire (1694–1778) is believed to have once lived here, and the building was a popular meeting place for artists during the 19th century.

At 17 quai d'Anjou is the **Hôtel Lauzun** ⑥, its Louis XIV interior decoration still almost entirely intact. As with other *hôtels particuliers* along the quays of the Ile St-Louis, the layout of this mansion and its grounds is the reverse of the usual Paris ground-plan (the main block is on the Seine side, with the courtyard and outbuildings behind it). Le Vau also designed this palace, which at one time belonged to the Richelieu family. In the mid-19th century, the poets Charles Baudelaire and Théophile Gautier also lived here.

Since 1946, quai des Orfèvres, the police HQ and home to the fictional Maigret, has lent its name to a literary prize for detective novels. The prize's jury is made up of real-life police and magistrates.

elegant square is home to 32 white-stone town houses built around a triangular courtyard. Famous past residents include singer Yves Montand and his actress partner, Simone Signoret. There are several pleasant cafés and restaurants here.

Other Sights

Other attractions on the island include the colourful **Marché aux Fleurs** on place Louis Lépine, opposite the Préfecture de Police on quai des Orfèvres and Haussmann's **Hôtel Dieu**, the oldest hospital in Paris. The market is an array of small glasshouses selling flowers and plants underneath old-fashioned, black street-lamps. On Sunday, the stalls become a market for caged birds. Look out, too, on rue de la Colombe, for the remains of the Gallo-Roman wall in the pavement.

Ile St-Louis

Across the pedestrian bridge, Pont St-Louis, at the eastern end of the Ile de la Cité, is the upmarket **Ile St-Louis**. The island developed from two mudbanks, owned by the cathedral chapter and handed over by royal command in 1614. From 1618 craftsmen began to settle on the islands, and it became a popular building site for rich nobles, who erected their *hôtels particuliers* (private mansions) here to escape the unhealthy confines of the city centre. One such building, to the east of the island is the rococo-fronted **Hôtel Chenizot** at 51 rue St-Louis-en-l'Ile.

Below: gilded angels in Sainte-Chapelle.

Louvre, Tuileries and Concorde

O ver the centuries, the Louvre has functioned as a fortress, prison, palace, administration centre and world-class museum and art gallery. Stretching out in front of it, the ornamental Jardin des Tuileries extends to place de la Concorde, providing a green lung for the city. At the Concorde end of the gardens are the Jeu de Paume and Orangerie museums, the former currently used for photography exhibitions and the latter housing Monet's dreamy *Water Lilies*.

See Atlas Pages 151 – 152

The Louvre ①

Originally built as a fortress in 1190 by King Philippe-Auguste, to protect a weak link in his city wall, the Louvre was transformed into a royal *château* in the 1360s by Charles V. Successive monarchs demolished, rebuilt and extended various sections, until Louis XIV decamped to Versailles in 1682.

Squatters, including Guillaume Coustou, sculptor of the **Marly Horses** (now one of the Louvre's most prized exhibits), consequently took up residence in the palace, and a vibrant artistic community grew out of the decaying passageways and galleries. In the 18th century the fine arts academy, which had joined the Académie Française and other academic bodies in the royal apartments, established salons for artists to exhibit their work here, a tradition that lasted for over 120 years.

Above: the Louvre's most famous exhibit, *Mona Lisa*.

PALACE TO MUSEUM

During the Revolution the rebels decided to inaugurate the palace as a museum, which, ironically, fulfilled the plans of Louis XVI, the king they had just beheaded. Opened in August 1793, the museum benefited from the growing collection of royal treasures, augmented by Napoleon's efforts to relocate much of Europe's artistic wealth, following his victorious military campaigns in Italy, Austria and Germany.

After Napoleon was defeated at Waterloo in 1815, many of the stolen masterpieces were reclaimed by their rightful owners. But a large number remained.

In 1981, President Mitterrand commissioned a massive renovation of the Louvre, one of his *grands projets*, transferring in the process the Finance Ministry from the Richelieu Wing to Bercy, in eastern Paris, to free up more space for the vast collection. When it was finally finished, the 'Grand Louvre', already a vast museum, had doubled in size, making it the biggest in the world.

SEE ALSO ARCHITECTURE, P.33; MUSEUMS AND GALLERIES, P.88

Left: I.M. Pei's pyramid entrance to the Louvre.

with an equestrian statue. In 1755, building work began on place de la Concorde, based on plans by the architect Ange-Jacques Gabriel. The monument to the king was erected in 1763, and the square named place Louis XV.

After the storming of the Bastille in 1789, the square became the focal point for revolutionary action. In 1792 it was renamed place de la Révolution, and the equestrian statue of the king was melted down to make copper coins; it was replaced with the guillotine that beheaded Louis XVI, Marie-Antoinette and thousands of others. During the Directory, in 1795, the square received its present name.

At the centre of the square is an **obelisk** from Luxor. On the north side are two magnificent 18th-century palaces by Gabriel: one is the **Hôtel de Crillon**; the other houses a government ministry. On the west side, the start of the Champs-Elysées, is heralded by copies of Guillaume Coustou's *Marly Horses*, the originals of which can be seen in the Louvre.
SEE ALSO HOTELS, P.71; MONUMENTS, P.87

The Tuileries ②

West of the Louvre is one of the city centre's main green spaces, the 28-hectare (69-acre) **Jardin des Tuileries**, named after a 13th-century tile factory once situated there, and finely landscaped by André Le Nôtre. Attractions in the park include modern sculpture, cafés, boating on the lake (popular with children) and two art galleries, the **Jeu de Paume** ③ (showcase for the Centre National de la Photographie) and the **Musée de l'Orangerie** ④, home to eight of Claude Monet's vast water-lily paintings.
SEE ALSO MUSEUMS AND GALLERIES, P.94, 102; PARKS AND GARDENS, P.122

The entrance to the Jardin des Tuileries from the Louvre is through the rather incongruous Arc de Triomphe du Carrousel, a mini version of the Arc de Triomphe.

Palais Royal ⑤

On the north side of the gardens is **rue de Rivoli**, named after Napoleon's victory over the Austrians in 1797. Over 500 houses were torn down in 1811 when construction work finally started on the street. The work was only completed in 1833, long after the emperor's 1814 abdication. The arcaded passageways now contain shops, which, thanks to the opening of **Marc Jacobs'** Parisian flagship store, are currently very much à la mode.

Right opposite the western end of the Louvre is the **Palais Royal**, built for Cardinal Richelieu as a subsidiary palace to the Louvre.
SEE ALSO FASHION, P. 57; PALACES, P.117

Place de la Corcorde ⑥

After the Treaty of Aachen in 1748, which ended the Austrian War of Secession, Paris decided to honour Louis XV

Below: the fountain on place de la Concorde.

9

Opéra and Grands Boulevards

North of the Louvre and Tuileries are the Grands Boulevards, wide avenues running from west to east, laid out when Louis XIV felt secure enough to tear down the city's medieval walls and replace them with broad, tree-lined streets. In the 19th century Haussmann extended development westwards, and the western end became the preserve of the rich. Today, the central boulevards are dominated by high-street chains, although traces of the Second Empire extravagance can still be seen.

Haussmann's Legacy

There is the unmistakable stamp of Gallic grandeur in the area that runs from place de la Madeleine in the west to boulevard Sébastopol in the east. The monuments are imposing, and the *boulevards* wide and busy, showing off Paris's striking ability to combine the historic with the present; to remain a city both lived in and living.

Weaving through these loud and crowded streets are shoppers darting up to the *Grands Magasins* (department stores), bankers racing to the Bourse (stock exchange), and tourists dipping in and out of bistros and bars.

Below: Galeries Lafayette, a temple to shopping.

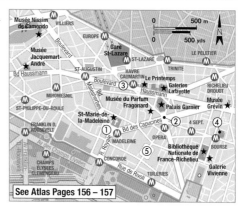

See Atlas Pages 156 – 157

Place de la Madeleine ①

The **Eglise de la Ste-Marie-de-la-Madeleine** was the fruit of anguished debate for 80 years in the 18th and 19th centuries. It was mooted as a stock exhange, library and railway station, before Napoleon Bonaparte lost patience with the wrangling and ordered that it become a place of worship.

The church is a now a landmark, sitting in the centre of a square that is the setting for a flower market, as well as the biggest branches of France's best-known delicatessen chains, **Hédiard** and **Fauchon**.

SEE ALSO CHURCHES, MOSQUES AND SYNAGOGUES, P.46; FOOD AND DRINK, P.64

Place de l'Opéra ②

Boulevard de la Madeleine leads into boulevard des Capucines, which opens into the wide expanse of place de l'Opéra. Stand in the middle of the square – or, better still, walk down avenue de l'Opéra – to get a view of the magnificent **Palais Garnier**. With its intricate façade and marbled halls, the opera house is the most exuberant example of Second Empire architecture.

Behind place de l'Opéra is rue Scribe, named after the prolific 19th-century playwright, Eugène Scribe. Here is the 1862 Grand Hotel and the **Musée du Parfum Fragonard**, which traces 3,000 years of perfumery.

Left: the sumptuous corridors of the Palais Garnier.

best examples of these arcades is the elegant **Galerie Vivienne**; others include **Passage des Panoramas**, with its philatelists, and, on the northern side of the Grands Boulevards, **Passage Jouffroy**, where the Paris waxworks museum, the **Musée Grévin** is situated. Also in this area is the **Bibliothèque Nationale de France – Richelieu**.
SEE ALSO ARCHITECTURE, P.30; MUSEUMS AND GALLERIES, P.97; SHOPPING, P.141

Faubourg St-Honoré

Place Vendôme ⑤ is the heart of one of Paris's most elegant quarters, the Faubourg St-Honoré. The square's centrepiece originally had an equestrian statue of Louis XIV, erected in 1699. This was destroyed in the Revolution and later replaced by Napoleon with the **Colonne de la Grande Armée**, modelled on Trajan's Column in Rome. The square has survived revolution and insurrection with remarkably little damage. Today it is home to banks, exclusive jewellers, the salons of leading dress designers, and the **Ritz** hotel.
SEE ALSO HOTELS, P.72; MONUMENTS, P.86

SEE ALSO MUSEUMS AND GALLERIES, P.104; MUSIC, P.108

Grands Boulevards

North of place de l'Opéra is the boulevard named after the town planner Baron Georges-Eugène Haussmann who, with his network of wide tree-lined avenues, brought better health and light to the city, as well as making it more difficult for the post-Revolutionary mob to barricade the streets. Nowadays **boulevard Haussmann** ③ is best known for its department stores, **Le Printemps** (No. 64) and **Galeries Lafayette** (No. 40).

Further west on boulevard Haussmann are some imposing Belle-Epoque mansions, built at the same time that the roads were widened. These include the magnificent home of the **Musée Jacquemart-André**, showcasing an exceptional art collection, and the mansion now housing the **Musée Nissim de Camondo**.

By the 19th century the Grands Boulevards were the centre of Parisian theatreland, but also of Parisian gangsterism. This earned them the nickname Criminal Boulevard. Fortunately, only the theatres now remain.

SEE ALSO MUSEUMS AND GALLERIES, P.98, 104; SHOPPING, P.143

Around La Bourse

Southeast of the opera house, between the boulevards and **La Bourse** ④ (stock exchange), is an area little explored by most tourists, but which holds a number of delights. Here you'll find some of the finest bistros in Paris and some of the city's most unexpected passageways and squares.

Don't miss the small, ornate shopping arcades that date from the 19th century, in which bars, cafés and boutiques still flourish. One of the

Below: the Opéra auditorium.

11

Beaubourg and Les Halles

Sandwiched between the Louvre and Palais-Royal to the west and the Marais to the east, this central chunk of the Right Bank is one of the city's busiest commercial and cultural centres. The area is dominated by the Forum des Halles, a vast and unsightly shopping and leisure complex, something of a poor relation to the monumental Louvre. The other landmark building here is the Centre Pompidou, Paris's modern art museum; unlike the 1980s' architectural disaster of Les Halles, this mass of pipes, ducts and scaffolds painted in primary colours is strangely alluring, and is one of the city's most-visited sites.

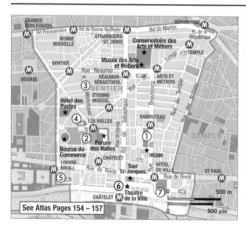

Above: the Stravinsky Fountain outside IRCAM.

Centre Pompidou

Known locally as Beaubourg, this area's highlight is the **Centre National d'Art et de Culture, Centre Georges-Pompidou** ①. Its architects, Richard Rogers and Renzo Piano, placed all the escalators, lifts, ducts, etc, on the outside. The high-tech design caused an uproar when the building opened in 1977, but its popularity soon silenced the critics. It houses an important modern art collection as well as a number of other cultural amenities. Close by is the avant-garde music institute **IRCAM**.
SEE ALSO MUSEUMS AND GALLERIES, P.92; MUSIC, P.107

Les Halles

Adjacent is **Les Halles** ②, a quarter that owes its name to the historic food market that stood from 1183 to 1969 on the spot now occupied by a vast shopping complex.

> Combined with a massive RER/metro interchange, the Forum des Halles has acquired a grim reputation. After a number of years, the Mairie de Paris has now decided on a design to redevelop the Forum; it has a huge glass canopy covering the re-landscaped squares and gardens. The regeneration project started in 2009, with completion estimated for 2012.

Large-scale construction has been a feature of the area since 1851, when Napoleon III ordered architect Victor Baltard to design ten huge cast-iron hangars to go over the market. By the 1960s the site had become impractical to manage. The market decamped to the suburbs of Rungis, and the hangars were tragically pulled down, leaving a gaping hole that became a national joke. It was filled in the 1980s by the **Forum des Halles**, an underground shopping mall with shops, a cinema and an Olympic-sized swimming pool.
SEE ALSO CINEMA, P.51; SPORT, P.145

Left: inside-out infrastructure of the Centre Pompidou.

rior. South of the Bourse du Commerce, facing the Louvre, is the church of **St-Germain-l'Auxerrois** ⑤.

SEE ALSO CHURCHES, MOSQUES AND SYNAGOGUES, P.46

Châtelet

Further east is **place du Châtelet** ⑥. Flanked by two theatres (**Théâtre du Châtelet** and **Théâtre de la Ville**), the square lies above a huge metro interchange. To the northeast, rises the Gothic **Tour St-Jacques**, a lone belfry from a church destroyed during the Revolution.

SEE ALSO CHURCHES, MOSQUES AND SYNAGOGUES, P.47; DANCE, P.52–3; MUSIC, P.107

Hôtel de Ville

Opening out at the eastern end of avenue Victoria is the wide esplanade of the **Hôtel de Ville** ⑦, the ornate neo-Renaissance home of the city council. In medieval times, place de l'Hôtel de Ville was the site of macabre executions. Today, however, the pedestrianised square is a lovely place for a stroll, especially in the evening, when the fountains and town hall are impressively floodlit.

SEE ALSO ARCHITECTURE, P.32

RUE MONTORGUEIL ③

Surrounding the market area are remnants of a bygone age, with brasseries staying open around the clock (the clientele no longer formed by hard-working market porters in the early hours, but by exhausted partygoers) and sleazy rue St-Denis, the age-old domain of prostitutes.

The best place for a glimpse of Les Halles of old is rue Montorgueil. This narrow pedestrian precinct is extremely popular, with cafés, bistros and open-fronted fruit and vegetable shops.

Sentier and St-Eustache

Immediately to the north of Les Halles is **Sentier**, a centre for wholesale clothing. Northwest is a garden with glass pyramids full of palms, papayas and banana trees. Metal walkways lead to the **Bourse du Commerce**, a circular building erected in the 18th century as a corn

> Rue Montorgueil is home to the unmissable *pâtissier*, Stohrer, where the *baba au rhum* is said to have been invented in 1730.

exchange, now housing the city's chamber of commerce.

Nearby, on rue St-Eustache, is **St-Eustache** ④, a colossal church modelled on Notre-Dame, with flying buttresses outside and a splendid Renaissance inte-

Below: artisan food shop in des Halles.

The Marais and Bastille

Although originally a marsh *(marécage)* on the outskirts of the city, nowadays the Marais is one of the most attractive areas of the city, home to an eclectic mix of grandiose and small-scale buildings, quaint boutiques, cosy cafés, hip bars and bistros, and several notable museums. The best way to explore its narrow streets is simply to wander and let yourself fall haphazardly upon hidden gems. Adjacent is the Bastille *quartier*, for years run down, resting only on its revolutionary notoriety. The area was given a shot in the arm by the construction of a new opera house in the late 20th century and has since become a potent symbol of urban regeneration.

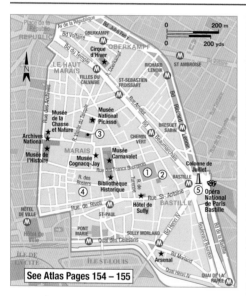

See Atlas Pages 154 – 155

Rue Oberkampf is the trendiest limb of the 11th *arrondissement*, especially at the upper end, east of avenue de la République, where there is a high concentration of cafés and bars and some independent shops. If you are looking for some of the old flavour of the area, wander down the side streets off rue Oberkampf.

XIV moved the court to Versailles, the Marais was abandoned by the upper classes. It wasn't until the 1960s that the *quartier* began to regain its prestige, thanks to a regeneration programme. Today, it is one of the most sought-after parts of the city, with a proliferation of museums, fashionable bars, restaurants and boutiques, and is the focus of gay life in Paris.

Many former private mansions are now museums. The Hôtel Carnavalet and Hôtel le Peletier de St-Fargeau house the **Musée de l'Histoire de Paris**, which documents the history of Paris; the Hôtel de Sully is a branch of the **Centre National de la Photographie**; the Hôtel Salé is home to the **Musée National Picasso** ③; the Hôtel Donon has the **Musée Cognacq-Jay**; and the Hôtel Guéné-

The Marais

The golden age of the Marais began in the reign of Henri IV (1553–1610), with the magnificent **place des Vosges** ① as a showcase for his court. Inaugurated as place Royale in 1612 by Henri's son, Louis XIII, the square comprised a garden surrounded by 36 arcaded residences. Following the Napoleonic Wars it was renamed after the first *département* to have paid its war taxes, Vosges.

Today, the arcades house restaurants and expensive commercial art galleries. In the southeast corner is the **Maison de Victor Hugo** ②, the writer's Paris home for 15 years, now a small museum.

Just as the place des Vosges was thriving, numerous *hôtels particuliers* (private mansions) were erected across the Marais, owners competing for the grandest architecture and decor. From 1682, however, when Louis

Left: walking is the best way to explore the Marais.

SEE ALSO LA VILLETTE TO BERCY, P.20; MONUMENTS, P.86; MUSIC, P.107

REGENERATION

The Bastille has changed enormously over the past 20 years. Backstreets have been gentrified, and the old inhabitants are increasingly moving out. You could try looking for what edgy attraction remains on streets such as rue de Lappe, rue de Charonne and rue Keller to the east of the square, yet the influx of the upwardly mobile has led to an epidemic of dimly lit bistro-bars that lure what are referred to as *les bobos* – bourgeois bohemians.

Oberkampf and République

This area just north of Bastille has come a long way in recent years. Around the turn of the millennium this was just another run-down district, but is now one of the hippest neighbourhoods in town, albeit urban cool rather than glamour.

Below: a Jewish *kippah* for sale in the Marais.

gaud, the **Musée de la Chasse et Nature**.
SEE ALSO GAY AND LESBIAN, P.66; MUSEUMS AND GALLERIES, P.94, 97, 98, 103

The Jewish Quarter ④

At the southern edge of the Marais is **rue des Rosiers**, the hub of what remains of the Jewish quarter. Kosher delis and shops selling religious artefacts line this narrow street. On rue du Temple, the **Musée d'Art et d'Histoire du Judaïsme** documents Jewish history. The **synagogue**, in rue Pavée, has an Art Nouveau façade by Hector Guimard.
SEE ALSO CHURCHES, MOSQUES AND SYNAGOGUES, P.47; MUSEUMS AND GALLERIES, P.96

> On 14 July 1789, when crowds stormed the prison, freeing the inmates (all seven of them), Louis XVI was unimpressed, writing in his diary, 'Today – nothing.'

Le Haut Marais

In recent years, people talk about the Marais having moved north into the third *arrondissement*, an area referred to as 'Le Haut Marais' (Upper Marais). The 3rd is in the midst of transition, with a busy market street (rue de Bretagne), some great North African restaurants and a smattering of shops.

The Bastille

First-time visitors should be warned – there is nothing to see of the prison at **Bastille** ⑤; the stronghold was entirely dismantled in the Revolution. The medieval Bastille covered the present place de la Bastille and the **Arsenal** complex to the south. The modern square is a busy thoroughfare with the **Colonne de Juillet**, commemorating the victims of the 1830 and 1848 revolutions, in the middle, and the **Opéra National de Paris Bastille** dominating the southeast.

15

Champs-Elysées, Trocadéro and West

After over a decade of regeneration, 'Les Champs' is the spine of a thriving, glamorous district of Paris. *Haute cuisine* and *haute couture* reign supreme. Attractions are big and bold, from the Belle-Epoque Grand and Petit Palais, both showcases for fine art, to the monumental Arc de Triomphe. Further west, around the Trocadéro, in an area developed for the 1937 World Fair, are museums of modern art, naval history and architecture. Adjacent is the upmarket 17th *arrondissement*, home to Parc Monceau.

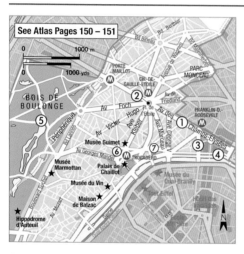

See Atlas Pages 150 – 151

From Pont de l'Alma, look towards the Seine for the Zouave, a statue used as a river marker. If his toes get wet, Paris is put on flood alert. If his ankles go under water, roads adjacent to the river are closed, and if his hips are wet, an emergency flood plan is put into action.

Determined to resurrect the area, Jacques Chirac, at that time mayor of Paris, budgeted €75 million to beautify the Champs: street parking was replaced by underground car parks; pretty flagstones were laid; and the number of trees doubled.

Champs-Elysées

First initiated by Louis XVI in 1667, the **Champs-Elysées** ①, or 'Elysian Fields' were laid out by landscape architect André Le Nôtre as an extension of the **Jardin des Tuileries**, running west from the Louvre. The wide street lined with gardens and trees later continued its development after the completion in 1836 of the Arc de Triomphe ②, celebrating Napoleon Bonaparte's military triumphs.

By the beginning of the 20th century the Champs had reached a zenith of popularity, attracting stylish, monied types from across the world to its chic café terraces.

The sophistication of the avenue evaporated during World War I, before making a brief comeback in the 1920s. Soon, however, came the Depression, then World War II, then congestion, thanks to the postwar popularity of the car. The Champs shifted from a luxury address to a commercial one, and by the 1980s it had none of its former glitz.

On average, around 1 million people pass along the Champs every Saturday.

Not surprisingly, the Parisians gave the avenue a second look. A turning point was 1999, when **Ladurée**, the venerable Parisian tea-room in rue Royale, opened a second branch at No. 75, and Louis Vuitton set up glamorous shop at No. 101.

The even more recent revival of streets such as the once blandly bourgeois **avenue Montaigne**, a fashion strip leading southwest from the Champs, has further increased the area's appeal.

SEE ALSO PARKS AND GARDENS, P.122; RESTAURANTS, P.133; SHOPPING, P.140

Left: the Champs-Elysées marks the end of *Le Tour*.

Many people venture to the 16th to visit its museums. **Place du Trocadéro** ⑥ houses the **Musée National de la Marine** and the **Cité de l'Architecture et du Patrimoine** (the world's biggest architecture centre) in the Art Deco **Palais de Chaillot**, built for the World Fair of 1937. Further down avenue du Président Wilson is the **Palais de Tokyo** ⑦, built as the Electricity Pavilion for the same World Fair and now home to the **Musée d'Art Moderne de la Ville de Paris**.

Others include the **Musée Guimet**, a showcase for Asian arts, the **Maison de Balzac**, erstwhile home of the novelist, the **Musée du Vin**, the **Musée Marmottan** with its Monet collection, and the **Musée de la Mode et du Costume** in the 1890s Palais Galliera.

SEE ALSO ARCHITECTURE, P.32; MUSEUMS AND GALLERIES, P. 96, 99, 100, 102; PARKS AND GARDENS, P.120

CULTURAL ATTRACTIONS

On the southern side of the Champs, between place Clemenceau and the river, is the glass-domed **Grand Palais** ③, constructed for the 1900 World Fair, now host to art exhibitions. The colossal building is also home to the **Palais de la Découverte** science museum. Across avenue Winston Churchill is the **Petit Palais** ④, which houses the art collection of the Musée des Beaux-Arts de la Ville de Paris.
SEE ALSO MUSEUMS AND GALLERIES, P.94, 105

L'ETOILE

Crowning the Champs-Elysées is a memorial to megalomania, the **Arc de Triomphe**, commissioned by Napoleon in 1806. In the Second Empire, place de l' Etoile, as the roundabout is officially called, and the streets radiating away from it were all redesigned by Haussmann.
SEE ALSO MONUMENTS, P.84

The 16th

The large 16th *arrondissement*, like the 7th, is full of smart, expensive residences. Just adjacent (though outside the Périphérique) is another Haussmann creation, the **Bois de Boulogne** ⑤, an 860-hectares expanse of woods and gardens. This is one of the reasons that the 16th has long been popular with Parisians; upmarket **avenue Foch**, leads right to its gates.

The 17th

This wealthy *arrondissement* is characterised by tree-lined boulevards, the former homes of Belle-Epoque plutocrats and the chic **Parc Monceau**.
SEE ALSO PARKS AND GARDENS, P.125

Below: Eiffel Tower from the Pont Alexandre.

Montmartre and Pigalle

Named the 'Mount of Martyrs' after the martyrdom of St-Denis, Montmartre is now a mount of tourism: it is second only to the Eiffel Tower as a destination for international visitors. Its narrow cobbled streets, meandering up and down the hill (or 'Butte', as it is known), its many stairways and its discreet but numerous islets of green all give the area a unique atmosphere. And, of course, there's the view: the panorama from the Sacré-Cœur will leave you even more breathless than the climb up to it. Back down the bottom of the hill is Pigalle, Paris's red-light district, once seedy, now increasingly respectable and cool.

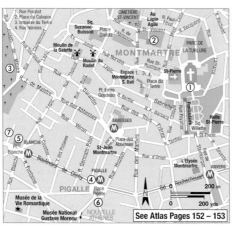

See Atlas Pages 152 – 153

Above: Montmartre is still romantic.

Montmartre

Sitting atop a hill overlooking the city, Montmartre has always stood apart from the rest of Paris. Legend has it that in AD287, the Romans decapitated St-Denis, first bishop of Paris, on the site of the Chapelle du Martyr (11 rue Yvonne Le Tac). St Denis calmly picked up his head and carried it to where the basilica of St Denis now stands.

The village of Montmartre ('martyr's mount') was not incorporated into the city boundaries until 1860. Today its most striking symbol is the **Sacré-Cœur** ① basilica, begun after France's defeat in the 1870 Franco-Prussian War, and completed in 1914.

In 1871, Montmartre saw the start of the Paris Commune, when the Montmartrois, led by Louise Michel, stood up to the right-wing government of Adolphe Thiers. SEE ALSO CHURCHES, MOSQUES AND SYNAGOGUES, P.47

Opposite the Lapin Agile, at the corner of rue St-Vincent and rue des Saules, look out for the city's last surviving vineyard, the tiny Clos de Montmartre, which produces a wine that reputedly 'makes you jump like a goat'.

ARTISTIC HERITAGE

At the end of the 19th century, artists, including Toulouse-Lautrec, began settling in the district and depicting its bars and cabarets. Suzanne Valadon (and later her son Maurice Utrillo) had their studio in the entrance lodge of what is now the **Musée de Montmartre** ②. In the early 20th-century, Montmartre nurtured the birth of Cubism, when Pablo Picasso painted *Les Demoiselles d'Avignon* in his studio in the Bateau Lavoir (13 place Emile Goudeau).

Left: the imposing white bulk of Sacre-Cœur.

Nouvelle Athènes ⑥

South of boulevard de Rochechouart and boulevard de Clichy, the area known as **Nouvelle Athènes** is being rediscovered. In the mid-19th century 'New Athens' drew writers, artists and composers, among them Chopin and George Sand. The houses on place St-Georges, the **Musée de la Vie Romantique** and the exclusive villas off rue des Martyrs give an idea of a grander past. The **Musée National Gustave Moreau** conjures a particularly vivid atmosphere with its remarkable studio, packed with his Symbolist paintings.
SEE ALSO MUSEUMS AND GALLERIES, P.101

Batignolles

West of place de Clichy, the area of **Batignolles** ⑦ is very different from the grand mansions and apartment blocks not far away in the 17th. Sliced through by huge railway depots, now due for redevelopment, it still retains its old working-class cafés, budget hotels, craft workshops and interesting alleys and courtyards, but it is increasingly being colonised by quirky boutiques and arty bistros.

At 22 rue des Saules, stands the legendary cabaret, **Au Lapin Agile**, the HQ of the avant-garde in the 1900s. Here, Renoir and Paul Verlaine laid tables, and Guillaume Apollinaire sang with fellow Surrealist poet Max Jacob. Picasso paid for a day's meals at the Lapin with one of his *Harlequin* paintings. By the 1920s most artists had moved across the river to Montparnasse, where rents were lower, but numerous studio buildings remained, and some are still occupied by artists today.

Pay tribute to Truffaut, Guitry, Dumas *fils*, Dalida, Berlioz, Degas and more in the shady groves of the **Cimitière de Montmartre** ③, on avenue Rachel.
SEE ALSO MUSEUMS AND GALLERIES, P.99

THE HIGHLIGHTS
Nowadays, **place du Tertre** sadly abounds in overpriced tourist bistros, gift shops and bad would-be artists. Leave the hordes on the square and strike out into the Butte's backstreets, many of which are still villagey, sheltering gorgeous ivy-clad cottages, cobbled squares and good, atmospheric eateries.

Pigalle ④

Back down below the Butte, Pigalle, the city's red-light district, is shedding its seedy reputation: it was the core of the Parisian sex trade for decades. Though sleaze still exists here, the cabarets that once occupied rue des Martyrs are being taken over by music clubs, such as **Le Divan du Monde** at No. 75.

Among the cabaret survivors is **Chez Michou** on rue des Martyrs, home of Parisian drag artists, and the **Moulin Rouge** ⑤, which has long since cleaned up its act and is now more cheesy than sleazy.
SEE ALSO MUSIC, P.109; NIGHTLIFE, P.110

Below: the Moulin Rouge.

La Villette to Bercy

There are two big sights in this part of the city: Père Lachaise cemetery and the leisure complex at La Villette. There are otherwise few major tourist attractions in these eastern neighbourhoods, but they are nonetheless fascinating for more off-the-beaten-path excursions and as evidence of the impending gentrification of formerly working-class areas of Paris. Do as the Parisians do: go for a stroll along the tree-shaded Canal St-Martin, take a breather at the top of rue de Belleville, then look downhill for an exceptional view of the Eiffel Tower, or spend time in Bercy, erstwhile home to the city's wine wharfs and now a popular spot for shopping and dining.

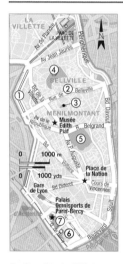

Above: artists mural in Belleville.

By Canal to La Villette

To the northeast of the city centre is a network of waterways built by Napoleon in the early 19th century to channel water into Paris. The **Canal St-Martin** ① begins at Pont Morland by the Seine, disappears undergound at Bastille (supposedly to allow troops faster access to subdue uprisings), then emerges in the 10th *arrondissement* at place François-Lemaître. It leads up to place de Stalingrad, before continuing east as the Canal de l'Ourca

across the **Parc de la Villette**.

In the 19th century warehouses were erected along parts of the canal to cope with the massive growth in freight haulage, but by the 20th century the development of road and rail haulage caused the area to fall into decline. Since the late 1980s, however, regeneration has taken place, and the canals are now used for recreation.

SEE ALSO PARKS AND GARDENS, P.125

Belleville ②

Ever since it was incorporated into the city in 1860, Belleville has been a vibrant place. At one time a forge of working-class agitation, it is now home to more than 60

nationalities and, with its vendors of felafels and bagels, noodles and couscous, the area retains a laid-back charm, despite the encroaching gentrification.

Earlier in the 19th century Belleville was a fertile country village, whose springs were tapped to channel water into Paris. There still remain a few old stone *regards* (control stations for the aqueducts), particulary

One of the nicest ways to tour the canal is to take a barge trip between Bastille and the Parc de la Villette. Some boats also stop at the Port de l'Arsenal, which is just a hop from the Parc de Belleville. See www.canauxrama.com for further details.

Left: a barge waits in a canal lock.

Legend has it that singer Edith Piaf was born under a lamppost at 72 rue de Belleville. The plaque over the doorway reads, 'On the steps of this house, on 19 December 1915, was born, in the greatest poverty, Piaf whose voice would later take the world by storm.' The tiny **Musée Edith Piaf** at 5 rue Crespin-du-Gast is a tribute to the queen of French chanson.

PARC DE BERCY

The long quai de Bercy is backed by the vast **Parc de Bercy** ⑦. On the north side of the park is the former American Center, designed by renowned architect Frank Gehry. It is now home to the trendy **Cinémathèque Française**.

The reclaimed area is also the site of the vast new headquarters of the Ministry of Finance, which extends out over the Seine as if it were meant to be a bridge. Close by is the pyramid-shaped **Palais Omnisports de Paris-Bercy**, a stadium for sports and concerts, seating 17,000 spectators.
SEE ALSO CINEMA, P.51; SPORT, P.144

around **Parc de Belleville** ③, a terraced crescent of green atop a hill with a panoramic view of Paris. The other park worthy of a detour is the **Parc des Buttes-Chaumont** ④, constructed under the aegis of Baron Haussmann.
SEE ALSO PARKS AND GARDENS, P.124

Ménilmontant

Due south of Belleville, and incorporating part of the trendy **rue Oberkampf**, the eastern district of Ménilmontant is another hotbed of alternative culture and also home to many of the city's more recent immigrants.

The draw for tourists is the **Cimetière du Père-Lachaise** ⑤, at 5 boulevard de Ménilmontant. Named after Louis XIV's confessor, the Jesuit Père de la Chaise, it is one of the most illustrious resting places in Paris. Famous people buried here include Abélard and Héloïse,

Apollinaire, Balzac, Edith Piaf, Oscar Wilde, Molière, Proust, Sarah Bernhardt, Frédéric Chopin and Doors singer Jim Morrison.

Bercy

For centuries wine was brought to Paris by boat from Burgundy, to the riverport of Bercy. Today, it is Paris's newest neighbourhood, connected by bridge to the **'New Left Bank'** across the river.

Old stone warehouses and cobbled streets have been reborn in the shape of **Bercy Village** ⑥, a carfree zone, centred on cour St-Emilion, busy with boutiques, restaurants and cafés. The futuristic **Ciné Cité** is Paris's biggest multiplex cinema, with 18 screens showing mainstream and art-house films, usually in their original language with subtitles.
SEE ALSO MONTPARNASSE AND BEYOND, P.27

Below: reading beside the canal.

21

The Latin Quarter and St-Germain

East of boulevard St-Michel is the Latin Quarter, a maze of ancient streets and the stomping ground of students for almost eight centuries. Lectures were given in Latin, hence the area's nickname, although Napoleon put a stop to that after the Revolution. West of boulevard St-Michel is St-Germain-des-Prés, the historical centre of literary Paris and café society. High fashion is increasingly replacing the more cerebral pursuits here, but both areas maintain their charm in tree-lined streets and manicured parks.

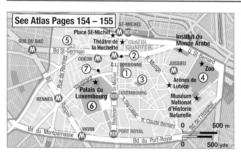

See Atlas Pages 154 – 155

Two monuments to the district's literary heyday, the Café de Flore and Les Deux Magots still provide fascinating, although expensive, venues for people watching.

The Latin Quarter

In 1968 the area around the **Sorbonne** ①, the great seat of learning founded by Robert de Sorbon in 1253, was the centre of the student uprisings that shook the country. Nowadays, accommodation here is too expensive for most students, and the book shops that previously dominated the area are gradually being taken over by fashion houses.

Northeast of place St-Michel is the Quartier de la Huchette. Of note on the otherwise unpleasant rue de la Huchette is the **Théâtre de la Huchette**, where Eugène Ionesco's *La Cantatrice Chauve* (The Bald Soprano) has been performed nightly since 1957. Avoid the restau-

rants on this street, as they are overpriced tourist traps. SEE ALSO LITERATURE AND THEATRE, P.83

HIGHLIGHTS

The most important museum in the Latin Quarter is the **Musée National du Moyen Age** ②, a showcase for treasures from the Roman and medieval periods, and most

renowned for its spectacular *The Lady and the Unicorn* tapestry cycle. Further evidence of the city's Roman past can be seen on the rue Monge, site of the **Arènes de Lutèce**, an amphitheatre where gladiators once fought, though now a setting for summer concerts.

Other key sights include the **Panthéon** ③, where the great and the good of the French nation are buried for posterity, and architect Jean Nouvel's **Institut du Monde Arabe**, home to a collection of treasures from the Islamic Arab world. Nearby is the **Mosquée de Paris**. SEE ALSO CHURCHES, MOSQUES AND SYNAGOGUES, P.48

If the pace gets too much, take refuge in the **Jardin des Plantes** ④, formerly the royal botanic gardens, where plants were cultivated to soothe the royal health. The gardens are home to the **Muséum National d'Histoire Naturelle** and a bucolic zoo.

One of the best ways to enjoy this characterful area

Right: books for sale on the Left Bank.

Left: boulevard St-Germain des Prés.

Lagerfeld and Rykiel.

For a real sense of the charm of St-Germain explore the quaint little **place Fursten-berg**, where the painter **Eugène Delacroix's** studio can be visited. The artist moved here in 1857 when he began painting the murals in the church, **St-Sulpice**, close by.

South of St-Sulpice is the **Jardin du Luxembourg** ⑥, where children play with sand and float boats. There is also a gallery for major art exhibitions in the former **Orangerie**. SEE ALSO CHURCHES, MOSQUES AND SYNAGOGUES P.49; MUSEUMS AND GALLERIES, P.100; PARKS AND GARDENS, P.121

L'Odéon

In the side streets around the traffic-congested Odéon crossroads you can find many cinemas, some showing films all day and all night. Down one little street, rue de l'Ancienne Comédie, is **Le Procope** (at No. 13), which purports to be the oldest café in the city. Nearby is place de l'Odéon, dominated by the Neoclassical **Odéon – Théâtre de l'Europe** ⑦. SEE ALSO LITERATURE AND THEATRE, P.83

is simply to wander, taking pleasure in some of the oldest streets in Paris: **rue Mouffe-tard**, for example, notable for its food market. A second food market is held on place Maubert. Nearby is rue de Bièvre, where the late president Mitterrand lived. A stroll down to the river leads to the book sellers that line the *quais* back to place St-Michel. SEE ALSO ARCHITECTURE, P.33; FOOD AND DRINK, P.64; MUSEUMS AND GALLERIES, P.95, 101, 102; PARKS AND GARDENS, P.122

to fashion gurus Karl Lagerfeld and Sonia Rykiel. This is reflected in the local shops, where Armani, not Aristotle, is now the *lingua franca*.

The changing face of the *quartier* is the subject of heated debate, and in 1997 an association was formed to preserve its intellectual credibility. The group was led by *chanteuse* Juliette Gréco and also, rather ironically,

St-Germain

Adjacent to the Latin Quarter is **St-Germain**, at the heart of which is **St-Germain-des-Prés** ⑤, the oldest church in Paris. The surrounding streets were once the essence of café society, but the crowd has changed from poets Paul Verlaine and Arthur Rimbaud and writers Jean-Paul Sartre, Simone de Beauvoir and Albert Camus

Below: a literary café on the Left Bank.

The 7th

When the Parisian nobility moved out of the Marais in the 18th century, and Versailles tumbled, the rich and famous built new town houses across the river from the Tuileries, in the 7th *arrondissement*. Not only is this chic district rich in fine buildings and smart restaurants, but it also has a wealth of visitor attractions, including the Eiffel Tower, Musée d'Orsay, École Militaire and Invalides, Musée du Quai Branly and Musée Rodin. It is not all museums and mansions, however: the market on the convivial rue Cler is especially lively early in the morning, when the local stallholders and shopkeepers are in full voice.

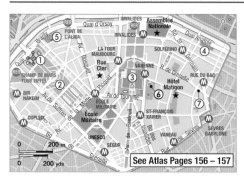

See Atlas Pages 156 – 157

Above: the dome of the Eglise du Dôme.

The Eiffel Tower ①

Dominating the skyline of the 7th is Gustave Eiffel's iron-constructed **Eiffel Tower**. When the structure was chosen as the centrepiece of the World Fair of 1889, the engineer claimed enthusiastically, 'France will be the only country with a 300-metre flagpole!'

His designs were initially met with a barrage of opposition, but the Parisian public loved the new tower, and only a few years later it was being lauded by writers and artists such as Apollinaire, Cocteau, Dufy and Utrillo. Surviving a proposal for its dismantling in 1909, when the placing of a radio transmitter at the top saved the day, the tower is now swarmed over by more than 6 million visitors a year.

Champs de Mars

Beneath the Eiffel Tower are the crowded gardens of the **Champs de Mars** ②, for centuries the site of a market garden supplying vegetables to Parisians. In 1752 however, Louis XV commissioned architect Ange-Jacques Gabriel to build a military college, the **Ecole Militaire**, intended to

> The return of Napoleon's body from St Helena came after seven years of negotiation with the British by Louis-Philippe, King of France. On 8 October 1840, 19 years after Napoleon's death, the coffin was exhumed and opened for two minutes before transport to France aboard the frigate La Belle Poule. Reputedly, the body was perfectly preserved.

help men of little means learn the art of soldiering. Napoleon Bonaparte completed the two-year course in just one, in 1784. The market gardens were turned into a military exercise ground, with capacity for 10,000 men.

The Invalides

To the east of the Champs de Mars is the **Hôtel des Invalides** ③, a masterpiece of French Classical architecture. The 17th-century buildings behind it were commissioned by Louis XIV to house and care for retired and wounded soldiers. The complex has also served as the royal arsenal, from which, in 1789, revolutionaries commandeered 30,000 rifles for the storming of the Bastille.

SEE ALSO MONUMENTS, P.86

Left: relaxing in the Eiffel Tower gardens.

Designed by architect Jean Nouvel and opened in 2006, it exhibits art from Africa, South America and the Pacific.

At the end of rue de Varenne, next to Les Invalides, is the Hôtel Biron, better known as the **Musée National Rodin** ⑥. The sculptor came to live in the mansion in 1908 and stayed until his death in 1917, paying his rent with sculptures. Not far away, on rue de Grenelle, is the Hôtel Bouchardon, where poet Alfred de Musset lived 1824–39. It is now the **Musée Maillol – Fondation Dina Vierny** ⑦, showcasing the works of Maillol alongside Cézanne, Degas and Matisse.
SEE ALSO MUSEUMS AND GALLERIES, P.92, 98, 103, 104

Napoleon, whose wars kept the hospital full, restored the institution to its former glory, making the church, the **Eglise du Dôme**, a necropolis for his own tomb and regilding its dome.

Spread across either side of the cour d'Honneur is the **Musée de l'Armée**. In a separate wing, the **Musée de l'Ordre de la Libération** commemorates the Resistance fighters who received the Order of Liberation, France's highest honour, created by Charles de Gaulle in 1940.

Stretching down to the Seine, the grassy Esplanade des Invalides is used by strollers, joggers, dog walkers and rollerbladers. Just to the west, on the river front by the Pont de la Concorde, is the colonnaded **Assemblée Nationale**, the parliament.
SEE ALSO ARCHITECTURE, P.30; CHURCHES, MOSQUES AND SYNAGOGUES, P.49; MUSEUMS AND GALLERIES, P.96

Museums

The 7th possesses several world-class museums. On the riverfront to the east of the *quartier* is the **Musée d'Orsay** ④. Formerly a railway station, it has now been converted to house the French national collection of art from 1848 to 1914. Also on the river front, but this time to the west, is Paris's newest museum, the **Musée du Quai Branly** ⑤.

Below: the Musée du Quai Branly was Jacques Chirac's *grand projet*.

Other Attractions

The backstreets of the 7th are worth exploring; many have beautifully preserved mansions, often housing ministries and embassies. The most famous is the residence of the French prime minister, **Hôtel Matignon**. This house has the largest private garden in the city. Another street worth investigating is rue Cler, with its tumultuous food market.

Montparnasse and Beyond

This once-hilly area was christened Mount Parnassus (after the home of Apollo and his muses) by a local poetry society during the 17th century. In the 20th century, between the wars, it was populated by revolutionaries and artists, who decamped from Montmartre due to the latter's inflated rents. Their legacy lives on, amid the modern tower blocks, in a thriving bar and café culture. Further east is the 13th, home to the villagey Buttes-aux-Cailles quarter, Chinatown and the regenerated 'New Left Bank'. The last has its own 'Latin Quarter', housing 30,000 students on a new campus centred around the rehabilitated Grands Moulins de Paris.

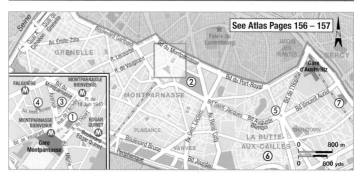

See Atlas Pages 156 – 157

Montparnasse

It was not until the 20th century that this once-rural area southwest of the Jardin du Luxembourg made its mark on Parisian history. In the 1920s it became a magnet for artists, composers and revolutionaries, who rented studios in the newly built-up area, and gathered in cafés and brasseries such as Le Select, Le Dôme, La Rotonde and La Coupole, situated around the lively Carrefour Vavin, now place Pablo Picasso.

After World War II, writers and philosophers such as Jean-Paul Sartre, Simone de Beauvoir and Louis Aragon moved in, patronising the same spots. Their legacy is safe in the thriving local cafés.
SEE ALSO CAFÉS AND BARS, P.39; RESTAURANTS, P.139

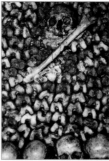

MAIN SIGHTS

Dominating the district's skyline is the 59-storey **Tour Montparnasse** ①. The building is lumbering and rather ugly, but there are wonderful views of Paris from the top (accessible by lift).

On boulevard Edgar Quinet, which has good cafés

Left: gruesome remains in the catacombes.

and a lively morning market on Wednesday and Saturday, is the **Cimetière du Montparnasse** ②. Among those buried here are the sculptor Bourdelle, composer Saint-Saëns and writers Baudelaire, Maupassant, Sartre and the Irish writer Samuel Beckett, who spent many years in Paris.

If you're still in macabre mood after a walk through the graveyard, pay a visit to the **catacombes**, below place Denfert-Rochereau.
SEE ALSO ARCHITECTURE, P.33

MUSEUMS

Most of the museums in Montparnasse focus on aspects of the area's artistic heritage. These include the

Left: colourful mural in Montparnasse.

bars. The hub of activity is around the cobbled rue de la Butte-aux-Cailles and rue des Cinq-Diamants.

CHINATOWN

Close by, roughly bordered by avenue d'Italie and avenue d'Ivry, is Chinatown. The area is a mini-city of skyscrapers and streets lined with kitsch gift shops, Thai groceries, Vietnamese noodle bars and Chinese tearooms.

'NEW LEFT BANK'

The 'new' Rive Gauche, formerly characterised by disused factories, runs south along the river from the Gare d'Austerlitz. The area's architectural centrepiece is the **Bibliothèque Nationale de France, François Mitterrand** ⑦, designed by Dominique Perrault and opened in 1997. Its 90-m high glass towers are meant to evoke four open books. This, and the extension of the metro, have sparked regeneration, with art galleries, upmarket cafés, restaurants and boutiques all moving in.

The existing side streets have been extended to the banks of the Seine, and the river banks have been landscaped to create Paris's hottest new nightlife area, with a flotilla of barges, where you can eat, drink and dance. Another popular evening attracton is the sweeping MK2 Bibliothèque multiplex cinema.
SEE ALSO ARCHITECTURE, P.30; CINEMA, P.51

Musée de Montparnasse ③, the **Musée Zadkine** ④ and the **Musée Bourdelle** ⑤.
SEE ALSO MUSEUMS AND GALLERIES, P.97, 99, 105

The 13th

Place d'Italie is one of the main traffic hubs of the 13th *arrondissement*, a neighbourhood where historic districts alternate with soulless tower blocks thrown up in the 1960s. Les Gobelins is the oldest part of the neighbourhood. Traces of a Gallo-Roman necropolis were discovered here last century, as well as the tomb of the

Behind the Tour Montparnasse is the Gare Montparnasse, serving northwestern France. In the mid-19th century thousands arrived at this station from Brittany, fleeing rural poverty and famine, hence the many Breton *crêperies* in the area today.

On boulevard Raspail stands Rodin's *Statue de Balzac*. The sculpture so shocked the Société des Beaux-Arts when unveiled at the 1898 Salon that it was turned down, and only finally cast and installed here in 1939.

first archbishop of Paris, St Marcel. The district owes its name to the **Manufacture Nationale des Gobelins** (42 avenue des Gobelins), a tapestry factory founded in 1662. Today visitors can still watch weavers at work here.

LA BUTTE-AUX-CAILLES

Just south of place d'Italie, still in the 13th, is the tranquil *quartier* of **La Butte-aux-Cailles** ⑥. Until the 20th century, the hill was covered with working wind and water mills. The narrow, cobbled streets of this traditional workers' neighbourhood offer some of Paris's friendliest, cheapest

In the New Left Bank, rue Louise-Weiss is the focus of a small gallery scene, where, in an unusual display of solidarity, the galleries have synchronised openings.

Outside the Périphérique

Just on the outer side of the Parisian ring road, the famously traffic-clogged Périphérique, are, to the northwest, the business park at La Défense, dominated by Johann-Otto van Spreckelsen's Grande Arche, and, to the west of the city, Paris's largest green space: the Bois de Boulogne. A little further afield, but still on the metro or RER lines, are Louis XIV's lavish palace at Versailles and Joséphine's chic imperial residence at Malmaison. Further afield still (but accessible by rail) are Henri II's château at Fontainebleau, the palace and racecourse at Chantilly, the palace of Vaux-le-Vicomte, and the water-lily pond that inspired Claude Monet.

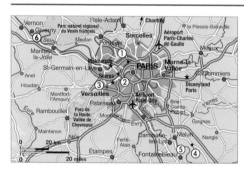

Just 32km (20 miles) east of Paris is Disney's ambitious and hugely popular theme park. Hosts Mickey and Minnie Mouse, Goofy, Donald Duck and Pluto wander around in their familiar costumes, posing with visitors (*see also Children, p.43*).

Just Outside the Périphérique

LA DÉFENSE ①

West of the city, at the end of the metro line, is the sky-scraping business district of **La Défense**. The area is named after the bronze sculpture by Louis-Ernest Barrias (1841–1905) that was erected on the square here in 1883 to commemorate the defence of Paris against the Prussian Army in 1870. Nowadays, approximately 150,000 people work in the district, and more than 20,000 people live here.

The area's focal point is Danish architect Johann-Otto von Spreckelsen's **Grande Arche**, a hollow cube so huge that it could straddle the Champs-Elysées and tuck Notre-Dame underneath it. The two 'legs' contain

Above: the modern cityscape of La Défense.

offices, while the roof houses conference rooms and exhibition spaces. Bubble lifts whisk you up through a fibre-glass-and-Teflon 'cloud', held by steel cables.
SEE ALSO ARCHITECTURE, P.32

BOIS DE BOULOGNE ②

In western Paris, butting up against the upmarket 16th *arrondissement*, is the capital's biggest park: 900 hectare (2,224 acres) of grassland, lakes and woods. Within the park is a museum, boating lake, an amusement park with attractions for children and two racecourses.
SEE ALSO CHILDREN, P.41; PARKS AND GARDENS, P.120

Versailles and Malmaison

If time is limited, but you want to explore just outside the city centre, a trip to **Versailles** ③ is an obvious first choice. The palace, the third most popular tourist attraction in France, is 23km southwest of Paris, and can be reached via RER line C5.

Another short hop, and an excellent option for a half-day trip, is the palace at **Malmaison**. Only 15km (9 miles) southwest of the city, en route to St-Germain-en-

Left: Monet's lily pond at Giverny inspired his painting.

Nicolas Fouquet. It is especially notable for André Le Nôtre's beautiful garden *à la française*, the first in this style.

The town of Fontainebleau, 15km (9 miles) from Vaux-le-Vicomte, is dominated by the first purpose-built royal château, residence of French sovereigns from François I to Napoleon III. Each ruler added something, creating a mixture of styles, but Napoleon I outdid them all by building an ornate throne room.
SEE ALSO PALACES, P.114

GIVERNY ⑥
A visit to the small village house where painter Claude Monet lived and worked for 43 years until his death, in 1926 aged 86, requires a full day. Set on a hill side above the Seine, the house (now the **Fondation Claude Monet**) is decorated in the colours favoured by the father of Impressionism. The highlight of a trip, however, is the garden, including the Japanese bridge and the water lilies on the pond that inspired so many of Monet's paintings.

Laye, the palace was the favourite home of Napoleon Bonaparte's first wife, Joséphine, and where she lived after their divorce.
SEE ALSO PALACES, P.115, 116

Other Day Trips

Options for days out include trips to other *châteaux* within the Ile-de-France region, a visit to Giverny, erstwhile home of Impressionist painter Claude Monet, and, if you have children, Disneyland, which attracts over 12 million visitors per year.

CHANTILLY
Roughly 50km (30 miles) north of Paris, Chantilly is famous for horse racing, but also offers a sumptuous palace, a magnificent park created by André Le Nôtre and the splendid 18th-century, palatial Grandes Ecuries, stables built by Prince Louis-Henri de Bourbon, who believed that he would be reincarnated as a

horse. **Vaux-le-Vicomte** ④ **and Fontainebleau** ⑤
The 17th-century *château* of Vaux-le-Vicomte and the palace at Fontainebleau make a good day trip combined, as the former is en route to the latter. Vaux, which is around 40km (25 miles) south-east of Paris and accessible by train, then a short taxi ride, was built by Louis XIV's royal treasurer,

Below: Versailles' stunning painted ceilings.

Architecture

Paris is one of the world's most centrally planned cities, moulding a variety of styles, from Gothic to Modernist, into a harmonious whole. Although invasions, sieges and insurrections have destroyed a number of the capital's early masterpieces, the contributions of architects and town planners including Pierre de Montreuil, Jules Hardouin-Mansart, Baron Georges-Eugène Haussmann, Ange-Jacques Gabriel, Hector Guimard, Le Corbusier and I.M. Pei continue to draw admirers. Included in this section are buildings of architectural value that do not easily fit into the other classifications in this book.

Assemblée Nationale – Palais Bourbon

33 bis quai d'Orsay, The 7th; tel: 01 40 63 60 00; www.assemblee-nationale.fr; visits on Sat at 10am, 2pm, 3pm, closed during sessions, proof of identity required; free; metro: Assemblée Nationale; map p.151 E1

The riverfront Assemblée Nationale is the Lower House of the French Parliament, workplace of the 491 *députés* (Members of Parliament). The neo-Grecian columns facing the river were grafted on to the earlier 18th-century palace by Napoleon to complement the **Eglise de la Madeleine** across the river.
SEE ALSO CHURCHES, MOSQUES AND SYNAGOGUES, P.46

Bibliothèque Nationale de France

François Mitterand

10 quai François Mitterrand, 13th; tel: 01 53 79 59 59; www.bnf.fr; Mon 2–7pm, Tue–Sat 9am–7pm, Sun 1–7pm; admission charge; metro: Bibliothèque François Mitterrand

The last of François Mitterrand's *grands projets (see*

Above: Baron Haussmann.

box, above right) was designed by Dominique Perrault and opened in 1997. The library cost over €1 billion to build and is more expensive to maintain than the Louvre. Its 90-m high glass towers evoke open books.

Together, the two national library buildings *(see also Bibliothèque Nationale Richelieu, below)* house a copy of every book published in France since 1500, with the bulk of the collection archived here. The library's book collection is one of the biggest in the world and includes Charlemagne's illuminated Bible and original

manuscripts of François Villon, François Rabelais, Victor Hugo and Marcel Proust.

Richelieu

58 rue Richelieu, 2nd; tel: 01 53 79 53 79; www.bnf.fr; Cabinet des Médailles Mon–Fri 1–5.45pm, Sat 1–4.45pm; free; metro: Bourse; map p.152 B1

The original national library building, tucked away behind the Palais Royal, the Richelieu houses dedicated departments for drawings, maps, music and manuscripts. The main reading room, designed by Henri Labrouste in 1863, is an architectural masterpiece. Downstairs, the permanent museum, the **Musée du Cabinet des Médailles**, contains *objets d'art* from the royal collections that were seized during the Revolution.

The Conciergerie

2 boulevard du Palais, 1st; tel: 01 53 40 60 97; www.monum.fr; Mar–Oct: daily 9.30am–6pm, Nov–Feb: 9am–5pm; admission charge; metro: Cité; map p.154 B3

The Conciergerie, part of the Palais de la Cité with the

Left: outside the Louvre's pyramid.

President François Mitterrand (1981–95) made his mark on the Paris skyline with a series of imposing works (his *grands projets*): the Louvre pyramid, the Grande Arche at La Défense, the Opéra-Bastille, the Institut du Monde Arabe and the national library that bears his name.

Fondation Le Corbusier

8–10 square du Docteur Blanche, 16th; tel: 01 42 88 41 53; www.fondationlecorbusier. asso.fr; Mon 1.30–6pm, Tue–Fri 10am–12.30pm and 1.30–6pm (Fri until 5pm), Sat 10am–5pm; admission charge; metro: Jasmin

Palais de Justice law courts and the architecturally breathtaking **Sainte-Chapelle**, looks like an intimidating castle, its towers rising imposingly above impenetrable walls. It was built as a palace, but when Charles V moved to the Hôtel Saint-Pol, it was used to accommodate Comte des Cierges, hence the name.

The *comte* was in charge of the king's lodgings and taxes, until the Conciergerie became a prison in the 14th century, when his job changed to that of chief gaoler. SEE ALSO CHURCHES, MOSQUES AND SYNAGOGUES, P.45

The Revolution

The Capetian palace came into its own during the Revolution, when it housed nearly 2,600 prisoners (including Marie-Antoinette), awaiting the guillotine. Ironically, the queen's prosecutor, Danton, also resided here before he met the guillotine, as did his nemesis Robespierre. In the merry-go-round of retribution, 1,306 heads rolled in one month at place de la Nation (now place de la Concorde).

KEY SIGHTS

The tower at the back is called Bonbec ('the squealer'), for it was here, from the 11th century, that torture victims told all. At the front is the 14th-century clock tower housing the first public clock in Paris, still ticking today. Inside, the original kitchens are still intact. They were built to feed up to 3,000 people using four huge fireplaces and have a Gothic canopied ceiling supported by buttresses. The adjacent Salles des Gens d'Armes is a vast four-aisled Gothic hall where the royal guards, or men-at-arms, used to live.

Although Le Corbusier (1887–1965) developed his brand of Modernism in the interests of providing better living conditions for residents of crowded cities, he has been heavily criticised for inspiring the building of soulless tower blocks surrounded by featureless wasteland in cities across the world.

However, the two adjoining houses that make up the Fondation show how elegant and light his buildings could be. They contain an exhibition space for his drawings, architectural plans, furniture and

Below: the kitchen hall in the Conciergerie.

Left: the Grande Arche.

elaborate Neo-Renaissance building, with its splendid Mansard roof, carved façade and statues, was rebuilt after the original 17th-century town hall was destroyed by fire during the 1871 Commune. The most notable features inside are the majestic Salle des Fêtes, a magnificent staircase and numerous chandeliers, providing a fitting backdrop for the city's governing powers.

Palais de Chaillot

Place du Trocadéro, 16th; *see Cité de l'Architecture*; metro: Trocadéro; map p.150 A1–B1

Dominating place du Trocadéro is the Palais de Chaillot, built for the 1937 World Fair. The imposing Art Deco palace was designed by architects Boileau, Carlu and Azema in the shape of an amphitheatre, with its wings following the original outline of the old Trocadéro palace in graceful symmetry. The buildings are decorated with quotations by the poet Paul Valéry.

The building holds three museums (the **Musée National de la Marine** and **Musée de l'Homme** in the west wing and the **Cité de l'Architecture**, *see below*, in the east wing) and the **Théâtre National de Chaillot**. Following restoration, all of the above have now reopened, except the Musée de l'Homme (closed until 2012).

SEE ALSO LITERATURE AND THEATRE, P.83; MUSEUMS AND GALLERIES, P.102

Cité de l'Architecture et du Patrimoine

Tel: 01 53 58 51 52 00; www.citechaillot.fr; Mon, Wed–Sun 11am–7pm, Thur until 9pm; admission charge; map p.150 B1

paintings (reminiscent of Pablo Picasso), as well as a library, and his archives of written and photographic material.

It is also possible to visit the apartment occupied by Le Corbusier 1933–65 in the nearby Immeuble Molitor (24 rue Nungesser et Coli, 16th; Wed 9am–noon, Sat 2–5pm).

Grande Arche

1 parvis de la Défense; tel: 01 49 07 27 57; www.grande arche.com; Apr–Aug: daily 10am–8pm, Sept–Mar: daily 10am–7pm; admission charge; metro: La Défense

Rounding off the western end of the Louvre–Arc de Triomphe–La Défense royal axis is this monumental marble gate. Designed by Danish architect Johann-Otto van Spreckelsen, who died two years before it was completed, the arch measures 110m high (360 ft) and 106m (348 ft) wide. It is given over to office space, but for tourists there are two glass 'bubbles' that zoom up to the roof; the lifts even cut through the 'cloud', a canvas net designed to reduce wind resistance.

Hôtel de Ville

29 rue de Rivoli, 4th; tel: 01 42 76 43 43; www.paris.fr; Mon–Sat 10am–7pm; free; metro: Hôtel de Ville; map p.155 C3

In medieval times, the square on which this ornate city council building stands was the site of hangings and macabre executions. The

The giant forecourt of La Défense is something of an open-air art museum, with works by Miró, Calder, Utshori, and an imposing bronze thumb by César.

Opened in 2007, this institute is now the world's largest architecture centre. It combines the city's original architecture museum with the Institut Français d'Architecture and serves as both a public museum and a research centre for professionals.

The Panthéon

Place du Panthéon, 5th; tel: 01 44 32 18 00; www.monuments-nationaux.fr; Apr–Sept: daily 10am–6.30pm, Oct–Mar: daily 10am–6pm; admission charge; metro: Cardinal Lemoine; map p.154 C1

The domed Panthéon stands on the small rise of the ancient Mons Luticius, consecrated to the patron saint of Paris, Ste Geneviève, in the Middle Ages. In 1756 the foundation stone for an ambitious new building, modelled on St Peter's in Rome, was laid. Architect Jacques-Germain Soufflot died 10 years before its completion in 1791.

Almost as soon as the building was finished, the revolutionary authorities decided to make the church a last resting place for national heroes. Voltaire's remains were moved to the crypt that same year. The honour has since been granted to, among others, Jean-Jacques Rousseau, Victor Hugo, Emile Zola, and Pierre and Marie Curie.

In addition to viewing the tombs, visitors can see **Foucault's Pendulum**, which hangs from the centre of the dome, and frescoes by 19th-century symbolist painter Puvis de Chavanne.

Pyramide du Louvre

Palais du Louvre, Cour Napoléon, 1st; metro: Palais Royal-Musée du Louvre; map p.154 B4

Probably the most controversial of François Mitterrand's

> Contrary to popular myth, the pyramid's steel structure does not contain the satanic number of 666 panes of glass, but rather 673 segments (603 rhombus-shaped and 70 triangular).

grands projets, this structure in the courtyard of the Louvre provides an entrance for the multitude of visitors, plus light and ventilation for the lower-ground level of the museum.

Despite these practical advantages and the pyramid's popularity in many quarters, the structure still has its critics, who fulminate against Sino-American architect I.M. Pei's uncompromising design set in this historically sensitive context.

SEE ALSO MUSEUMS AND GALLERIES, P.88

Tour Montparnasse

33 avenue du Maine; tel: 01 45 38 52 56; www.tourmontparnasse56.com; Apr–Sept: daily 9.30am–11.30pm, Oct–Mar: Sun–Thur 9.30am–10.30pm, Fri and Sat 9.30am–11pm, last lift 30 mins before closing; admission charge; metro: Montparnasse; map p.157 E1

Dominating the skyline south of St-Germain is the Tour Montparnasse. When built (1969–72), it was the tallest building in Europe at 210m (689ft). However, it was heavily criticised for not relating to its context, and, two years after its construction, new skyscrapers were prohibited in the city centre. The tower is mostly used as office space, but visitors can go up to a viewing platform at the top.

In 1995, instead of taking the lift, a Frenchman, Alain 'Spiderman' Robert, scaled the building's exterior using only his bare hands and feet and without any safety equipment. Not advisable.

Unesco

7 place de Fontenoy, 7th; tel: 01 45 68 10 10; www.unesco.org; Mon–Fri 9.30am–5.30pm; tours Mon–Fri 3pm, in English on Tue; free; metro: Ecole Militaire, Ségur; map p.157 C3

On the south side of place de Fontenoy is the Y-shaped Unesco building (1958), designed by American architect Marcel Breuer, Frenchman Bernhard Zehrfuss and Italian Pier Luigi Nervi. Artists including Picasso, Arp and Miró were commissioned to produce works for the interior. A more recent addition is the minimalist Japanese Garden by architect Tadao Ando.

Below: the Panthéon's sculptural and scientific heritage; Foucault's Pendulum still hangs from the ceiling.

Cafés and Bars

In a city where wine is often cheaper than bottled water, and the local café is regarded as a home from home, forum for discussion or even as an office, there is plenty of choice of places in which to drink and snack. There is some cross-over here with other chapters: '*Restaurants, p.126–39*' covers places that focus on food, while bars that also run regular music nights are included in either '*Nightlife, p.110–13*' or '*Music, p.106–9*', (the former for dance bars; the latter for jazz clubs). Otherwise, look below for classic cafés, wine and cocktail bars, genteel tearooms, historic literary haunts and more.

The Islands

Berthillon
29–31 rue St-Louis-en-l'Île, 4th; tel: 01 43 54 31 61; www.berthillon-glacier.fr; Wed–Sun 10am–8pm; metro: Pont Marie; map p.155 D2
Sample the frosty delights of this legendary ice-cream maker, on the lovely Ile St-Louis. The tearoom and shop are adjacent.

Louvre, Tuileries and Concorde

Angelina's
226 rue de Rivoli, 1st; tel: 01 42 60 82 00; Mon–Fri 8am–7pm, Sat and Sun 9am– 7pm; metro: Tuileries; map p.154 B3–4
Famed Parisian tearoom that is also good for lunch. Serves great squishy meringues and African hot chocolate.

Bar du Crillon
Hôtel de Crillon, 16 rue Boissy d'Anglas, 8th; tel: 01 44 71 15 39; Mon–Sat 11am–2am; metro: Concorde; map p.151 E2
This is where Ernest Hemingway drank, when he had the money. The turn-of-the-20th-century décor has been given a designer facelift by Sonia Rykiel. No admittance wear-

Above: inside the Louvre's Café Marly.

ing jeans or trainers.
SEE ALSO HOTELS, P.71

Café Marly
Palais du Louvre, 93 rue de Rivoli, 1st; tel: 01 49 26 06 60; daily 8am–2am; metro: Palais Royal Musée du Louvre; map p.154 B4
Rest from your labours at the Louvre in the Marly's lavish, utterly chic Second Empire-style rooms or covered terrace facing the Pyramid. Nice for breakfast.
SEE ALSO MUSEUMS AND GALLERIES, P.88

Le Fumoir
6 rue de l'Amiral-de-Coligny, 1st; tel: 01 42 92 00 24; www.lefumoir.fr; daily 11am–2am;

metro: Louvre Rivoli; map p.154 B3–4
This 'smoking room' feels more like a club than a bar. Regulars sit in plush leather chairs sipping rum-based Cuban mojitos, while perusing something from the 3,000-plus books in the library or newspaper racks.

Juvénile's
47 rue de Richelieu, 1st; tel: 01 42 97 46 49; Mon 4–11pm, Tue noon–11pm; metro: Palais Royal Musée du Louvre; map p.152 B1
Friendly wine bar owned by a Scot who serves tapas-style dishes with a wide selection of reasonably priced wine, sherry and – of course – Scotch malt whisky.

Le Rubis
10 rue du Marché St-Honoré, 1st; tel: 01 42 61 03 34; Mon–Fri noon–10.30pm, Sat noon–4pm, closed Aug; metro: Tuileries; map p.152 A1
This is the place to be when the Beaujolais Nouveau comes out in November. At other times of the year, it is a pleasant place for lunch with a glass of excellent wine. Popular *plats du jour* include

Left: classic Parisian zinc-topped bar.

01 40 39 07 36; Mon–Fri 8am–2am, Sat 4pm–2am; metro: Sentier; map p.152 B1
This bustling corner café, decorated with kitsch paraphernalia, is typically crammed with an eclectic mix of people. A great place for a cheap beer and a natter.

Harry's New York Bar
5 rue Daunou, 2nd; tel: 01 42 61 71 14; www.harrys-bar.fr; daily 10.30–4am; metro: Opéra; map p.152 A1
A Parisian landmark, said to have been the birthplace of the Bloody Mary. Writer F. Scott Fitzgerald was a regular in the 1920s. Still popular today, it attracts plenty of interesting characters.

Beaubourg and Les Halles

Café Beaubourg
25 rue Quincampoix, 4th; tel: 01 42 77 48 02; Mon–Fri 8am–1am, Sat–Sun 8am–2am; metro: Rambuteau, Hôtel de Ville; map p.155 C4
Designer café opposite the Centre Pompidou. Ideal for a light bite and people-watching. Gaze out from the terrace on to the Pompidou forecourt or turn your gaze inward, to the café's habitués.

Café des Initiés
3 place des Deux-Ecus, 1st; tel: 01 42 33 78 29; www.lecafedes inities.com; Mon–Fri 7.30am–

> For a proper cup of tea in Paris, go to a tearoom, where, especially in the Asian salons, it is virtually an art form. By contrast, tea is almost always a disappointment in cafés, where a pot of hot water and tea bag on the side costs a fortune.

classic dishes such as bœuf bourguignon and lentils with salt pork.

Willi's Wine Bar
13 rue des Petits-Champs, 1st; tel: 01 42 61 05 09; www.willis winebar.com; Mon–Sat noon–11pm; metro: Pyramides; map p.152 B1
Chic bar attracting a mixed business and fashion crowd. Wonderful selection of French wines, mainly from the Rhône Valley.

Opéra and Grands Boulevards

A Priori
35–7 Galerie Vivienne, 2nd; tel: 01 42 97 48 75; Mon–Fri 9am–6pm, Sat 9am–6.30pm, Sun noon–6.30pm; metro: Bourse; map p.152 B1
Froufrou tearoom in a beautiful arcade away from the

hubbub of the city at large. Tea and large home-made cakes recommended.
SEE ALSO SHOPPING, P.141

Café Jacquemart-André
158 boulevard Haussmann, 8th; tel: 01 45 62 04 44; daily 11.45am–5.30pm; metro: Miromesnil; map p.151 D3
The sumptuous café in the Musée Jacquemart-André pulls in local residents as well as museum-goers. While waiting for your lunch salad (smoked salmon, breast of duck, etc) to arrive, look up and admire the *trompe l'œil* ceiling by Tiepolo.
SEE ALSO MUSEUMS AND GALLERIES, P.98

Le Café Noir
65 rue Montmartre, 2nd; tel:

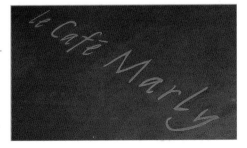

Left: a mouthwatering selection of *pâtisserie*.

salads and light dishes, and some nice wines at the bar. Come on your own and read a book – plenty of people do.

Au P'tit Garage

63 rue Jean-Pierre-Timbaud, 11th; tel: 01 48 07 08 12; daily 6pm–2am; metro: Parmentier; map p.155 E4

Rue Jean-Pierre-Timbaud is bar-hopping heaven – the whole street is a string of (largely good) drinking dens. This one is possibly the best: a jumble of junk-shop furniture, cool crowd, nice cheap drinks and good music.

Bar à Nénette

26 rue de Lappe, 11th; tel: 01 48 07 08 18; www.lebaranenette. com; daily 5pm–2am; metro: Bastille; map p.155 E2

Rue de Lappe is another street full of bars, and there's never a shortage of people lurching along it come sundown. Nénette has a happy hour until 10pm, plates of sausages or cheese, and a friendly clientele.

La Belle Hortense

31 rue Vieille-du-Temple, 4th; tel: 01 48 04 71 60; www.cafeine. com; daily 5pm–2am; metro: Hôtel de Ville; map p.155 C3

This gorgeous little place right in the heart of the Marais combines a wine bar with a book shop. Heaven for bohemian bookworms.

Bistrot à Vins Mélac

42 rue Léon-Frot, 11th; tel: 01 43 70 59 27; www.melac.fr; Tue–Sat noon–midnight; metro: Bastille; map p.155 D2

This wine bar-cum-wine shop-cum-'vineyard' (there are a few vines on the exterior wall), just west of place de la Bastille, is crowded with workers at lunchtime. The food is mostly cheese and specialities from the Auvergne region.

2am, Sat–Sun 9am–2am; metro: Les Halles; map p.154 B4

Crumbling old corner café turned trendy hangout, this fashionable drinks purveyor has ergonomic red-bench seating, a long zinc bar, swish black lamps and elegant flower arrangements in glass vases. Friendly, too.

Le Tambour

41 rue Montmartre, 2nd; tel: 01 42 33 06 90; Tue–Sat noon–6am, Sun–Mon 6pm–6am; metro: Sentier; map p.152 B1

There is nowhere else in Paris quite like this all-night bar. Inside it looks like a junk shop, its décor a melding of all manner of old metro signs, stray statues, old books and even older customers (there are lots of students, too). The moustachioed owner is usually on hand, swapping animated bar-room philosophies with the regulars. Priceless.

Marais and Bastille

L'Abreuvoir

103 rue Oberkampf, 11th; tel: 01 43 38 87 01; Mon–Sat 5pm–2am; metro: Oberkampf; map p.155 E4

The 'watering trough' is one of the relatively quiet gems on the Oberkampf scene. Candlelit tables, a bar decorated with rock 'n' roll posters and knick-knacks, and a range of unusual beer-based cocktails (including *Casse-Tête*, which is beer, rum and peach liqueur) make it a good place to spend a few hours.

L'Apparrement Café

18 rue des Coutuers-St-Gervais, 3rd; tel: 01 48 87 12 22; Mon–Sat noon–2am, Sun noon– midnight; metro: St-Sébastien Froissart; map p.155 D3

This relaxed spot – distressed armchairs, jazz soundtrack, a low hubbub of conversation – feels like someone's artfully bohemian flat, which is precisely the intention. There are

Drinks prices often vary in a café: they're cheapest at the bar, more at a table and even more sitting outside. There may be a further increase, generally about 50 cents, after 10pm.

Café Charbon
109 rue Oberkampf, 11th; tel: 01 43 57 55 13; Mon–Thur and Sun 9am–2am, Fri and Sat 9am–4am; metro: Parmentier; map p.155 E4

This former coal (charbon) shop with its fin-de-siècle atmosphere – lofty ceilings, ornate mirrors and red-leather sofas – is a fixture of east Paris café culture.

Le Café du Passage
12 rue de Charonne, 11th; tel: 01 49 29 97 64; Mon–Fri, Sun 6pm–2am, Sat noon–6pm; metro: Bastille; map p.155 E2

A comfortable spot that's good to drop into if you want a bite to eat. Food ranges from risotto to andouillette à la crème (tripe sausages in cream), and the wine selection is reliable: there are around 400 bottles from the Côtes du Rhône alone. Excellent malts, too.

Les Couleurs
117 rue St-Maur, 11th; tel : 01 43 57 95 61; daily 9am–2am; metro: Parmentier; map p.155 E4

Arty hangout near Oberkampf, where kitsch meets distressed chic (tacky mural, bare brick, bare light-bulbs) and potent cocktails.

Le Loir dans la Théière
3 rue des Rosiers, 4th; tel: 01 42 72 90 61; Mon–Fri 11.30am–7pm, Sat–Sun 10am–7pm; metro: St-Paul; map p.155 D3

Tea, cake, comfy sofas and armchairs, and a friendly, relaxed ambience. Little wonder the place is always full.

La Perle
78 rue Vielle-du-Temple, 3rd; tel: 01 42 72 69 93; daily 8am–

2am; metro: Hôtel de Ville; map p.155 C3

This is a straightforward and non-exclusive neighbourhood café, and none-the-worse for that, which serves good salads and omlettes. DJs often play in the evenings.

Rosso
4b is rue Neuve-Popincourt, 11th; tel: 01 49 29 06 36; ww.lerosso.com; Tue–Sun 6pm–2am; metro: Parmentier; map p.155 E4

The arty Rosso is a newish bar, a sister operation to Le Zéro Zéro (89 rue Amelot, tel: 01 49 23 51 00), a short distance away. The bar's eponymous cocktail is vodka, triple sec and framboise; there are also daiquiris of various flavours and a handful of beers.

Stolly's
16 rue Cloche-Perce, 4th; tel: 01 42 76 06 76; daily 4.30pm–2am; metro: St-Paul; map p.155 D3

Happy hour at this established Anglo bar is a good way to start a night out in the Marais. Choose between the cramped interior or the small terrace for, surprisingly, a steady party vibe.

Champs-Elysées, Trocadéro and West

Bar du Plaza
Hôtel Plaza Athénée, 25 avenue Montaigne, 8th; tel: 01 53 67 66 65; www.plaza-athenee-paris.com; daily 6pm–2am; metro: Alma Marceau; map p.151 C2

Come here for the chic designer interior and off-the-wall cocktails, and mix with the fashion-forward Gucci- and Prada-clad crowd.

Café Le Nôtre
Pavillon Elysée Carré Marigny, 10 avenue des Champs-Elysées, 8th; tel: 01 42 65 85 10; Mon–Sat noon–midnight, Sun noon–4pm; metro: Champs-Elysées-Clemenceau; map p.151 D2

This pretty, wedding cake-style pavilion in the gardens of the Champs-Elysées offers everything from breakfast to lunch, dinner, tea and snacks. Famous for its pastries.

Culture Bière
65 avenue des Champs-Elysées, 8th; tel: 01 42 56 88 88; www.culturebiere.com; daily nonstop; metro: George V, Franklin D. Roosevelt; map p.151 C2–3

It is an unusual pitch – a 'beer

Below: leftish reading matter in Montmartre.

37

bar' on the increasingly glitzy Champs-Elysées – but this innovative boutique-lounge-gallery-restaurant concept from Heineken is pretty sleek itself, and good value with it. Try the beer sorbet or the *crêpes* topped with *confit de bière*. Alternatively, just have one of the dozens of beers.

The Honest Lawyer

176 rue de la Pompe, 16th; tel: 01 45 05 14 23; http://honest-lawyer.com; daily 8am–midnight; metro: Rue de la Pompe; map p.150 A2

A short walk from place Victor Hugo, this yuppie pub has three televisions and reasonably priced pub grub. A convivial jazz brunch is served on Sundays.

Montmartre and Pigalle

Dok's Café

46 rue Lamartine, 9th; tel: 01 53 16 32 49; Mon–Fri 8.30am–8.30pm, Sat 9.30am–8.30pm; metro: Cadet; map p.152 B3

Dok's, in the Montmartre foothills, describes itself as a 'contemporary *salon de thé*', for which read relaxed lounge

Below: *un café*.

How do you like your coffee? Ask for *serré* if you prefer your coffee more concentrated, and *allongé* if you like a 'longer' more American-style drink. For decaffeinated coffee, ask for *déca*.

Right: café life in Montmartre.

with a handsome selection of coffees and, especially, teas. The menu includes dishes such as *pomme d'amour*, which contains caramelised apple and maraschino cherry. They don't serve alcohol, but they do serve cakes and tarts.

La Fourmi

74 rue des Martyrs, 18th; tel: 01 42 64 70 35; Mon–Thur 8.30am–2am, Fri–Sat 8.30–4am, Sun 10am–2am; metro: Abbesses; map p.152 B4

This retro-industrial bar was once a bistro, but has now been given a modish modern makeover. The big windows pour light into the sand-coloured interior, and the attractive zinc counter is lit by industrial lamps. They play good music, and the piles of flyers for local gigs and club nights make it a good source of nightlife tips.

Le Sancerre

35 rue des Abbesses, 18th; tel: 01 42 58 08 20; daily nonstop; metro: Abbesses; map p.152 B4

Le Sancerre is one of the cornerstones of the Montmartre bar scene. The terrace is always packed, the music (sometimes live) always loud, the crowd largely young and hip. There is a good choice of beers and standard cocktails; food-wise, choose from decent salads and a variety of daily specials.

Xtremes Bar

10 rue Caumartin, 9th; tel: 01 44 94 05 64; daily till 2am; metro: Haussmann-St-Lazare; map p.152 A2

This place has something for everyone, with a lounge and chill-out music on the top floor, and live sports broadcast in the bar on the ground floor.

La Villette to Bercy

La Flèche d'Or

102bis rue de Bagnolet, 20th;

tel: 01 44 64 01 02; www.flechedor.com; Mon–Thur 8pm–2am, Fri and Sat 8pm–6am; metro: Gambetta

A hip mecca for eastern Paris, the 'Golden Arrow' occupies the premises of a former railway station. Free concerts on weeknights at 8pm. For details, see website.

Le Jemmapes

82 quai des Jemmapes, 10th; tel: 01 40 40 02 35; Mon, Wed–Sun 11am–2am, Tue 7pm–2am; metro: République; map p.153 D3

Unusual flavoured vodkas are the speciality at this ever-popular canal-side café-bar, which gets packed at the weekends, especially its terrace in summer. Good beers and a relaxed vibe are two more reasons to pay a visit.

The Latin Quarter and St-Germain

Le Bar Dix

10 rue de l'Odéon, 6th; tel: 01 43 26 69 83; daily 6pm–2am; metro: Odéon; map p.154 B2

A two-level favourite with students and the economy-

minded for decades, this bar has a cramped upper bar done out with old Jacques Brel record sleeves, and a basement that is made even more romantic by candles. The drinks of choice are cheap reds by the glass or home-made *sangria*.

Café de Flore
172 boulevard St-Germain, 6th; tel: 01 45 48 55 26; www.cafe-de-flore.com; daily 7.30am–1.30am; metro: St-Germain-des-Prés; map p.154 A2
Grand historic café with an Art Deco interior of red seating, mahogany and mirrors. In its less expensive days and when, perhaps, the food was better, it was frequented by Jean-Paul Sartre and Simone de Beauvoir, who met here to discuss philosophy. To keep the literary connection going, the café awards an annual literary prize, the Prix de Flore, to promising talent.

Les Deux Magots
6 place St-Germain-des-Prés, 6th; tel: 01 45 48 55 25; www.lesdeuxmagots.fr; daily

7.30am–1am; metro: St-Germain-des-Prés; map p.154 A2
Great rival to Café de Flore, and also once habituated by Sartre and de Beauvoir, as well as Hemingway, Picasso and Gide, among others. Like many places that have become an institution, it is unfortunately also overpriced and overcrowded. Light food served all day.

La Fourmi Ailée
8 rue du Fouarre, 5th; tel: 01 43 29 40 99; daily noon–midnight; metro: Maubert-Mutualité; map p.154 C2
Atmospheric, inexpensive tearoom-cum-restaurant that was formerly a women's library (the walls are still lined with books). A relaxing haven in which to recuperate after the crowds around Nôtre-Dame.

Rhubarb
18 rue Laplace, 5th; tel: 01 43 25 35 03; daily 5pm–2am; metro: Luxembourg, Maubert-Mutualite; map p.154 C1
An excellent bar in a crumbling Latin Quarter cellar, with a laid-back atmosphere and great cocktails, notably, the now-famous apple Martini (they also do chocolate and melon varieties).

The 7th

Le Café Constant
139 rue St-Dominique, 7th; 01 47 53 73 34; www.cafeconstant.com; Tue–Sat 8.30am–10.30pm; metro: Ecole Militaire; map p.157 C4

Busy and unfaddish, this café does good food and wine at a very fair price. The blackboard menu announces daily fare such as poached eggs with salad or steak tartare.

Le Café du Marché
38 rue Cler, 7th; tel: 01 47 05 51 27; Mon–Sat 7am–midnight, Sun 7am–4.30pm; metro: Ecole Militaire; map p.157 C4
Rue Cler is a market street, hence the name of this ever-popular café, which is ideal for a break in the middle of a spot of shopping. The house wine, served by the carafe, is good; the food is tasty.

Montparnasse and Beyond

Rosebud
11 bis rue Delambre, 14th; tel: 01 43 35 38 54; daily 7pm–2am; metro: Montparnasse; map p.157 E1
The décor is a throwback to the 1930s, when the likes of Sartre drank here. It now draws an older crowd of mostly arty and media types.

Les Tontons
38 rue Raymond-Losserand, 14th; tel: 01 43 21 69 45; Mon–Sat 8am–midnight; metro: Montparnasse
Traditional café with late opening hours and a zinc bar. Food offerings have a regional flavour – that of the southwest – and run to huge salads and 10 different varieties of *tartare*.

Below: bill and tip at Le Café du Marché.

Children

Disneyland might be the obvious attraction for children in or around Paris, and the reason for many special trips to the Ile-de-France, but there's plenty, too, to keep them happy in the capital itself. There are parks with boats to sail and puppet shows to watch, zoos for animal-lovers, and child-friendly museums, including one dedicated solely to children. In addition, there are fun sports facilities, rides along the Seine and around the city on open-topped buses and unique experiences such as a trip up the Eiffel Tower. The following is a selection of ideas on how to keep the little ones busy.

Accommodation

Most hotels have family rooms. For those with babies, a cot *(lit bébé)* can often be provided for a small supplement, but do check this before booking.

Babysitting

Baby Sitting Services
Tel: 01 46 21 33 16; www.babysittingservices.com; open 24 hours; charge per hour
Offers babysitting services, which can be arranged at just a couple of hours' notice.

Eating Out

Taking your children out to a restaurant should not be a problem (although check beforehand with the more up-market places). French children are used to eating out from an early age and are therefore generally well behaved in restaurants.

Many eateries offer a children's menu. If not, they may be happy to split a *prix-fixe* menu between two. With very young children, just request an extra plate and give them food from your own. Alternatively, order a simple dish,

Children under three are usually allowed free entry into most museums. Those under 13 (sometimes older) generally only have to pay half price. A reduction for families *(familles nombreuses)* applies in some museums.

such as an omelette, *croque-monsieur*, sandwich or soup. With the bread that comes automatically to a French table, and ice cream or fruit to follow, most children will be well fed.

Museums and Galleries

SEE MUSEUMS AND GALLERIES, P.88–105
The following are particularly suited to children:
Centre Pompidou – Galerie des Enfants
This has displays and workshops aimed at children. Entry is free to anyone under 18.
Château de Chantilly
Attractions include boat trips in the palace grounds and dressage shows at the nearby Musée Vivant du Cheval (Equestrian Museum).
SEE ALSO PALACES, P.114

Cité des Enfants

At the **Parc de la Villette**, the Cité des Enfants has lots of fun, interactive attractions for the little ones, with areas divided according to age (3–5 and 5–12 year olds).
SEE ALSO PARKS AND GARDENS, P.125

Musée Grévin

The waxworks museum is ever popular with children, with recent figures including Britney Spears and Spider-man. Free for the under 6s.

Musée du Louvre

This heavyweight may not be an obvious choice for children, but it puts on a special programme for them, including performances, readings and workshops.

Musée National de la Marine

Model boats and an area where boat renovators can be watched at work. Free for the under 6s; reduced price for the 6–18s.

Musée de la Poupée

Impasse Berthaud, 3rd; tel:01 42 72 73 11; www.museedela poupeeparis.com; admission charge; Tue–Sun 10am–6pm; metro: Rambuteau; map p.155 C4

Left: a merry-go-round by the Eiffel Tower.

Jardins du Ranelagh
Avenue du Ranelagh, 16th; daily, Mon–Fri: from 8am, Sat, Sun: from 9am; metro: La Muette, Ranelagh

These gardens are aimed at children, with a wonderful old wind-up merry-go-round, puppet shows and donkey rides.

Parc des Buttes-Chaumont
Attractions for kids include a playground, pony rides (summer only) and puppet shows.

Parc de la Villette
Themed gardens, with bright-red *folies*, are fun for the kids.

This small museum traces the evolution of French dolls, from the Second Empire to the current day. Next door is a doll shop and hospital.

Muséum National d'Histoire Naturelle
Attractions here include dinosaurs in the Galeries de Paléontologie, stuffed animals in the Grande Galérie de l'Evolution and interactive fun in the Salle de Découverte. Free for under 4s and reduced price for those under 13.

Palais de la Découverte
The planetarium is fun for scientifically minded children.

Parks and Gardens
SEE PARKS AND GARDENS, P.120–5

Jardin d'Acclimatation
Bois de Boulogne; tel: 01 40 67 90 82; www.jardindacclimatation. fr; May–Sept: 10am–7pm, Oct–Apr: 10am–6pm; entrance charge; metro: Porte Dauphine, Les Sablons or Porte Maillot

In the **Bois de Boulogne** this is an amusement park for youngsters. Attractions include a hall of mirrors, zoo, go-kart racing, wooden fort, theatre and puppet show

(Wed, Sat and Sun at 3pm and 4pm). There is even a pretty little historic train (built in 1880) that you can catch from Porte Maillot every 20 minutes from 10.15am.

Jardin du Luxembourg
Attractions include puppet shows, playgrounds, a merry-go-round, tennis courts and a pond on which motorised boats (for hire in the gardens) can be sailed.

Jardin des Tuileries
Lots to keep the kids happy, including sailing boats, puppet shows and a big Ferris wheel (in summer).

Puppet Shows and Circuses

Cirque d'Hiver Bouglione
110 rue Amelot, 11th; tel 01 49 29 09 78; www.cirquedhiver. com; entrance charge; shows Oct–Feb; metro: Filles du Calvaire; map p.155 E4

Shows at this historic circus include acrobats, clowns, ventriloquists, trapeze artists and horse dressage.

PUPPET SHOWS
In addition to the puppet shows in the main parks *(see above)*, there are also regular performances at:

Below: the Jardin des Plantes has a small zoo aimed at children.

Marionettes du Champ de Mars
Champs de Mars (between avenues Risler and Motte Piquet), 7th; tel: 01 48 56 01 44; entrance charge; Wed, Sat, Sun 3.15pm, 4.15pm; metro: Ecole Militaire; map p.165 C3
Six shows a week on the Champ de Mars.

Marionettes des Champs-Elysées
Rond Point des Champs-Elysées (between avenues Matignon and Gabriel), 8th; entrance charge; Wed, Sat, Sun 3pm, 4pm, 5pm; metro: Franklin D. Roosevelt; map p.151 D2
Historic puppet shows half way up the Champs-Elysées.

Shopping

Apache
84 rue du Faubourg-St Antoine, 12th, tel: 01 53 46 60 10; www. apache.fr; metro: Bastille; map p.155 E2
Toy shop with an activities studio and cybercafé.

La Boutique de Floriane
17 rue Tronchet, 8th; tel: 01 42 65 25 95; metro: Havre Caumartin; map p.152 A2
Quality children's clothes, plus Babar the Elephant toys.

Chantelivre
13 rue de Sèvres, 6th; tel: 01 45 48 87 90; metro: Sèvres-Babylone; map p.154 A2
Children's book shop. Also sells CDs, paints, stationery.

Les Cousines d'Alice
36 rue Daguerre, 14th; tel: 01 43 20 24 86; metro: Denfert-Rochereau
Stuffed animals, books, construction games and more.

Les Deux Tisserins
36 rue des Bernardins, 5th; tel: 01 46 33 88 68; metro: Maubert Mutualité; map p.155 C2

Lots of wooden toys, plus clothing and accessories.

fnac Junior
19 rue Vavin, 6th; tel: 01 56 24 03 46; www.fnacjunior.fr; metro: Vavin
Educational games, toys, DVDs and CDs for kids.

Pain d'Epices
29 passage Jouffroy, 9th; tel: 01 47 70 08 68; www.pain depices.fr; metro: Bourse; map p.152 B2
Paradise for doll enthusiasts.

Petit Bateau
26 rue Vavin, 6th; tel: 01 55 42 02 53; www.petit-bateau.com; metro: Vavin
Children's and women's underwear, T-shirts and sleepwear in soft cotton.

Sport

In addition to the swimming pools listed below, watery attractions include Paris-Plage (see p.61), when the banks of the Seine are transformed into a beach. Temporary ice-skating rinks are set up in front of the Hôtel de Ville and Tour Montparnasse in winter. Skating is free; charge for skate hire.
SEE SPORT, P.144–5

Aquaboulevard
4–6 rue Louis Armand, 15th; tel: 01 40 60 10 00; www.aqua boulevard.com; Mon–Thur 9am–11pm, Fri 9am–midnight, Sat 8am–midnight, Sun 8am–11pm; entrance charge; metro: Balard
Massive water world with waves, flumes and indoor and outdoor pools.

Bowling-Mouffetard
73 rue Mouffetard, 5th; tel: 01 43 31 09 35; www.bowlingmouffetard.fr; entrance charge (shoe hire extra); Mon–Fri 3pm–2am, Sat–Sun 10am–2am; metro: place Monge; map p.155 C1
Eight bowling lanes should appeal to older children.

Piscine Joséphine Baker
The main pool here has a

Below: exploring and learning at the Cité des Enfants.

> Disneyland's official language is English, but French is widely spoken.

retractable roof, and there's also a children's pool.
SEE ALSO SPORT, P.145

Theme Parks

Disneyland Resort Paris/ Walt Disney Studios Park

Marne-la-Vallée; tel: 08 25 30 60 30 (in France); 0870 503 0303 (in the UK); www.disneyland paris.com; Disneyland: Sept–mid-July: Mon–Fri 10am–8pm, Sat, Sun 9am–8pm mid-July–Aug: daily 9am–11pm; Studios Park: winter: Mon–Fri 10am–6pm, Sat, Sun 9am–6pm, summer: daily 9am–6pm; entrance charge (various tickets available, see web for details); free for infants under 3 years; RER/train: Marne-la-Vallée-Chessy

French reaction to the arrival of Disney was mixed, even though Disney researchers had identified Walt's ancestors originating from the French town of Isigny (D'Isigny = Disney). The park receives around 12.5 million visitors a year, however, which is firm confirmation of its resounding success.

It consists of five worlds: **Fantasyland**, the most popular land for younger children; **Main Street US**, representing the early 1900s with ragtime and Dixieland bands; **Frontierland**, evoking dreams of the Wild West; **Adventureland**, with characters such as Captain Hook; and futuristic **Discoveryland**, which has a Space Mountain and several attractions with a French theme, such as an underwater trip that pays homage to Jules Verne's *20,000 Leagues Under the Sea*.

There's also Walt Disney Studios, which gives visitors an insight into the world of

Above: the easy way to tour the city.

Hollywood special effects. There are numerous restaurants and hotels on site.

Parc Astérix

60128 Plailly; tel: 08 26 30 10 40; www.parcasterix.fr; Apr–Jun: daily 10am–6pm, July–Aug: daily 9.30am–7pm, Sept–Oct: Wed, Sat and Sun 10am–6pm; entrance charge; free for infants under 3 years; reduced price for children aged 3–11; RER: Roissy Charles de Gaulle, then shuttle bus

Located 35km (22 mlies) north of Paris is this theme park based on the adventures of the cartoon-strip character, Asterix (by Albert Uderzo and René Goscinny).

Split up into historical sections, the park includes rides (notably the biggest wooden roller coaster in Europe), adventure playgrounds, live acts and animals, including dolphins. There is also an on-site hotel.

Tours

Bâteaux-Mouches

Pont de l'Alma, 8th; tel: 01 40 76 99 99; www.bateaux-mouches. fr; summer: daily 10am–11pm, departures every 30–45 mins, winter: daily 11am, 2.30, 4, 6, 9pm; entrance charge; metro:

Pont de l'Alma; map p.150 C1
Leaving from the Pont de l'Alma, boat tours along the Seine, with the longest-running Parisian riverboat firm, offer fun sightseeing for kids.

Canauxrama

Northbound boat: Port de l'Arsenal (opposite 50 boulevard de la Bastille), 12th; metro: Bastille; map p.155 E2; southbound boat: Bassin de la Villette, 13 quai de la Loire, 19th; tel: 01 42 39 15 00; www.canauxrama.fr; entrance charge; daily 9.45am, 2.30pm; metro: Jaurès; map p.153 E4

Tours along the Canal St-Martin and Canal de l'Ourq are a less touristy alternative to the busy boats on the Seine and a fun way to reach the Parc de la Villette. Boats run in both directions; see website for details.

Cityrama

2 rue des Pyramides, 2nd; tel: 01 44 55 61 00; www.cityrama. fr; times vary, see website for details; entrance charge; free for the under 4s; reduced price for children aged 4–11; metro: Palais Royal, Pyramides; map p.154 A4

Tour the city on an open-top bus and hop on and off at any of the 50 stops along four set routes. Good multilingual commentaries. Passes for one and two days available.

> **4 Roues sous 1 Parapluie**
> Office at 12 rue Chabanais, 2nd; tel: 06 36 67 32 26 68 (from France), 0800 800 631 (from abroad); www.4roues-sous-1parapluie.com
> The quirky way to tour the city, in an iconic soft-topped Citroen 2CV (hence the name, meaning four wheels under an umbrella). Each car can hold a maximum of three passengers. Pick-up from your hotel can be arranged; otherwise meet at Opéra. Choose from several themed tours.

Churches, Mosques and Synagogues

The proliferation of sacred buildings in the city is testament not only to the importance of Christianity but also to the many different religions in its history. It is impossible to give a full listing of Paris's 170 churches and temples here. There follows a selection of the most historically important or architecturally noteworthy places of worship of various denominations and faiths.

The Islands

Cathédrale Notre-Dame de Paris

Place du Parvis-Notre-Dame, 4th; tel: 01 42 34 56 10; www.notredamedeparis.fr; cathedral: daily 8am–6.45pm; crypt: Tue–Sun 10am–6pm; towers: Oct–Mar: daily 10am–4.45pm, Apr–Sept: daily 9am–6.45pm; free except towers and crypt; metro: Cité; map p.154 C2

Notre-Dame dominates the Ile de la Cité. In Roman times a temple to Jupiter stood here; in the 4th century AD, St-Etienne, a Christian church, was built on the site, joined two centuries later by a second church, dedicated to Notre-Dame. Norman raids left them both in a sorry state, and, in the 12th century, Bishop Maurice de Sully decided that they should be replaced by a cathedral.

The main part of Notre-Dame, begun in 1163, took 167 years to finish. Its transition from Romanesque to Gothic has been called a perfect representation of medieval architecture; an opinion that has attracted dissenters: Cistercian monks

Above: the rose window.

protested that such a structure was an insult to the godly virtue of poverty.

The original architect is unknown, but Pierre de Montreuil was responsible for much of the 13th-century work. The present look of the cathedral is due to Eugène Viollet-le-Duc, who from 1845 to 1863 restored it following the ravages of the 18th century, caused more by pre-Revolutionary meddlers than by revolutionaries who stripped it of religious symbols. Popular support for the expensive restoration was inspired by Victor Hugo's novel *Notre-Dame de Paris*.

POMP AND CIRCUMSTANCE

The cathedral has witnessed momentous occasions over the centuries, including, in 1239, the procession of Louis IX, during which the pious king walked barefoot carrying what was believed to be Christ's crown-of-thorns.

In 1594 Henri IV made his politically motivated conversion to Catholicism here to reinforce his hold on the French throne. Napoleon crowned himself emperor at Notre-Dame, upstaging the Pope, who had come to Paris expecting to do it (the scene is depicted in Jacques-Louis David's vast painting, *The Consecration of Napoleon*, now in the Louvre, *see p.88*).

More recent occasions include General de Gaulle marking the 1944 liberation of Paris with a Mass here, and in 1970 his death was similarly commemorated.

THE WEST FRONT

Across the three doorways of the west front, the 28 statues of the **Galerie des Rois** repre-

Left: looking over the city from Sacre-Cœur.

Ste-Chapelle

4 boulevard du Palais, 1st; tel: 01 53 40 60 80; www.monum. fr; Mar–Oct: daily 9.30am– 5.30pm, Nov–Feb: daily 9am– 4.30pm; entrance charge; metro: Cité, RER: St-Michel Notre-Dame; map p.154 B3

In 1245–8 the devout Louis IX (later St Louis) had his original palace chapel converted by architect Pierre de Montreuil into an elaborate shrine to house holy relics acquired from the Emperor of Byzantium in 1239; these relics include the so-called crown-of-thorns. Such a treasure had to be closely guarded, and the king was the only person with a key to the reliquary chapel. Each Good Friday he would display its holy contents to the people in the Cour du Mai; for the rest of the year they were locked away. During the French Revolution the reliquary was melted down to make coins, the relics were moved – the crown-of-thorns is now in Notre-Dame – and the chapel was damaged. Work to restore the chapel began in 1846.

The exterior consists mainly of high tracery win-

Excavations beneath the square in front of Notre-Dame have revealed walls and foundations from the Gallic, Roman and medieval eras, which now form part of an exhibition on early Paris, on show in the crypt.

---

sent the kings of Judah. These are 19th-century restorations: the originals were torn down during the Revolution because they were thought to depict kings of France (21 of them were recently re-discovered and are in the **Musée National du Moyen Age**).

The central rose window depicts the Redemption after the Fall. Two more outsized rose windows illuminate the transept; the northern one retains most of its 13th-century glass. A 14th-century Virgin and Child is to the right of the choir entrance.

Napoleon III's town planner Haussmann greatly enlarged the *parvis*, or cathedral forecourt, diminishing the impact of the towering west front.
SEE ALSO MUSEUMS AND GALLERIES, P.102

THE TOWERS

The 255-step climb up the north tower is rewarded with glorious views of Paris and close-ups of the roof and Notre-Dame's famous gargoyles. Cross over to the south tower – and another 122 steps – to see the 13-tonne bell, the only one still remaining (the Revolutionaries melted down the others to make cannon). The bell was re-cast in the 1680s. A further 124 steps lead to the top of the south tower for more spectacular views.

Below: the magnificent west front of Notre-Dame.

dows with pointed gable roofs and narrow flying buttresses between them.

Inside, the ground-floor chapel, the Chapelle Basse (Lower Chapel), was used by the royal court for prayers. More impressive, however, is Sainte-Chapelle's upper storey, or Chapelle Haute (Upper Chapel), reached via a spiral staircase. This single-aisled chapel is a masterpiece of High Gothic architecture and was used exclusively by the royal family and the canons. The magnificent 13th-century stained glass, which depicts 1,134 scenes from the Bible in 85 major panels, is without equal anywhere in Paris.

St-Louis-en-l'Ile
19 bis rue St-Louis-en-l'Ile, 4th; tel: 01 46 34 11 60; Tue–Sun 9am–noon, 3–7pm; free; metro: Pont-Marie; map p.155 D2
The only church on the picturesque Ile St-Louis was built between 1664 and 1765. Its lavish baroque interior makes a fine venue for occasional classical concerts.

Louvre, Tuileries and Concorde

St-Germain-l'Auxerrois
2 place du Louvre, 1st; tel: 01 42 60 13 96; www.saintgermain

Below: St-Louis-en-l'Isle.

> Sainte-Chapelle is unique among Gothic buildings for its medieval frescoes, which have all been restored.

auxerrois.cef.fr; Mon–Sat 8am–7pm, Sun 8am–8pm; metro: Pont Neuf, Louvre Rivoli; map p.154 B3
At midnight on 24 August 1572, the bells of this former royal church rang as the signal to start the St Bartholomew's Day Massacre, when thousands of Protestants were butchered on the orders of Catholic Catherine de Médici. Inside there's an magnificent canopied bench, carved by Le Brun for the royal family.

St-Roch
296 rue St-Honoré, 1st; tel: 01 42 44 13 20; www.saintroch. esqualite.com Mon–Sat 9am–7pm, Sun 9am–8.30pm; free; metro: Tuileries; map p.152 A1
In 1653, in the ancient street of rue St-Honoré, Louis XIV laid the foundation stone for this church. It was consecrated to St Roch, the patron saint of plague victims.

St-Roch was once the finest Baroque church in all Paris, but most of its exceptional sculpture and façade decoration was lost in the Revolution. Nevertheless, the church still owns a rich collection of excellent religious works of art, brought there in 1819 from demolished Paris churches. It is also the resting place of France's most celebrated landscape gardener, André Le Nôtre, and of writers Corneille and Diderot.

Opéra and Grands Boulevards

Eglise de la Ste-Marie-de-la-Madeleine
Place de la Madeleine, 8th; tel: 01 44 51 69 00; www.eglise-lamadeleine.com; daily 9.30am–7pm; free; metro: Madeleine; map p.151 E2

Place de la Madeleine is dominated by this church, commonly referred to as 'La Madeleine'. In 1764, Louis XV laid the foundation stone for the present structure, which initially was intended to resemble the Panthéon. Construction was slow, and in 1805 Napoleon decided to turn the half-finished church into a temple of glory for his grand army. In 1808 the structure assumed its present neoclassical appearance, but work stopped on it after the fall of Napoleon; the church was only consecrated in 1845.

The bare, uninviting interior is in the shape of a long hall vaulted by three domes. The apse contains a neoclassical fresco, showing Christ, St-Madeleine and historical figures including Napoleon.

Beaubourg and Les Halles

St-Eustache
Rue du Jour, 1st; tel: 01 42 36 31 05; www.st-eustache.org; daily 9.30am–7pm; free; metro: Les Halles; map p.154 B4
North of the Forum des Halles is St-Eustache, a vast church modelled on Notre-Dame (note the flying buttresses) and built 1532–1640. The interior is a Renaissance feast of columns, arches and stained glass. Berlioz and Liszt played here in the 19th century, and concerts on the church's 8,000-pipe organ are still held weekly, at 5.30pm on Sunday. Outside the church,

> On 5 October 1795 several rebellious royalists who had barricaded themselves into St-Roch were summarily shot on the church steps on the orders of Napoleon Bonaparte. Bullet holes and other traces from the battle can be seen on the church wall.

Above: the high altar of the Madeleine.

a sculpture of a giant head and cupped hand by Henri de Miller attracts children and pigeons to its benign seat.

St-Merri
78 rue St-Martin, 3rd; tel: 01 42 71 93 93; www.saintmerri.org; Mon–Sat 3–7pm; free; metro: Hôtel de Ville; map p.155 C3

The richly adorned Flamboyant-Gothic church of St-Merri dates mostly from the 16th century, but its bell dates to 1331, making it the oldest in Paris. The organ used to be played by Saint-Saëns.

Tour St-Jacques
Square de la Tour St-Jacques, 4th; closed to the public; metro: Châtelet; map p.154 C3

This Gothic bell tower is the only remaining part of the St-Jacques-La-Boucherie church built 1508–22. At the base is a statue of scientist and philosopher Blaise Pascal (1623–62), who carried out pioneering experiments on atmospheric pressure from the top of the tower (where there is still a weather station).

The Marais and Bastille

St-Gervais-St-Protais
Place St-Gervais, 4th; tel: 01 48 87 32 02; various opening times, phone for details; free; metro: Hôtel de Ville; map p.155 C3

This 17th-century church, with a triple-tiered classical façade, a flight of Italianate steps, a Gothic rear and some monstrous-looking gargoyles, is renowned for its 18th-century organ, and concerts are frequently held here. As a parting shot at the end of World War I, the church was shelled by the German Army, killing almost 100 worshippers.

St-Paul-St-Louis
99 rue St-Antoine, 4th; tel: 01 42 72 30 32; www.saintpaulsaint louis.com; Mon–Sat 8am–8pm, Sun 9am–8pm; free; metro: St-Paul; map p.155 D3

An ancient passageway leads from rue St-Paul to the church of St-Paul-St-Louis (an amalgamation of two parishes), constructed by Jesuits in 1627 to mimic the Gesù church in Rome. Here, the hearts of Louis XIII and Louis XIV were embalmed and kept as relics until the Revolution, when they were removed and sold to an artist who crushed them to mix with oil for a varnish for one of his pictures.

Later he gave what was left of Louis XIII's heart to the newly installed King Louis XVIII, in return for a golden snuffbox. Highlights include Delacroix's *Christ in the Garden of Olives*.

Synagogue
10 rue Pavée, 4th; tel: 01 48 87 21 54; visits by request only; free; metro: St-Paul; map p.155 D3

At the heart of the Jewish quarter in the Marais, the synagogue is notable for its 1913 Art Nouveau façade by Hector Guimard, who also designed the furnishings inside. The building was severely damaged by a bomb (along with six other Parisian synagogues) during anti-Semitic demonstrations on the evening of Yom Kippur 1941. It has been restored and is now a French national monument.

Montmartre

Sacré Cœur
35 rue du Chevalier-de-la-Barre,

Below: the Tour St-Jacques.

47

If you don't fancy the climb to the top of Sacré Cœur's hill, you could opt for the Funiculaire tramway. Be warned that the queues tend to be long.

18th; tel: 01 53 41 89 00; www.sacre-coeur-montmartre. com; basilica: daily 6am–10.30pm, crypt and dome: summer 9am–6.45pm, winter 10am–5.45pm; free except crypt and dome; metro: Anvers and funicular; map p.152 B4
This basilica was planned in 1870 by a group of Catholics, who vowed to build a church to the Sacred Heart if Paris was delivered safely from the Prussian siege (the heart of one of the men, Alexandre Legentil, is in a stone urn in the crypt). The Church took on responsibility for the project in 1873, and work started two years later. Architect Paul Abadie based his design on the Romano-Byzantine cathedral of St-Front in Périgueux. It

was completed in 1914 but not consecrated until 1919.
The dome offers a stunning view over Paris, up 237 narrow spiral steps. From the stained-glass gallery beneath there is a good view of the cavernous interior, which, apart from the massive mock-Byzantine mosaic of Christ (1912–22) by Luc Olivier-Merson on the chancel's vaulted ceiling, has little else to offer.
The building's mediocre architecture, added to its symbolic censure of a popular uprising, has rendered the Sacré-Cœur one of the Parisians' least favourite monuments. However, the steps in front of the church afford one of the best views of Paris.

St-Pierre de Montmartre
2 rue du Mont Cenis; tel: 01 46 06 57 63; daily 8.30am–7.00pm; free; metro: Abbesses; map p.152 B4
Next to the Sacré-Cœur is this simple church, the second oldest in Paris. It dates from

The bone-white colour of the Sacré Cœur comes from its Château-Landon stone, which secretes calcite when it rains, bleaching the walls.

1133 and is the only remaining vestige of the Abbey of Montmartre, where the Benedictine nuns once lived. The church was abandoned after the Revolution until it was reconsecrated in 1908. The graveyard behind the church is only open to the public on 1 November.

The Latin Quarter and St-Germain
Mosquée de Paris
2 place du Puits de l'Ermite, 5th; tel: 01 45 35 97 33; www. mosquee-de-paris.net; tours daily 9am–noon and 2–6pm; entrance charge; metro: Monge, Jussieu, Censier; map p.155 C1
The city's green-and-white main mosque was built in the Hispano-Moorish style in 1922 by three French architects to commemorate North African participation in World War I. Incorporating the **Institut Musulman**, the complex of buildings includes a museum of Muslim art, a large patio inspired by the Alhambra in Granada and an impressive selection of carvings and tiles. There is also a library, a restaurant, a good *salon de thé*, and a Turkish bath.
SEE ALSO PAMPERING, P.119

St-Etienne-du-Mont
Place Ste-Geneviève, 5th; tel: 01 43 54 11 79; Mon noon–7.30pm, Tue–Sun 8.45am–7.30pm; free; metro: Cardinal Lemoine, RER: Luxembourg; map p.154 C1
Behind the Panthéon is the church of St-Etienne-du-Mont. Formerly the parish church of the Abbey of St-Geneviève, there is a

Left: the imposing St-Suplice.

Above: the *salon de thé* at the Mosque de Paris.

shrine to her here, as patron saint of Paris (she saved the city from Attila the Hun in 451). Also noteworthy here is the only Renaissance rood screen (1541) in Paris.

St-Germain-des-Prés
3 place St-Germain-des-Prés; tel: 01 55 42 81 33; www. eglise-sgp.org; daily 10.30am– noon and 2.30– 6.45pm, except Mon and Sat am; free; metro: St-Germain-des-Prés; map p.154 A2
The church takes its name from St Germain, cardinal of Paris in the 8th century. On his death he was buried in the 6th-century abbey of Ste-Croix-St-Vincent, now St-Germain-des-Prés. The church has the oldest bell tower in Paris and was the only Romanesque church to survive the 1789 revolution.

St-Sulpice
Place St-Sulpice; tel: 01 42 34 59 98; www.paroisse-saint-sulpice-paris.org; daily 7.30am–7.30pm; free; metro: St-Sulpice; map p.154 A2
The eastern side of place St-Sulpice is dominated by Jean-Baptiste Servandoni's vast Italianesque church, notable for its towers, one of

which is higher than the other. Highlights inside include, in a chapel at the back of the church, Eugène Delacroix's massive frescoes, completed two years before his death. If the frescoes whet your appetite for Delacroix's work, visit the nearby **Musée National Eugène Delacroix**, set within his delightful former home and studio.
SEE ALSO MUSEUMS AND GALLERIES, P.100–1

Val-de-Grâce
Place Alphonse-Laveran, 5th; tel: 01 40 51 47 28; Tue, Wed, Sat, Sun noon–6pm; entrance charge; RER: Port Royal
Anne of Austria vowed to build this church if she had a son, and, after the safe birth of the future Louis XIV, the commission went to François Mansart. His original plans, however, were altered by his successor on the scheme, Jacques Lemercier. The building's façade is celebrated for its architectural harmony. Mansart's interior shows a strong Italian influence, in the nave and transepts, in the majestic dome, and in the large baldachin altar with barley-sugar columns. The adjacent monastery building houses a cloister, a school for army doctors and, attached to it, a medical museum.

The 7th

Eglise du Dôme
Esplanade des Invalides, 7th; tel: 01 44 42 40 69; www. invalides.org; Apr–Sept: daily 10am–6pm, Oct–Mar: daily 10am–5pm, closed first Mon of month; entrance charge; metro: Les Invalides, Varenne, La Tour Maubourg; map p.157 D4
Part of the Invalides complex, the Eglise du Dôme contains the tomb of Napoleon. The emperor's body was returned to the city from St Helena in 1840

with much pomp and ceremony, and laid to rest in the church crypt. The mausoleum is fittingly overblown.

Outside the Périphérique

Basilique Cathédral de St-Denis
1 rue de la Légion d'Honneur; tel: 01 48 09 83 54; www. monuments-nationaux.fr; Apr–Sept: daily 10am–6.15pm, Oct–Mar: Mon–Sat 10am–5.15pm, Sun noon–5.15pm; entrance charge; metro: Basilique de Saint-Denis
The burial place of France's kings and queens, the magnificent Gothic St-Denis was mainly built by Abbot Suger in the 12th century on the site of an abbey church. According to legend, this is the spot reached by St-Denis when he walked out of Paris carrying his head, after being decapitated in Montmartre. Monarchs from Dagobert I (628– 37) are buried here, and the sculptures are some of the finest in France.

Below: Eglise du Dôme.

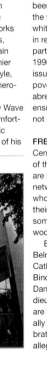

Cinema

Generations of directors, from Louis Malle, Claude Chabrol and François Truffaut to Jean-Luc Godard and Mathieu Kassovitz, have been beguiled by the photogenic and romantic qualities of the French capital. Following World War II, the city achieved iconic status in American films such as *Funny Face* and *An American in Paris*. Although now portayed in a variety of lights, the city is often shown as the home to troubled or oddball characters, whether in the tragic *Les Amants du Pont-Neuf*, the dark 1980s *Subway*, the gritty *La Haine*, or the nostalgic, sugary-sweet, *Amélie*.

French Film

Although the Lumière Brothers made their first film in Lyon in 1885, the first flowering of French cinema was in the 1930s, marked by the films of director Jean Renoir. This era was only surpassed by innovative New Wave cinema of the late 1950s and early 1960s.

Since then, French cinema has come to be equated with the unique artistic vision of the *auteur*, with directors such as Alain Resnais, Godard, Claude Chabrol and

Below: the Cinémathèque Française.

François Truffaut having no qualms about considering themselves creative artists.

Since the New Wave heyday, the best French films have tended to be intimate, small-scale works on conventional themes, distinguished by a certain artistry. Bertrand Tavernier is a champion of this style, believing in 'the minor heroism of daily life'.

The veterans of New Wave cinema also appear comfortable with this humanistic approach. Truffaut said of his

creed, 'The best of the permanent subjects is love.'

Many of these same French film makers have been criticised for seeing the world through privileged white bourgeois eyes. As if in response, French cinema, particularly since the early 1990s, has confronted social issues such as Aids, crime, poverty and race, keeping abreast with the times and ensuring that its renown is not exclusively artistic.

FRENCH ACTORS

Central to the strong identity of the French film industry are its players, a tight-knit network of actors, many of whom retain their passion for their national cinema, even, sometimes, in spite of Hollywood success.

Brigitte Bardot, Jean-Paul Belmondo, Yves Montand, Cathérine Deneuve, Juliette Binoche, Isabelle Huppert, Daniel Auteuil, Gérard Dépardieu and Emmanuelle Béart are some of the internationally renowed actors celebrated for their strong allegiance to French film.

Left: scene from Coco before Chanel.

Forum des Images
Porte St-Eustache, Forum des Halles, 1st; tel: 01 44 76 62 00; www.forumdesimages.net; Tue–Sun 1–9pm; metro: Les Halles; map p.154 C4
With four screens, this forum within Les Halles not only shows films but is also home to an archive of Paris on film. You can watch items from the collection on the small screen.

Géode
Parc de la Villette, 19th; tel: 01 39 17 10 00; www.lageode.fr; charge; daily 10.30am–8.30pm, Mon till 6.30pm; metro: Porte de la Villette
One of the attractions in the Parc de la Villette, La Géode is a giant silver ball containing a wraparound cinema for 3D films. Great for kids.

mk2 Bibliothèque
128–62 avenue de France, 13th; tel: 08 92 69 84 84; www.mk2.com; daily 11am–10pm; metro: Bibliothèque François Mitterrand
This multiplex cinema on the emerging 'New' Left Bank has 14 screens, four restaurants and three shops, a big draw on evenings and weekends.

La Pagode
57 bis rue de Babylone, 7th; tel: 01 45 55 48 48; metro: St-François-Xavier; map p.157 D3
For a unique experience and arthouse films visit this extraordinary 19th-century copy of a Japanese pagoda. Wonderfully lavish interior and pretty, overgrown garden.

> Ticket prices across Paris are often reduced by up to 30 percent on Monday.

Film Festivals

Although Cannes, on the French Riviera, is the undisputed showcase of international cinema, Paris holds its own with the **Fête du Cinéma**, held over three days in June (usually the last weekend). Movie-goers pay the full price of one ticket and are then given a 'passport' that allows them entry to as many other films as they want during the festival for only €2.

Cinemas

Paris has a high concentration of multiscreens showing the latest films, but if you'd rather see a French classic than the most recent blockbuster, there are good retro and art-house cinemas too.

Cinemas on the Champs-Elysées and around Odéon in St-Germain-des-Prés often show recent releases in *vo (see box right)*, as do the Latin Quarter arts

cinemas for old movies. The following is a selection of the best screens:

Accattone
20 rue Cujas, 5th; tel: 01 46 33 86 86; daily 1–9pm; RER: Luxembourg; map p.154 B1
A quintessential Latin Quarter establishment: a slightly louche atmosphere, an audience of Left Bank aficionados and a programme of classic art-house cinema.

Le Balzac
1 rue Balzac, 8th; tel: 01 45 61 10 60; www.cinemabalzac.com; daily 1–9pm; metro: George V; map p.150 C3
Stylish retro cinema showing the latest films (sometimes preceded by a short speech from the manager).

Cinémathèque Française
51 rue de Bercy, 12th; tel: 01 71 19 33 33; www.cinematheque francaise.com; daily except Tue, see website; metro: Bercy
On the north side of the Parc de Bercy, in the former American Center designed by Frank Gehry, is the new headquarters of French cinema, home to a museum, research centre, repertory cinema, restaurant and archive.

> Most cinemas in the city centre show films in their original language with French subtitles (*vo*, or *version originale*), though once you get out of the city centre, mainstream films are usually dubbed (*vf*, or *version française*).

Dance

Paris has a long, distinguished dance tradition. It was home to the world's first ballet academy, the Académie Royale (est. 1661), the birthplace of the cancan and Rudolph Nureyev's base after his defection from Russia to the West in 1961. Vaslav Nijinsky, who took Paris by storm with Sergei Diaghilev's Ballets Russes, is buried at Père Lachaise cemetery, as is Isadora Duncan, considered by many to be the mother of modern dance. It's not all old news, however: classical dance still flourishes in the French capital, and the contemporary scene, with some excellent venues, is thriving.

Major Venues

Ballet de l'Opéra National de Paris Bastille
120 rue de Lyon, 12th; tel: 08 92 89 90 90; www.operadeparis.fr; metro: Bastille, RER: Gare de Lyon; map p.155 E2

Palais Garnier
Place de l'Opéra, 9th; tel: 08 36 69 78 68; www.operadeparis.fr; metro: Opéra, RER: Auber; map p.152 A2

Around 180 performances per year of classics and new productions are staged by the Ballet de l'Opéra, mostly in the sumptuous surroundings of the renovated 19th-century Palais Garnier, although some pieces are staged at the more modern Opéra Bastille.

The current dance director is Brigitte Lefèvre, while stars include Aurélie Dupont, Marie-Agnès Gillot, Agnès Letestu, Delphine Moussin,

Above: Paris has a strong tradition of classical dance.

Clairemarie Osta, Laëtitia Pujol, Jean-Guillaume Bart, Kader Belarbi, Mathieu Ganio, Manuel Legris, Nicolas Le Riche, José Martinez, Hervé Moreau, Benjamin Pech and Wilfried Romoli.
SEE ALSO OPÉRA AND GRANDS BOULEVARDS, P.10; THE MARAIS AND BASTILLE, P.14; MUSIC, P.107

Centre National de la Danse
1 rue Victor-Hugo, Pantin; tel: 01 41 83 27 27; www.cnd.fr; metro: Hoche

Dance was given a boost in 2004 with the opening of this national centre. The atmosphere is intimate, with performances in small studios. Facilities include an archive and rehearsal spaces.

Théâtre du Châtelet
1 place du Châtelet, 1st; tel: 01 40 28 28 40; www.chatelet-theatre.com; metro: Châtelet; map p.154 C3

Concerts, opera and ballet are staged at this historic theatre. Dance productions include works by international groups such as the American Ballet and shows by regional troupes.

Théâtre National du Chaillot
Palais du Chaillot, 1 place du Trocadéro, 16th; tel: 01 53 65 30 00; www.theatre-chaillot.fr; metro: Trocadéro; map p.150 A1

Productions of global dance such as tango and flamenco pull in the crowds here.
SEE ALSO LITERATURE AND THEATRE, P.83

In 1961 Russian premier dancer Rudolf Nureyev (1938–93) defected while on tour with the Kirov Ballet. He was Director of the Paris Opera Ballet 1983–9.

Left: probably the dance for which Paris is best known.

Dance Lessons

Centre de Danse du Marais
41 rue du Temple, 4th; tel: 01 42 77 58 19; www.parisdanse. com; Mon–Fri 9am–9pm, Sat 9am–8pm, Sun 9am–7pm; metro: Rambuteau; map p.155 C3
A wide range of classes, seven days a week, from classical ballet to belly dancing, jazz, samba and tango.

Studio Harmonic
5 passage des Taillandiers, 11th; tel: 01 48 07 13 39; www.studioharmonic.fr; Mon–Fri 9.30am–10pm, Sat 9am–7.30pm; metro: Bastille; map p.155 E2
Founded in 1988, this trendy dance school has over 1,000 sq m of space and 80 teachers. Classes include classical ballet, jazz, tap, hip-hop, African dance, tango, flamenco and Egyptian dance.

Below: Nijinsky in *Le Spectre de la Rose* for the Ballets Russe.

On the façade of the Theatre des Champs-Elysées *(see p.108)* is a bas-relief called The Dance by sculptor Emile-Antoine Bourdelle. The piece was inspired by free-spirited Californian-born dancer Isadora Duncan (1877–1927), who lived for some time in Paris. Duncan is now remembered for her freakish death: she was nearly decapitated when her fashionably long scarf got caught in the open spoke of a wheel of a car in Nice on 14 September. She is buried in Père Lachaise cemetery.

Théâtre de la Ville
2 place du Châtelet, 4th; tel: 01 42 74 22 77; www.theatredelaville-paris.com; metro: Châtelet; map p.154 C3
This is Paris's leading contemporary dance venue with a busy programme of national and international companies and productions, here and at the sister venue, the newly renovated **Théâtre des Abbesses** in Montmartre (31 rue des Abbesses, 18th; tel: 01 42 74 22 77; metro Abbesses; map p.152 B4).

Fringe Venues

L'Etoile du Nord
16 rue Georgette-Agutte, 18th; tel: 01 42 26 47 47; www.etoiledunord-theatre.com; metro: Guy Môquet
Located just north of the Cimetière de Montmartre, this is a good venue for contemporary dance shows.

Ménagerie de Verre
12–14 rue Léchevin, 11th; tel: 01 43 38 33 44; www.menagerie-de-verre.org; closed July, Aug; metro: Parmentier; map p.155 E4
Puts on contemporary, mostly experimental, dance shows and classes.

Théâtre de la Bastille
76 rue de la Roquette, 11th; tel: 01 43 57 42 14; www.theatre-bastille.com; metro: Bastille, Voltaire; map p.155 E3
This venue stages cutting-edge contemporary dance and theatre.

Théâtre de la Cité Internationale
17 boulevard Jourdan, 14th; tel: 01 43 13 50 50; www.theatredelacite.com; RER: Cité Universitaire
Contemporary dance productions and workshops.

53

Essentials

Paris is an easy city to negotiate. Here is all the practical information you need on how to understand Parisian postcodes, what to do in an emergency, how to understand the currency and where to find the tourist office. There are also details on health care, telecommunications, time differences and visas. For additional information, visit the useful websites www.parisinfo. com, www.franceguide.com, www.paris.org and www.paris.fr. Government travel advice is available at www.fco.gov.uk/travel (UK) or www.travel. state.gov (US). For the weather forecast, take a look at www.meteo.fr.

Addresses

Paris is divided into numbered districts, called *arrondissements* because they fan out in a 'round' pattern, clockwise from the city centre. Officially they are labelled by a five-digit postcode (75001, 75002, etc), but most people refer to them by their abbreviated form (1st, 2nd, 3rd, 4th, etc). There are 20 in total.

Embassies/Consulates

Australia
4 rue Jean-Rey, 15th; tel: 01 40 59 33 00
Canada
35 avenue Montaigne, 8th; tel: 01 44 43 29 00
Republic of Ireland
Embassy: 12 avenue Foch, 16th; tel: 01 44 17 67 00; Consulate: 4 rue Rude, 16th
UK
Embassy: 35 rue du Faubourg St-Honoré, 8th; tel: 01 44 51 31 00; Consulate: 18 bis rue

Metric to Imperial Conversions
Metres–Feet 1=3.28
Kilometres–Miles 1=0.62
Hectares–Acres 1=2.47
Kilograms–Pounds 1=2.2

Above: ask a *gendarme*.

d'Anjou, 8th; tel: 01 44 51 31 02
US
Embassy: 2 avenue Gabriel, 1st; tel: 01 43 12 22 22; Consulate: 2 rue St-Florentin, 1st; tel: 08 36 70 14 88.

Emergencies

Ambulance (SAMU): 15
Fire brigade (*pompiers*): 18
Police (*police secours*): 17
From a mobile phone: 112

Health

EU NATIONALS
If you are an EU national and you fall ill in France, you can receive emergency medical treatment from doctors, dentists and hospitals. You will have to pay the cost of this treatment, but are entitled to claim back up to 70 per cent of your medical expenses.

To receive a refund you must have a European Health Insurance Card. For UK citizens, these are available by going online at www.dh. gov.uk or from post offices. For more information tel: 0800 555777.

NORTH AMERICANS
International Association for Medical Assistance to Travellers (IAMAT)
40 Regal Road, Guelph, Ontario N1K 1B5, Canada; tel: 519 836 0102; www.iamat.org
This is a non-profit-making group that offers members fixed rates for medical treatment. Members receive a passport-sized medical record completed by their doctor and a directory of English-speaking IAMAT doctors in France, who are on call 24 hours a day. Membership is free, but donations are appreciated.

Left: universal symbols.

France is mostly GMT +1 hour (+2 hours Apr–Oct). When it is noon in Paris, it is 6am in New York.

the east and north pillars), 7th; 11 rue Scribe, 9th; 18 rue de Dunkerque, 10th; 20 boulevard Diderot, 12th; 21 place du Tertre, 18th.

ABROAD
French Travel Centre (UK)
Lincoln House, 300 High Holborn, London WC1V 7JH; tel: 0906 824 4123 (60p per min); www.franceguide.com; Mon–Fri 10am–4pm
Maison de la France (US)
825 Third Avenue, 29th Floor, NY-10022; tel: 514 288 1904; 9454 Wilshire Boulevard, Suite 715, 90212, Beverly Hills, CA; tel: 514 288 1904; www.franceguide.com

Visas

All visitors to France require a valid passport. No visa is required by visitors from the EU, the US, Australia, Canada or Japan. Nationals of other countries may need a visa; if in doubt (and, advisably, if visiting for over 90 days), check with the French Consulate in your home country.

Below: *les timbres pratiques.*

You'll need an adapter for most British and US plugs: French sockets have two round holes. Supplies are 220 volt, and US equipment will need a transformer.

HOSPITALS
American Hospital (Hôpital Américain de Paris)
63 boulevard Victor Hugo, 92200 Neuilly-sur-Seine; tel: 01 46 41 25 25; www.american-hospital. org; open 24 hours; metro: Porte Maillot, then bus 82
A private hospital with English-speaking staff.

Money

The currency of France is the euro, divided into 100 cents. Coins (*pièces*) come in 1, 2, 5, 10, 20 and 50 cents, and 1 and 2 euros. Banknotes (*billets*) come in 5, 10, 20, 50, 100, 200 and 500 euros.

The easiest way to take out money is to use a cashpoint (ATM), with a debit or credit card using your PIN. Most shops and restaurants and almost all hotels accept credit cards. The most common are Visa, American

Express (Amex), Diner's Club, Mastercard, Maestro and Cirrus. All are widely recognised.

Post

Main branches are open Mon–Fri 8am–7pm, Sat 8am–noon. The central post office is at 52 rue du Louvre (1st; tel: 01 40 28 76 00; www.laposte.fr). Stamps (*timbres*) are available at most *tabacs* (tobacconists).

Telephones

Most public phone boxes in Paris are card-operated. Phonecards, or *télécartes*, can be bought from kiosks, tobacconists and post offices.

Telephone numbers in Paris start with 01. The code for France is +33.

Tourist Information

IN PARIS
Main Paris Tourist Office
25 rue des Pyramides, 1st; tel: 08 92 68 3000; daily 9am–8pm; metro: Pyramides; map p.152 A1
Branches also at:
Carrousel du Louvre, 99 rue de Rivoli, 1st; Eiffel Tower (between

55

Fashion

Paris has long been the centre of European fashion, and has the shopping to match. The city's big couture houses are clustered mostly in the avenue Montaigne area, the Faubourg St-Honoré and St-Germain. The best areas for boutiques and more cutting-edge design are the Marais, the backstreets of Montmartre (such as rue des Abbesses), the Bastille and Oberkampf. Rue de Rivoli, Les Halles and the streets around Opéra and Grands Magasins are good for high-street fashion. The listings below focus on French brands and individual shops. For information on department stores, see 'Shopping'.

Left: an exquisite top.

Designer Fashion

Balenciaga
10 avenue George V, 8th; tel: 01 47 20 21 11; www.balenciaga.com; metro: Alma Marceau, George V; map p.150 C2
Head designer Nicolas Ghesquière has been blowing the dust off this illustrious Spanish fashion house, and it's now back at the top of the fashion tree. Its floaty fabrics and sharp cuts are popular with A-listers.

Chanel
31 rue Cambon, 1st; tel: 01 42 86 28 00; www.chanel.fr; metro: Concorde, Madeleine; map p.151 E2
You can still find that quilted bag and tailored suit, or Chanel No. 5 (first produced in 1921), but the classics are now displayed alongside Karl Lagerfeld's quirky take on leisurewear. The haute-couture atelier is still in this building, as

is the flat where the legendary Coco Chanel once lived.

Chloé
54–56 rue du Faubourg St-Honoré, 8th, tel: 01 44 94 33 00; www.chloe.com; metro: Concorde, Madeleine; map p.151 D2–3
She may have now left the design house, but Phoebe Philo's design aesthetic is still at the root of the delicate feminine creations with an urban edge, ever-popular.

Christian Dior
30 avenue Montaigne, 8th; tel: 01 40 73 73 73; www.dior.com; metro: Franklin D. Roosevelt; map p.151 C2
Join the well-heeled mothers, daughters and granddaughters vacuuming up flimsy, bias-cut outfits, gilded cosmetics and other knick-knacks at this chic boutique.

Something for Everyone

The fashion industry is still a tangible presence in Paris, even if French designers no longer dominate the world fashion stage. But between the couture tags and the high-street chains, you can find small boutiques with their own take on French style, street-wise retailers picking out exciting young talents, and the one-off boutiques of individual fashion designers. And at a number of *atelier-boutiques*, especially around Bastille and Montmartre, you can buy directly from designers and may even see the clothes being made in the back of the shop.

> Parisians traditionally go shopping after lunch on Saturday, so if you prefer to browse in relative peace, shop in the morning.

Left: Chanel on the catwalk.

Bohemian designs, for those who like their clothes effortlessly fashionable and discreetly sexy.

Jean-Paul Gaultier
6 rue Vivienne, 2nd; tel: 01 42 86 05 05; www.jeanpaulgaultier.fr; metro: Bourse; map p.152 B1
Outlandish tailoring by this wonderfully individual designer, for men and women, plus accessories.

Lagerfeld Gallery
40 rue de Seine, 6th; tel: 01 55 42 75 51; metro: Odéon; map p.154 B3
Designer Karl Lagerfeld's style laboratory, showcasing his fashion and photography. Check out the latest fashion and beauty press lying on the round table at the front.

Louis Vuitton
101 avenue des Champs-Élysées, 8th; tel: 08 10 81 00 10; www.vuitton.com; metro: George V; map p.150 C3
A label known mainly for its trademarked leather goods that attract queues of tourists.

Marc Jacobs
56–62 galerie de Montpensier, 1st; tel: 01 55 35 02 60; www.marcjacobs.com; metro: Palais Royal Musée du Louvre, Pyramides; map p.154 B4
The establishment of Jacobs' shop in the arcades of rue de

Christian Lacroix
73, rue du Faubourg St-Honoré, 8th; tel: 01 42 68 79 04; www.christian-lacroix.fr; metro: Franklin D. Roosevelt; map p.151 D3
Christian Lacroix's exuberant colours evoke the vibrant palettes of Provençal artists. At the time of writing, the label was on the verge of bankruptcy.

Comme des Garçons
54 rue du Faubourg St-Honoré, 8th; www.doverstreetmarket.com; tel: 01 53 30 27 27; metro: Madeleine, Concorde; map p.151 D2–3
Trends from once-reclusive designer Rei Kawakubo are displayed in chilli-pepper red interiors designed by Sir Richard Rogers' son, Abe, and partner Shona Kitchen.

Givenchy
3 avenue George V, 8th; tel: 01 44 31 51 09; www.givenchy.com; métro: George V, Alma Marceau; map p.150 C2
Couture by British designer Julien MacDonald. His Paris creations are less flamboyant than those for his eponymous London-based label.

The main sales *(soldes)* periods in France are January and July.

Hermès
24 rue du Faubourg St-Honoré, 8th, tel: 01 40 17 47 17; www.hermes.com; metro: Concorde, Madeleine; p.151 D2–3
Fogeys, old and young, are still well catered for with Hermès's silk scarves, Kelly bags and stylish saddle bags.

Isabel Marant
16 rue de Charonne 11th; tel: 01 49 29 71 55; www.isabelmarant.tm.fr; metro: Ledru-Rollin; map p.155 E2

Below: you can find everything from sharp tailoring to flowing bohemian silks.

Below: from outerwear to accessories and lingerie.

Rivoli has sparked a regeneration in the area. Girly dresses in pared-down neutrals, pretty frilled, cute ballerina pumps and even his gorgeous Gardenia perfume are as hip as muse Sofia Coppola.

Plein Sud
29 rue du Dragon, 6th; tel: 01 45 48 79 29; metro: St-Sulfice; map p.154 A2

Sexy fashion for women by top Moroccan designer, Fayçal Amor. The splits are high, the skirts short, and the necklines plunging.

Vanessa Bruno
25 rue St-Sulpice, 6th; tel: 01 43 54 41 04; www.vanessa bruno.com; metro: Odéon;

map p.154 B2

Vanessa Bruno's individual clothes have a gorgeous, quiet femininity. Delicate handbags complete the look.

Other Womenswear Labels and Boutiques
Abou Dhabi
10 rue des Francs-Bourgeois, 3rd; tel: 01 42 77 96 98; www.aboudabibazar.com; metro: St-Paul; map p.155 D3

The best of other designer boutiques (Paul et Joe, Isabel Marant, etc), all beautifully colour-coordinated.

Agnès b
2, 3, and 6 rue du Jour, 1st; tel: 01 45 08 56 56; www.agnesb.fr; metro: Les Halles; map p.154 B4

The French designer has pretty much colonised the rue du Jour; the street numbers above refer to stores for children's, men's and women's fashions respectively. A Parisian fashion institution for stylish clothes at mid-range prices.

Antik Batik
18 rue de Turenne, 3rd, tel: 01 44 78 02 00; www.antikbatik.fr; metro: St Paul; map p.155 D3

Clothes and accessories with an 'ethnic' influence but with a luxury finish. Hippy chic, Parisian style.

Antoine & Lili
95 quai de Valmy, 10th; tel: 01 40 37 41 55; www.antoineetlili.com; metro: Jacques Bonsergent, Gare de l'Est; map p.155 D2–3

Another outlet for the purveyors of hippy-chic. A&L's shocking-pink shop fronts are a familiar sight in Paris.

Barbara Bui
23 rue Etienne Marcel, 1st; tel: 01 40 26 43 65;

In addition to the listings here, see the department stores section in 'Shopping'. Several of the large stores have outlets entirely dedicated to men.

The majority of shops open from 9 or 10am until around 7pm. Few stores open on Sunday, except in the Marais and one or two on the Champs-Elysées. Some smaller shops close on Monday all day or in the morning until about 2pm. Many close throughout August for the traditional French summer holiday.

www.barbarabui.com; metro: Etienne Marcel; map p.154 C4

Beautiful garments with achingly clean cuts for the smart woman about town.

Corinne Sarrut
4 rue du 29 juillet, 1st; tel: 01 42 60 20 01; www.corinnesarrut.fr; metro: Palais des Tuileries; map p.154 A4

A very Parisian label, producing distinctly feminine, 1940s-style silhouettes in an original mix of materials and colours.

L'Habilleur
44 rue de Poitou, 3rd; tel: 01 48 87 77 12; metro: St Sebastien Froissart; map p.155 D4

End-of-line and ex-catwalk clothes from some of the top designers.

Maria Luisa
7 rue Rouget de Lisle, 1st; tel: 01 47 03 96 15; www.marialuisa paris.com; metro: Concorde; map p.151 E2

One of the hottest multi-label stores in Paris with an eye not only for the avant-garde but also for what is wearable. Menswear is sold round the corner, at 40 rue du Mont-Thabor.

Paul et Joe
62 rue des Saints-Pères, 7th; tel: 01 42 22 47 01 www. pauland joe.com; metro: rue du Bac, St-Germain-des-Prés; map p.154 A3

The fetish boutique of Parisian fashionistas is filled with weathered-looking creations that emulate the continuing vintage craze. Stylish menswear too.

Above: bold print on a silk halterneck.

Stella Cadente
93 quai de Valmy, 10th; tel: 01 42 09 27 00; www.stella cadente.com; metro: République; map p.153 D1–2

A light, airy boutique looking onto the Canal St-Martin with a lovely range of feminine clothes and imaginative accessories.

Lingerie

Alice Cadolle
4 rue Cambon, 1st; tel: 01 42 60 94 22; www.cadolle.com; metro: Concorde, Madeleine; map p.151 E2

Established by Hermine Cadolle, who invented the bra, this shop is now run by her great, great granddaughter, Poupie. Expensive but gorgeous creations.

Fifi Chachnil
68 rue Jean Jacques Rousseau, 1st; tel: 01 42 21 19 93; www.fifichachnil.com; metro: Les Halles; map p.154 B4

Froufrou girly undies in the vein of sexy British brand Agent Provocateur. Baby dolls, bows and frills.

Menswear

Charvet
28 place Vendôme, 8th, tel: 01 42 60 30 70; metro: Madeleine; map p.151 E2

Occupying a town house on this prestigious square, this venerable gentleman's outfitters is known for its shirts, but also sells ties, cufflinks, suits and other men's essentials.

Loft Design By
56 rue de Rennes, 6th; tel: 01 45 44 88 99; www.loftdesignby.com; metro: St-Sulpice; map p.154 A2

Fashion basics French-style, for men (and women), in neutrals of black, grey or white.

Madelios
23 boulevard de la Madeleine, 1st; tel: 01 53 45 00 00; www.madelios.com; metro: Madeleine; map p.151 E2

Everything a man might need under one vast roof. Two floors, with stylish, mostly contemporary-classic labels from Paul Smith to Dior, and a dedicated beauty salon.

Shoes and Accessories

Christian Louboutin
19 rue Jean-Jacques Rousseau, 1st; tel: 01 42 36 53 66; www.christianlouboutin.com; metro: Palais Royale-Musée du Louvre; map p.154 B4

Distinguished by their flame-red heels, Louboutin's sexy shoes are the footwear of choice with today's fashion-forward A listers.

J. Donegan
38 rue St-Dominique, 7th; tel: 01 45 51 69 15; metro: Latour Maubourg, Ecole Militaire; map p.159 C4

Don't be thrown by the Irish name. This men's shoe-maker, catering to the needs of well-heeled men-about-town, is very Parisian. Wonderful range of glazes and patinas.

Rodolphe Ménudier
14 rue de Castiglione, 1st; tel: 01 92 60 86 27; www.rodolphe menudier.com; metro: Concorde, Tuileries; map p.151 E2

Killer heels and sexy boots by this top designer are displayed like artworks in a striking black-and-silver boutique.

Roger Vivier
29 rue du Faubourg St-Honoré, 8th; tel: 01 53 43 00 00; www.rogervivier.com; metro: Concorde, Madeleine; map p.151 D2–3

The man credited with inventing the stiletto is enjoying something of a renaissance among the fashion pack. Classics by Vivier and new designs by **Bruno Frisoni**, who also has his own shop at 34 rue de Grenelle, 6th; tel 01 42 84 12 30; www.brunofisoni.fr; metro: rue du Bac).

Ursule Beaugeste
15 rue Oberkampf, 11th; tel: 01 48 06 71 09; metro: Parmentier; map p.155 E4

The brains behind this brand, Anne Grand-Clément, started off designing for Sonia Rykiel et al. These days she creates uniquely stylish bags, with distinctive detailing.

Below: ties at Charvet.

Festivals and Events

From bold displays of national pride on Bastille Day, to sporting events that finish with a bang on the Champs-Elysées, to gastronomic festivities, wine festivals, fireworks, fashion shows and free music and cinema, the Parisians certainly know a thing or two about celebrating in style. Indeed, festivals and special annual events are so passionately regarded here that several of them run right through the night. The following listing covers the main events and some of the more unusual ones.

Public Holidays

1 Jan, **Jour de l'An**; Easter Monday, **Lundi de Pâques**; 1 May, **Fête du Travail**; 8 May, **Victoire 1945**; Ascension Day, **L'Ascension**; Whit Monday, **Pentecôte**; 14 July, **Bastille Day**; 15 Aug, **L'Assomption**; 1 Nov, **La Toussaint**; 11 Nov, **L'Armistice**; 25 Dec, **Noël**.

Festivals and Events

JANUARY/FEBRUARY
Fête des Rois
6 Jan; various venues
Epiphany is celebrated with *galettes des rois* cakes.
Nouvel An Chinois
Jan/Feb; 13th; metro: Porte d'Ivry, Porte de Choisy
Chinese New Year.

MARCH
Le Printemps des Poètes
Mar; various venues; www. printempsdespoetes.com
National poetry festival.
Paris Fashion Week
Mar (also Oct); various venues; www.modeaparis.com
Haute-couture shows.
Printemps du Cinéma
Mar; various venues; www.printempsducinema.com
Three days of cut-price film.

Above: the Hôtel de Ville during the Nuit Blanche.

APRIL
Foire du Trône
Early Apr (until late May); Pelouse de Reuilly; free; metro: Porte Dorée
France's biggest funfair.
Paris Marathon
Avenue des Champs-Elysées, 8th, to avenue Foch, 16th; tel: 01 41 33 15 68; www.paris marathon.com; metro: start George V, finish Porte Dauphine; map p.150 C3
Over 30,000 runners take part in the Paris marathon.

MAY
Fête du Travail
1 May; various venues
Most places close on this workers' day bank holiday.
Printemps des Musées
All month; various venues; http://printempsdesmusees. culture.fr; free
Museum collections usually in reserve are open to the public.
La Nuit des Musées
Mid-May; various venues; www. nuitdesmusees.culture.fr; free
Key museums stay open late and hold special events.

JUNE
Le Printemps des Rues
All month; various venues; tel: 01 47 97 36 06; www. leprintempsdesrues.com
Street-theatre festival.
Fête de la Musique
21 June; various venues; tel: 01 40 03 94 70; www.fetede lamusique.fr; free
Huge music festival, with concerts through the night.
Gay Pride
End of the month; various venues; tel: 01 43 57 21 47; free
A day of celebrations with a parade ending at Bastille.

Left: Paris Plage.

OCTOBER
La Nuit Blanche
Early Oct; various venues; free
Stay up all night for free artistic events all over town.
Fête des Vendanges à Montmartre
Second weekend; rue des Saules, 18th; tel: 01 30 21 48 62; www.fetedesvendanges demontmartre.com; metro: Lamarck Caulaincourt
Celebrate the grape harvest at Montmartre's vineyard.
FIAC
End Oct; various venues; tel: 01 41 90 47 47; www. fiacparis.com; entrance charge
Internationally renowned contemporary art fair.

NOVEMBER
Fête du Beaujolais Nouveau
Third Thur; various venues; www.beaujolaisnouveau.com
The year's new vintage is tasted in bars and cafés.

DECEMBER
Nouvel An
31 Dec; various venues
Crowds fill the Champs-Elysées and Trocadéro for New Year's Eve fireworks.

Below: the delightful Montmartre vineyards.

When in Paris, French speakers should look out at crossroads for the digital signposts that read *'La Mairie de Paris vous informe...'*, giving details of current events.

JULY/AUGUST
Bastille Day
14 July; across Paris
Celebrations to mark the storming of the Bastille kick off on 13 July on place de la Bastille. At 10am on 14 July a military parade leaves the Champs-Elysées. Other festivities include fireworks at the Trocadéro.
Paris Quartier d'Eté
Mid-July to mid-Aug; various venues; free/charge; www.quartierdete.com
Summer arts festival.
Le Tour de France
End of July; avenue des Champs-Elysées, 8th; tel: 01 41 33 15 00; www.letour.fr; metro: Charles-de-Gaulle-Etoile; map p.150 B3
The world's most famous bicycle race sprints to a finish.
Paris-Plage
Mid-July till mid-Aug; Pont des Arts to Pont de Sully; tel: 08 20 00 75 75; www.paris.fr; free; metro: Sully Morland, Louvre Rivoli, Châtelet, Hôtel de Ville, Ponte Marie; map p.154–5
The beach comes to Paris with 2,000 tonnes of sand, parasols, paddling pools and beach huts along the Seine.
Cinéma en Plein Air
Mid-July till end Aug: nightly except Mon; Parc de la Villette, 19th; tel: 01 40 03 75 75; www.villette.com; free; metro: Porte de Pantin
Classic movies on a giant outdoor inflatable screen.

SEPTEMBER
Jazz à la Villette
Early Sept; Parc de la Villette, 19th; tel: 01 40 03 75 75; www.villette.com; entrance charge; metro: Porte de Pantin
Jazz festival.
Festival d'Automne
Mid-Sept till mid-Dec; various venues; tel: 01 53 45 17 17; www.festival-automne.com; entrance charge
Theatre, music and dance.
Journées du Patrimoine
3rd weekend; various venues; tel: 08 20 20 25 02; www.journeesdu patrimoine.culture.fr
Open house at otherwise off-limits buildings.

Food and Drink

Paris has the reputation of being one of the best food cities in the world, with a stellar gastronomic history. However, over the past ten years food critics have been hard on the French capital, claiming that, unlike in London, New York and Sydney, the culinary scene has been stubbornly slow to evolve: 'duck *à l'orange*, again?' There is some truth to these reproaches – France is conservative when it comes to food – but this attitude is not without benefits, especially for visitors in search of those fabulous classic dishes such as *bœuf bourguinon*, *tarte tatin* or *mousse au chocolate*.

French Food

An enormous fuss has been made in recent years about the death of French cuisine. Critics hail Spain as the 'new France', or London, Sydney, or New York; whereas Paris, they whine, is stuck in a rut.

It's not an entirely fair evaluation. French cooking may be slow to evolve, but this is because France is a country that truly knows its food. A new ingredient or dish will not be welcomed into the cuisine until it proves itself worthy. The French are highly protective, disciplined and judicious in the cultivation of their tradition.

THE CONTEMPORARY AND INTERNATIONAL SCENES

This is not to say that contemporary and international experiences are not to be found. In recent years, young chefs have been opening more fashion-conscious restaurants – impervious to Michelin ratings – serving French food, yet integrating (cautiously) more exotic flavours such as ginger, peanut, curry and lime.

Above: innovative bistro food at Le Square Trousseau.

The international scene, although perhaps not as widespread as elsewhere, is also an integral part of the city's taste experience. The greatest concentration of Chinese and Vietnamese restaurants is in the 5th and 13th *arrondissements* (the Latin Quarter and southeast), while Japanese eateries are concentrated in the 1st (Louvre, Palais-Royal and Châtelet).

The best Moroccan restaurants are peppered across Paris, but around the Bastille is a good place to start. There is excellent Lebanese food in the 8th and 16th (Madeleine, Grands Boulevards, Champs-Elysées and West), while good African food can be found around Pigalle and the East.

Places to Eat

Brasseries (breweries) were introduced to Paris in the 19th century, at about the time when modern methods of brewing were being perfected. They're a jolly experience: spacious, clamorous and festive, usually elaborately decorated in gracious Belle-Epoque style. Many serve Alsatian specialities, such as choucroute and Steins of beer; others specialise in shellfish. Outside the latter, you'll spot heaps of shellfish on beds of ice, and men in overalls shucking oysters from dawn till dusk.

Bistros are generally smaller-scale establishments and offer more or less the same menus wherever you go: *hareng pommes à l'huile* (smoked herring marinated in oil with warm potatoes), *blanquette de veau* (veal in a white sauce), *mousse au*

Left: delicious fresh produce.

natural shape. This is considered proper behaviour because it means the last person served won't be left with just the rind.

Drinks

It is usual to be offered an *apéritif*, such as a glass of Champagne, white wine, a *kir* (white wine with cassis, a blackcurrant liqueur) or white port, before a meal in France.

In the minds of the French, **wine** is the ever-present accompaniment to eating, whether by the bottle, by the glass or, cheaply, by the jug. *Un pichet de rouge* (a jug of red) will get you an inexpensive, potentially rough, but entirely drinkable red wine.

Beer is usually only ordered with sandwiches, Alsatian meals or quick Asian lunches. Cider accompanies Breton and Norman specialities such as *crêpes* or mussels.

Numerous mineral **waters** are on offer in all restaurants. Request *pétillante* for sparkling; *plate* for still; or *en carafe* for a jug of tap water.

Coffee in France is served after, rather than with, dessert. *Café* means espresso, strong and black; if you like milk

Below: chunky, ripe cheese.

The origin of the name 'bistro' supposedly lies in the days of the Allied occupation of Paris in 1814. The Russian military were forbidden to drink, so whenever they dived into a bar in Montmartre, they demanded their refreshments urgently – *'bistrot'* – to avoid being caught.

---

chocolat and *tarte tatin* (caramelised apple upside-down tart).

A number of bistros have a regional bent, and offer provincial specialities, including *foie gras* and duck (southwestern), hot pepper, salt cod and ham (Basque), and *ratatouille*, lamb and *bouillabaisse* (Provençale).

Cafés, in the traditional sense of the term, usually serve sandwiches, notably the ubiquitous *croque-monsieur* (grilled ham and cheese), as well as a variety of giant (not necessarily healthy) salads. More recent establishments may offer fuller menus with a Mediterranean slant.

Restaurants, whether Michelin-starred or not, range from being gloriously old-fashioned, with truffle-studded *foie gras* terrines and venison in grand old sauces, to being self-consciously cutting-edge, with hot-pepper sorbets to cleanse the palate between veal slow-cooked in orange juice, and desserts that show off milk or chocolate in five different ways. You can often try a tasting menu *(dégustation)* for a host of dishes in smaller-than-usual portions, so that there's room for them all.

Cheese

Between the main course and dessert comes the cheese trolley or platter, laden with a delectably smelly array. The number of options mean it can take years to become familiar with French cheeses. Just remember two rules: 1) in a cheese tasting, always start with the mildest cheese and work your way around to the strongest; and 2) never steal 'the nose' off a piece of cheese if you're serving yourself; always slice cheese in such a way as to preserve its request a *café noisette*. *Café crème* (a large milky coffee) is considered a breakfast drink; ordering it after dinner will raise eyebrows. Finally, if caffeine will keep you up all night, ask for a *café décaféiné* (*déca* for short), or for *une tisane* (herbal tea).

Food Markets

Bastille
Boulevard Richard-Lenoir (between rues Amelot and St-Sabin), 11th; Thur and Sun am; metro: Richard-Lenoir; map p.155 E3
Large street market with a vast range of produce.

Daumesnil
Avenue Daumesnil (place Félix-Eboué to rue de Charenton), 12th; Tue and Fri am; metro: Daumesnil, Dugommier
A large and varied 'roving' street market.

Marche St-Quentin
85 boulevard Magenta, 10th; Tue–Sat all day, Sun am: metro: Gare de l'Est; map p.153 C3
The best-preserved of the cast-iron covered markets.

Rue Mouffetard
Rue Mouffetard, 5th; stalls open Tue–Sat all day (long break for lunch) and Sun am; metro: Cardinal-Lemoine, Place Monge; map p.154 C1

Food shops with stalls that spill out onto the pavement.

Food Shops

Alléosse
13 rue Poncelet, 17th; tel: 01 46 22 50 45; www.fromage-alleosse.com; Tue–Sat 9am–1pm, 4.30–7pm (Fri, Sat till 7.30pm); metro: Ternes; map p.150 B4
Stocks around 200 cheeses and supplies numerous world-class restaurants.

L'Autre Boulange
43 rue de Montreuil, 11th; tel: 01 43 72 86 00; www.lautre boulange.com; Mon–Fri 7.30am–1.30pm, 4–7.30pm, Sat 7.30am–1.30pm; metro: Nation
Thirty kinds of organic bread, cooked in a wood-fired oven.

Dalloyau
99–101 rue Faubourg St-Honoré, 8th; tel: 01 42 99 90 00; www.dalloyau.fr; daily 8.30am–9pm; metro: St-Philippe du Roule, Miromesnil; map p.151 D3
Venerable house (est. 1802), whose specialities include mini macaroons and a huge variety of chocolate truffles.

L'Épicerie
51 rue St-Louis-en-L'Ile, 4th; tel: 01 43 25 20 14; www.epicerieparis.com; Oct–Apr: daily 10.30am–7pm, May–Sept: 11am–8pm; metro: Pont Marie,

> For a comprehensive list of Parisian markets, visit www.mairie-paris.fr.

Sully Morland; map p.155 D2
Around 100 varieties of jam, a similar number of mustards, plus oils and vinegars.

Fauchon
26 and 30 place de la Madeleine, 8th; tel: 01 70 39 38 00; www.fauchon.com; Mon–Sat 8am–9pm (No. 26) and 9am–8pm (No.30); metro: Madeleine; map p.151 E2
Spectacular displays of prepared dishes, pastries, chocolate, and fine wine.

Hédiard
21 place de la Madeleine, 8th; tel: 01 43 12 88 88; www.hediard.fr; Mon–Sat 8.30am–9pm; metro: Madeleine; map p.151 E2
Fauchon's great rival, on the other side of the square. Coffees, teas and spices are particularly recommended.

Maison de la Truffe
19 place de la Madeleine, 8th; tel: 01 79 35 01 57; www.maison-de-la-truffe.com; Mon–Sat 9.30am–8pm; metro: Madeleine; map p.151 E2
You can buy the sought-after fungus here, fresh from November to March.

Petrossian
18 boulevard de la Tour Maubourg, 7th; tel: 01 44 11 32 22; www.petrossian.fr; Mon–Sat 9.30am–8pm; metro: La Tour Maubourg; map p.157 D4
Caviar specialist.

Pierre Hermé
72 rue Bonaparte, 6th; tel: 01 43 54 47 77; www.pierreherme.com; Tue–Sun 10am–7pm (Sat till 7.30pm); metro: St-Germain des Prés; map p.154 A3
Architecturally constructed cakes and irresistibly delicious exotic chocolates.

Ryst Dupeyron
79 rue du Bac, 7th; tel: 01 45 48 80 93; www.vintageandco.com; Mon–Sat 11am–7pm; metro:

Below: whisks galore at E. Dehillerin (18 rue Coquillière, 1st, tel: 01 42 36 53 13), an Aladdin's cave, full of kitchen implements.

Above: patisserie is an art form.

Rue du Bac; map p.157 E3
Stock includes around 200
premiers crus Bordeaux, rare
whiskies and vintage ports.
Stohrer
51 rue Montorgueil, 2nd; tel: 01
42 33 38 20; www.stohrer.fr;
daily 7.30am–8.30pm; metro:
Les Halles; map p.154 C4
Established in 1730 and
reputedly the oldest patisserie in Paris. The originator
of *baba au rhum* (a rich cake,
soaked in rum).
Les Ultra Vins
16 rue Lacuée, 12th; tel:
01 43 46 85 81; Mon–Sat 9am–
8.30pm; metro: Bastille, Quai
de la Rappé; map p.155 E2
Small shop stocking almost
2,000 wines.

Useful Vocabulary

Meat (Viande)
bleu **rare**
à point **medium**
bien cuit **well done**
grillé **grilled**
rôti **roasted**
agneau **lamb**
andouille(tte) **tripe sausage**
bifteck **steak**
boudin **sausage**
boudin noir **black pudding**
caille **quail**
canard **duck**
carbonnade **casserole of
beef, beer and onions**
carré d'agneau **rack of lamb**
cervelle **brains**
côte d'agneau **lamb chop**
dinde **turkey**

entrecôte **beef rib steak**
escargot **snail**
faisan **pheasant**
farci **stuffed**
foie **liver**
grillade **grilled meat**
jambon **ham**
langue **tongue**
oie **goose**
pintade **guinea fowl**
porc **pork**
pot-au-feu **beef casserole**
poulet **chicken**
rognons **kidneys**
sanglier **wild boar**
saucisse **fresh sausage**
saucisson **salami**
veau **veal**

Fish (Poisson)
anchois **anchovies**
anguille **eel**
bar (or *loup*) **sea bass**
barbue **brill**
brandade **salt-cod purée**
cabillaud **cod**
calamars **squid**
coquillage **shellfish**
coquilles St-Jacques
scallops
crevette **shrimp**
daurade **sea bream**
flétan **halibut**
fruits de mer **seafood**
hareng **herring**
homard **lobster**
huître **oyster**
langoustine **large prawn**
limande **lemon sole**
lotte **monkfish**
morue **salt cod**
moule **mussel**
oursin **sea urchin**
raie **skate**
saumon **salmon**
thon **tuna**
truite **trout**

> Devoted to the culinary arts,
> the Librarie Gourmande book
> shop (4 rue Dante, 5th; tel: 01
> 43 54 37 27) is abuzz all year
> round owing to the fame of its
> proprietor Geneviève Baudon
> and her appetising collection
> of cookery books.

Above: fruity red wine.

Vegetables (Légumes)
ail **garlic**
artichaut **artichoke**
asperge **asparagus**
aubergine **aubergine/
eggplant**
avocat **avocado**
céleri rémoulade **grated
celery with mayonnaise**
champignon **mushroom**
cornichon **gherkin**
courgette **courgette/
zucchini**
chips **crisps/potato chips**
chou **cabbage**
chou-fleur **cauliflower**
concombre **cucumber**
crudités **raw vegetables**
épinards **spinach**
frites **chips, French fries**
haricot **dried beans**
haricots verts **green beans**
lentilles **lentils**
oignon **onion**
poireau **leek**
pois **peas**
pomme de terre **potato**
riz **rice**
salade verte **green salad**

Fruit (Fruit)
ananas **pineapple**
cerise **cherry**
citron **lemon**
citron vert **lime**
fraise **strawberry**
framboise **raspberry**
pamplemousse **grapefruit**
pêche **peach**
poire **pear**
pomme **apple**
raisin **grape**

Gay and Lesbian

The moniker is famous, but just how gay really is Paris? Although France has some way to go before gays have the same rights as heterosexuals, gays and lesbians are increasingly accepted in the capital, and this greater openness is being championed by the city's openly gay mayor Bertrand Delanoë. The Marais (4th *arrondissement*) is the most gay-friendly district, with gay-oriented restaurants, wine bars, boutiques, bookshops, beauty salons, hotels, bars and discos. The following is just a selection of venues; for more information check out the websites and magazines listed below.

Accommodation

SEE HOTELS, P.70–7
Gay Travel
236 rue St-Martin, 3rd; tel: 01 42 78 03 50; www.gaytravel france.com; metro: Hôtel de Ville, Rambuteau; map p.155 C4
This agency can arrange gay-friendly apartment rental and recommend hotels.
Hôtel Beaumarchais
Easy-going, gay-friendly hotel in trendy Oberkampf.
Hôtel Duo
This fashionable hotel in the Marais is very welcoming, although not exclusively gay.

Bars and Cafés

The main concentration of gay bars and cafés is found in the Marais, on and between rue des Archives and rue Vieille-du-Temple.
Eagle
33 bis rue des Lombards, 1st; tel: 01 42 47 00 67 15; Mon–Sun 6pm–4am; metro: Les Halles;

map p.154 C4
Popular hang-out for leather-men. Evenings may start off with tea and cake, but get steadily more full-on as the clientele gravitates towards the disco at the back.
Le Central
33 rue Vieille-du-Temple, 4th, tel: 01 48 87 56 08; www.hotel centralmarais.com; Mon–Fri 4pm–2am, Sat–Sun 2pm–2am; metro: Hôtel de Ville; map p.155 D3
A classic gay bar in a historic Marais town house. A good place to kick off an evening.
Le Cox Café
15 rue des Archives, 4th, tel: 01 42 72 08 00; www.cox.fr;

Sun–Thur 11am–2am, Fri, Sat 11am–4am; metro: Hôtel de Ville; map p.155 C3
Busy bar with café-style food and a mixed gay crowd.
L'Open Café
17 rue des Archives, 4th, tel: 01 42 72 26 18; www.opencafe.fr; Sun–Thur 11am–2am, Fri, Sat 11am–4am; metro: Hôtel de Ville Next door to the Cox *(see above)*, with the same vibe.
Les Scandaleuses
8 rue des Ecouffes, 4th, tel: 01 48 87 39 26; metro: St-Paul; map p.155 D3
The Marais's rue des Ecouffes is peppered with bars, cafés (including this

Left: Gay Pride Parade.

MAGAZINES

There are various free magazines you can pick up in gay bars in the 3rd and 4th *arrondissements*. The magazine **Têtu** (www.tetu.com) is a useful source of information, and can be bought at most news kiosks in the city.

SHOPS
Les Mots à la Bouche
6 rue Ste-Croix-la-Bretonnerie, 4th; tel: 01 42 78 88 30; www. motsbouche.com; Mon–Sat 11am–11pm, Sun 1–9pm; metro: Hôtel de Ville; map 155 D3
The capital's largest gay bookshop stocks literature from around the world, including an English-language section. A good place to find out what's going on in the local gay scene.

Pharmacie du Village
26 rue du Temple, 4th; Hôtel de Ville; tel: 01 42 72 60 71; Mon–Sat 8.30am–9.30pm, Sun 9am–8pm; map 155 C3
A dispensing chemist, but with a local twist: the staff are gay and can offer advice on subjects such as sexually transmitted diseases and street drugs as well as more standard pharmaceuticals.

one) and boutiques aimed at lesbians.

Le Troisième Lieu
62 rue Quincampoix, 4th; tel: 01 48 04 85 64; Mon–Sat 6pm–2am; metro: Rambuteau; map p.155 C4
Lesbian bar with something of a militant reputation. Great light food.

Clubs
SEE NIGHTLIFE, P.110–3
Pulp
25 boulevard Poissonnière, 2nd; tel: 01 40 26 01 93; www.pulp-paris.com; free Wed, Thur, entrance charge Sat–Sun; metro: Grands Boulevards; map p.152 B2
A 'club for girls that boys like a lot too', Pulp does popular themed nights and has big-name DJs on Wednesday nights. Glam French music-hall decor.

Le Queen
102 avenue des Champs-Elysées, 8th; tel: 01 53 89 08 90; www.queen.fr; daily midnight–6am; entrance charge varies; metro: George V; map p.150 C3
Not exclusively gay (midweek, particularly, it tends to

be mixed), but predominately a lesbian crowd. Big-name and local DJs play dance, disco and techno. Some drag shows and stripteases. Foam parties in summer.

Festivals
Gay Pride Parade
www.gaypride.fr
This annual parade, which takes place in June, gets bigger by the year. The revellers, many in outlandish costumes and make-up, bring traffic to a standstill across the city, ending with a bang at place de la Bastille.

Resources
Centre Gai et Lesbien
63 rue Beaubourg, 3rd; tel: 01 43 57 21 47; Mon–Sat 4–8pm; metro: Rambuteau; map p.155 C4
Opened in 1994, this centre for members of the gay and lesbian community houses a lending library (Tue, Fri 4–6pm), with around 2,000 volumes. It also advises on health, social and legal issues.

It's not all good news for equality. Although since 1999 co-habiting couples (of all persuasions) have had financial and legal rights in France through a Civil Solidarity Pact (PACS), same-sex marriages are not legally recognised. In March 2007 the country's first same-sex civil union, conducted in 2004 between Stéphane Charpin and Bertrand Charpentier, was deemed unlawful by the courts. Same-sex couples in France are not allowed to adopt children.

History

c.300 bc
A Celtic tribe, the Parisii, settle on the Ile de la Cité and found the settlement of Lutétia.

58–52 bc
Roman conquest under Julius Caesar.

c. ad 250
St Denis establishes the first Christian community in Paris. He is martyred in ad 287.

508
Clovis, King of Franks, makes Paris his capital.

987
Hugues Capet is elected King of France.

13th century
Founding of the Sorbonne.

1420
The English occupy Paris.

1431
Henry VI of England is crowned King of France.

1436
The English are expelled.

1682
Louis XIV moves his court to Versailles.

1789
Storming of Bastille starts French Revolution.

1793
Execution of Louis XVI and Marie-Antoinette; Reign of Terror.

1804
Napoleon Bonaparte becomes emperor, ushering in the First Empire.

1814–15
The fall of Napoleon heralds the restoration of the Bourbon monarchy.

1830
Bourgeois revolution; Louis-Philippe of Orléans becomes king.

1836
The Arc de Triomphe is completed.

1848
Revolution brings Louis-Napoleon to power. Second Republic.

1852–70
Baron Georges Haussmann undertakes a massive redesign of the city.

1855
First World Fair held in Paris.

1863
Manet's painting Le Déjeuner sur l'Herbe scandalises the Académie.

1866
Founding of Le Figaro newspaper.

1870–1
Franco-Prussian War. Paris surrenders to Prussia, and Napoléon III abdicates.

1871
Uprising by the Paris Commune, with 25,000 people killed, the Tuileries palace destroyed and the Hôtel de Ville burnt down.

1894–1906
The Dreyfus Affair.

1889
The Eiffel Tower is built for the World Fair. Pigalle's Moulin Rouge opens.

1909
First Paris Métro line opens.

1914–18
World War I.

1939–45
World War II. In 1940 the French Government capitulates, and the Germans occupy Paris until 1944.

1946
General Charles de Gaulle becomes president of the Fourth Republic.

1958
Algerian crisis topples the Fourth Republic. De Gaulle returns as president of the Fifth Republic.

1958–63
Construction of La Défense begins.

1962
End of the Algerian war.

1968
Student riots and workers' general strikes rock Paris and force de Gaulle to call an election. He wins but resigns a year later.

1969
Les Halles food market is moved to Rungis. Pompidou becomes president.

1977
Jacques Chirac becomes the first elected mayor since 1871. Centre Georges-Pompidou opens

1981–95
François Mitterrand's presidency, notable for his architectural grands projets.

1986
Opening of the Musée d'Orsay and completion of the Cité des Sciences at La Villette.

1995
Jacques Chirac is elected president.

1998
France wins the football World Cup.

2005
Urban unrest over immigration and racism, inflamed by comments of hard-line interior minister Nicolas Sarkozy.

2006
Protests over new youth employment law.

2007
Presidential election won by right-wing candidate Nicolas Sarkozy.

2008
Bertrand Delanoë is re-elected mayor.

2010
European Rugby Cup Final to be held in Paris.

Hotels

Hotels in Paris range from the positively palatial to the absolutely pitiful, seemingly always at elevated prices. In general, it's difficult to find anything decent, with its own bathroom, for less than 100 euros a night. In the middle range, the stress tends to be on style and charm rather than high-tech facilities. North Americans, in particular, may be astounded at the tiny lifts and lack of room space in a typical Parisian hotel. The following list, which covers a range of places to suit all budgets and tastes, is divided geographically into the same areas covered in the 'Areas' section of this guide.

The Islands

Henri IV
25 place Dauphine, 1st; tel: 01 43 54 44 53; €; metro: Pont Neuf; map p.154 B3
Some of the least-expensive rooms in Paris can be found at this modest hotel which has been popular with visitors on a budget for decades. The 21 rooms are somewhat old-fashioned, with shared bathrooms, but this pales into significance beside the fabulous location on place Dauphine. Only a short walk from Notre-Dame and St-Michel. Reserve well in advance. No credit cards.

Hôtel des Deux-Iles
59 rue St-Louis en-l'Ile, 4th; tel: 01 43 26 13 35; www.deuxiles-paris-hotel.com; €€; metro: Pont Marie; map p.155 C2
Set in a small, attractive 17th-century mansion on the main street of the Ile St-Louis, this hotel, with 17 soundproofed rooms, is comfortable, with friendly staff. Rooms are on the small size, but prettily decorated.

There's an attractive courtyard too. Facilities include wi-fi internet.

Hôtel du Jeu de Paume
54 rue St-Louis-en-l'Ile, 4th; tel: 01 43 26 14 18; www.jeude paumehotel.com; €€€; metro: Pont Marie; map p.155 C2
Delightfully set on the pretty Ile St-Louis, this hotel, with ancient beams and romantic decor, is great for a taste of old Paris. Facilities have been updated too, with new bathrooms, a sauna, and wi-fi internet. Breakfast is served in the mansion's 17th-century real-tennis court. Gym, library, billiards room, concierge and room service.

Hôtel de Lutèce
65 rue St-Louis-en-l'Ile, 4th; tel: 01 43 26 23 52, fax: 01 43 29 60 25; www.paris-hotel-lutece. com; €€; metro: Pont Marie; map p.155 C2
On the exclusive Ile St-Louis, this lovely hotel – under the same management as the Deux Iles – has 23 tiny rooms that are attractive and very quiet. Those on the sixth floor are the most romantic. Facilities include wi-fi Internet.

Above: outside elegant Hôtel de Crillon.

Left the luxurious
Hôtel Plaza-Athénée.

Note that prices can vary widely within a hotel, and may change according to the time of year. Rooms are often less expensive in August, when the Parisians traditionally take a month's holiday.

two notable restaurants: Michelin-starred **Les Ambassadeurs** (headed by chef Jean-François Piège) and the more affordable **L'Obélisque**. There's also the romantic Winter Garden for tea, coffee and cocktails. In the bedrooms, the decor is fittingly grand. Facilities include a gym, parking and room service.
SEE ALSO CAFÉS AND BARS, P.34

Louvre, Tuileries and Concorde

Hôtel Brighton
218 rue de Rivoli, 1st; tel: 01 47 03 61 61; www.brightonhotel paris.com; €€; metro: Tuileries; map p.151 E2
This grand 19th-century hotel, which owes its name to the thriving relations between France and England during Queen Victoria's reign, holds its own over the northern stretch of the Tuileries. The lounge, breakfast room and most of the bedrooms have been refurbished. Facilities include Internet access.

Hôtel Costes
239 rue St-Honoré, 1st; tel: 01 42 44 50 00; www.hotel costes.com; €€€€; Métro: Tuileries; map p.151 E2
This super-hip hotel is just off elegant place Vendôme in an exclusive neighbourhood lined with chic boutiques. The rooms are exquisitely decorated with baroque paintings, heavy drapes and antiques. Some bathrooms have clawfoot bathtubs and mosaic tiles. Owner Jean-Louis Costes dislikes electrial lighting, so the hallways are lit with candles; even the beautiful indoor pool, which has an underwater sound system, is dark. The Café Costes is one of the trendiest places in town. Other facilities include a bar, gym, restaurant, room service and parking.
SEE ALSO RESTAURANTS, P.126

Hôtel de Crillon
10 place de la Concorde, 8th; tel: 01 44 71 15 00; www.crillon. com; €€€€; metro: Concorde; map p.151 E2
This palatial world-renowned hotel forms part of the splendid neoclassical façade that dominates the north side of place de la Concorde. Known for its impeccable service (only to be expected at this price), it also has a legendary bar and

Opéra and Grands Boulevards

Four Seasons George V
31 avenue George V, 8th; tel: 01 49 52 70 00; www.fourseasons. com/paris; €€€€; metro: George V, Alma Marceau; map p.150 C2
One of the most famous hotels in Paris, just off the Champs-Elysées. The George V offers the height of opulence, with beautifully decorated, traditional-style rooms with modern touches and magnificent marble bathrooms. Exquisite service. Facilities include a fabulous spa inspired by the palace at Versailles, a bar, two restaurants and a business centre.

Hôtel Amour
8 rue Navarin, 9th; tel: 01 48 78 31 80; www.hotelamourparis.fr; €€; metro: St-Georges; map p.152 B3
Trendy boutique hotel hidden behind an anonymous facade in the 9th. The 20 rooms have been decorated by contemporary artists; some of them even feature art installations.

Price ranges, which are given as a guide only, are for a standard double room with bathroom, including service and tax but excluding breakfast (usually from around €5–20, depending on the rating of the hotel):
€   under €120
€€   €120–200
€€€   €200–350
€€€€   over €350

Above: Hotel Plaza Athene.

The bar has DJs, and the restaurant has a garden.

Hôtel Chopin

10 boulevard Montmartre, 46 passage Jouffroy), 9th; tel: 01 47 70 58 10; www.hotel breton-nerie.com; €; metro: Richelieu Drouot; map p.152 B2

Tucked away at the end of the historic glass-roofed Passage des Panoramas (see p.141), this is a quiet, friendly, simply furnished hotel, offering 36 rooms at a fabulous price for the location. Facilities are basic, but there are televisions in the rooms. Book well in advance.

Hôtel Edouard VII

39 avenue de l'Opéra, 2nd; tel: 01 42 61 56 90; www.edouard7 hotel.com; €€–€€€; metro: Opéra; map p.152 A1

Historic family-owned hotel on one of the grandest avenues

in Paris, just a stone's throw from the Palais-Garnier and the Louvre. Some rooms at the front have balconies with marvellous views of the opera house. The hotel features the smart **Angl'Opera** restaurant and a stylish, comfortable bar. Impressive lobby. Facilities include room service.

SEE ALSO RESTAURANTS, P.128

Hôtel Plaza-Athénée

25 avenue Montaigne, 8th; tel: 01 53 67 66 67; www.plaza-athe-nee-paris.com; €€€€; metro: Alma Marceau; map p.151 C2

This palatial hotel, with lavish Versace decor, has sound-proofed rooms, a club, restaurant and suites furnished in Louis XVI or Regency style. Super-chef Alain Ducasse is in charge of the restaurant. If you can't stretch to the price of a room, treat yourself to a

cocktail in the fashionable bar. Facilities include a gym and business centre.

SEE ALSO RESTAURANTS, P.127

Ritz

15 place Vendôme, 1st; tel: 01 43 16 30 70; www.ritzparis. com; €€€€; metro: Concorde, Opéra; map p.151 E2

One of the most prestigious addresses in the world, the Ritz has welcomed the most

Price ranges, which are given as a guide only, are for a standard double room with bathroom, including service and tax but excluding breakfast (usually from around €5–20, depending on the rating of the hotel):
€ under €120
€€ €120–200
€€€ €200–350
€€€€ over €350

Not all properties are wheelchair-accessible; even if a hotel does have a lift, for example, it is likely that it will be a fairly small one. Travellers with disabilities should check before reserving.

discriminating of guests, including Coco Chanel (who lived in a suite here for 37 years), the Duke and Duchess of Windsor, and Princess Diana and Dodi Al Fayed. Rooms are plush, decorated in Louis XV style with antique clocks and rich tapestries. The spa has a beautiful indoor pool, and there are two fine restaurants and a pleasant garden. All the facilities one would expect, including a gym and business centre.

Beaubourg and Les Halles

Hôtel du Cygne
3–5 rue du Cygne, 1st; tel: 01 42 60 14 16; www.cygne-hotel-paris.com; €; metro: Étienne Marcel; map p.154 C4
A good choice for those on a budget, this small central hotel is set within a 17th-century building on a pedestrianised street in the heart of Les Halles *quartier*. Rooms are basic but cosy.

Hôtel de Roubaix
6 rue Grenata, 3rd; tel: 01 42 72 89 91; www.hotel-de-roubaix.com; €; metro: Arts et Métiers, Réaumur Sébastopol; map p.154 C4
Another good choice for a centrally positioned budget hotel. Decor in the 53 rooms is typically French (florid wallpaper), and there are no frills, but it's clean, and the staff are friendly. Great value for money.

Marais and Bastille

Hôtel du Bourg Tibourg
19 rue du Bourg-Tibourg, 4th;

tel: 01 42 78 47 39; www.hotel bourgtibourg.com; €€€; metro: Hôtel de Ville; map p.155 C3
Situated on a charming narrow street in the heart of the Marais, this 17th-century building is home to a well-kept, affordable, mid-size hotel. Rooms are decorated in Gothic style, with a luxurious, over-the-top feel. Breakfast is served in a vaulted dining room with exposed stone. Facilities include wi-fi internet and room service.

Hôtel Caron de Beaumarchais
12 rue du Vieille du Temple, 4th; tel: 01 42 72 34 12; www.caron debeaumarchais.com; €€; metro: St-Paul, Hôtel de Ville; map p.155 C3
A gorgeous little hotel in an excellent location in one of the nicest streets in the Marais. Rooms are decorated in a romantic French 18th-century style with pretty chandeliers and antiques, in honour of the 18th-century playwright after whom the hotel is named. Very friendly management. There are only 19 rooms, so book in advance.

Hôtel Duo
11 rue du Temple, 4th; tel: 01 42 72 72 22; www.duoparis.com; €€; metro: Hôtel de Ville; map p.155 C3
Trendy hotel in an excellent

location in the Marais. The 58 rooms, which are quiet despite the central location, thanks to excellent soundproofing, are furnished in contemporary style, with good-sized bathrooms (unusual in Paris). Facilities include a bar, gym and sauna. Wi-fi internet access is available for free in the communal area.

Hôtel de la Place des Vosges
12 rue Birague, 4th; tel: 01 42 72 60 46; http://hotelplacedes vosges.com; €–€€; metro: St-Paul; map p.155 D3
An intimate hotel with only 16 rooms in former stables. It's popular and in a great location by the elegant place des Vosges, so book ahead. A successful marriage of old and new, although still slightly crumbly. Friendly staff.

Hôtel St-Merry
78 rue de la Verrerie, 4th; tel: 01 42 78 14 15; www.hotelmarais. com; €€–€€€; metro: Hôtel de Ville; map p.155 C3
Arguably the most original hotel in Paris, the St-Merry was once a 17th-century presbytery. Rooms have stained-glass windows and are decorated with mahogany church pews and iron candelabra and, in one, a carvedstone flying buttress. The phone booth is in a confes-

Below: the Pavillon de la Reine, *see overleaf*, is elegant and cosy.

sional. A Gothic masterpiece. Fancy facilities are few and far between: only the suite has a television, for example.

Pavillon de la Reine
28 place des Vosges, 3rd; tel: 01 40 29 19 19; www.pavillon-de-la-reine.com; €€€; metro: St-Paul; map p.155 D3

This romantic mid-sized hotel, located on the elegant place des Vosges, feels like a country *château*. Rooms vary greatly in size and price, but most have four-poster beds, exposed wooden beams and antiques. The cosy lobby bar has evening wine tasting, and there are manicured gardens.

Champs-Elysées, Trocadéro and West

Hôtel Daniel
8 rue Frédéric-Bastiat, 8th; tel: 01 42 56 17 00; www.hoteldanielparis.com; €€€; metro: St-Philippe-du-Roule, Franklin D. Roosevelt; map p.151 C3

A member of the prestigious Relais & Châteaux group, the upmarket Hôtel Daniel is wonderfully romantic, with 26 rooms exquisitely decorated with hand-painted chinoiserie wallpaper, plush carpets and pretty antiques. Facilities

include a bar, restaurant, wi-fi internet access, parking and room service. A great location for the Champs-Elysées and rue du Faubourg St-Honoré.

Hôtel Keppler
12 rue Keppler, 16th; tel: 01 47 20 65 05; www.hotelkeppler.com; €; metro: Georges V; map p.150 B2

The Keppler offers some of the best accommodation for the price in this posh neighbourhood. The 49 rooms are large and comfortably furnished; four have balconies. There is a spiral staircase, welcoming fireplace and a bar with room service. An impeccably managed, family-owned hotel. Facilities include wi-fi internet.

Hôtel Square
3 rue de Boulainvilliers, 16th; tel: 01 44 14 91 90; www.hotelsquare.com; €€€; metro: Passy; map p.156 A3

Stylishly decorated in contemporary fashion, this hotel has just 22 rooms. Facilities include the trendy **Zebra Square** restaurant, a bar with DJ, business centre, wi-fi internet, parking and room service.

There are other hotels in the same chain as the excellent Le Général. These include Le Quartier Bastille, Le Faubourg (9 rue de Reuilly, 12th; tel: 01 43 70 04 04; www.lequartier hotelbf.com), Le Quartier République and Le Marais (39 rue Jean-Pierre Timbaud, 11th; tel: 01 48 06 64 97; www.lequartierhotelrm.com).

Montmartre and Pigalle

Hôtel Ermitage
24 rue Lamarck, 18th; tel: 01 42 64 79 22; www.ermitagesacre coeur.fr; €; metro: Lamarck Caulaincourt

This small, 12-roomed hotel, located in an old residential neighbourhood close to Sacré-Cœur, is an excellent budget choice. The cosy, colourful bedrooms are decorated in French farmhouse style, and there's a pleasant courtyard and terrace, where breakfast is served in summer. No credit cards.

Kube Rooms & Bar
1–5 passage Ruelle, 18th; tel: 01 42 05 20 00; www.kubehotel.com; €€€; metro: La Chapelle; map p.153 D4

An achingly trendy designer hotel with a vodka bar in the multicultural Goutte d'Or *quartier*. Things are high-tech here: each room is equipped with a computer with which guests control facilities in their rooms; even opening the doors is done at the push of a button. Facilities include a gym, wi-fi internet access, parking and room service.

La Villette to Bercy

Le Général
5–7 rue Rampon, 11th; tel: 01 47 00 41 57; www.legeneral hotel.com; €€; metro: République; map p.153 D1

This hotel offers the boutique experience at reasonable prices. The rooms are beauti-

Below: the very cool vodka bar at the Kube Rooms.

Right: the Ermitage feels like a family home.

fully decorated, minimalist yet cosy. There's a gym, a sauna and a bar. Room service is available anytime, and there's wi-fi internet access too.

Hôtel Apollo
11 rue de Dunkerque, 10th; tel: 01 48 78 04 98; €; metro: Gare du Nord; map p.153 C3
Just opposite the Gare du Nord, this is a cheap and certainly cheerful hotel for your stop-off before or after a long journey. The 45 rooms are clean, safe and quiet.

Hôtel Beaumarchais
3 rue Oberkampf, 11th; tel: 01 53 36 86 86; www.hotelbeau marchais.com; €€; metro: Filles du Calvaire; map p.155 E4
The Hôtel Beaumarchais has been running since the early days of the rue Oberkampf regeneration. The brightly coloured fittings, the mosaics and wavy headboards feel a little dated now, but it's very clean, the staff are friendly, and the location is excellent. Facilities include wi-fi internet access and room service.

Mama Shelter
109 rue de Bagnolet, 20th; tel: 01 43 48 48 48; www.mama shelter.com; €€; metro: Gambetta; map p.156 C1
Recently opened designer hotel (by Philippe Starck) situated in the slightly gritty but cool east of Paris. The build-

Price ranges, which are given as a guide only, are for a standard double room with bathroom, including service and tax but excluding breakfast (usually from around €5–20, depending on the rating of the hotel):

€	under €120
€€	€120–200
€€€	€200–350
€€€€	over €350

ing was originally a multi-storey car park but is now kitted out with all that an urban hipster could wish for: pool table, bar, apple computers and table football.

The Latin Quarter and St-Germain

Abbaye St-Germain
10 rue Cassette, 6th; tel: 01 45 44 38 11; www.hotelabbaye paris.com; €€€; metro: St-Sulpice; map p.154 A2
This 17th-century abbey, a favourite haunt of writers and artists, is well situated between the Jardin du Luxembourg and St-Germain-des-Prés, and has been sensitively converted into a hotel. The charm of the old decor has been retained – some of the

46 rooms have beams and wood panelling – but there are the comforts of modernity too. Breakfast is served in the garden in summer by attentive staff. Facilities include wi-fi internet access, room service and a bar.

D'Angleterre
44 rue Jacob, 6th; tel: 01 42 60 34 72; www.hotel-dangleterre. com; €€; metro: St-Germain-des-Prés, Mabillon, Rue du Bac; map p.154 A3
The location couldn't be better, on a quiet, upmarket street lined with art galleries. This charming hotel was the site on which the Treaty of Paris, proclaiming the independence of the US, was signed in 1783; in the 19th century it was used as the

Above: the Hôtel Esmeralda may be a little worn around the edges but has some fabulous views.

British Embassy. Ernest Hemingway lodged here (in room 14) in 1921. Rooms are fairly small and furnished with antiques; only the top-floor doubles are spacious. The delightful terrace and garden is where breakfast is served in the summer.

Hotel des Deux Degrés
10 rue des Grands-Degrés, 5th; tel: 01 55 42 88 88; www.lesdegreshotel.com; €€; metro: St-Michel; map p.155 C2

Romantically furnished hotel in a fabulous location overlooking Notre-Dame (rooms 47 and 501 have views of the cathedral). The 10 rooms are exquisitely decorated with pretty antiques; original wooden beams add to the character. Book well in advance.

Hôtel Esmeralda
4 rue St-Julien-le-Pauvre, 5th; tel: 01 43 54 19 20; €; metro: St-Michel, Maubert Mutualité; map p.154 C2

The 17th-century Esmeralda, the ultimate in shabby chic, is one of those places you either love or loathe. Its 19 rooms have loud floral wallpaper, antique furniture and a rickety old staircase (no lift) that takes some negotiating with suitcases. In addition to the extremely low prices (rooms from around 40 euros for a single) and the undeniable character, an attraction is the incredible location; just under half of the rooms have views of Notre-Dame directly across the Seine.

Hôtel Familia
11 rue des Ecoles, 5th; tel:

01 43 54 55 27; www.familia hotel.com; €; metro: Jussieu, Maubert Mutualité; map p.155 C1

Location is one of the advantages of this mid-sized hotel, which is within a few minutes' walk of the islands and St-Germain des Près. The Familia offers solid comforts in smallish rooms for a modest price; rooms on the fifth and sixth floors have views of Notre-Dame. Another attraction for the hotel's many regular guests is the hospitable Gaucheron family, who live on the premises and take pride in every detail. Look out for the frescoes painted by a local artist.

Hôtel des Grandes Ecoles
75 rue du Cardinal-Lemoine, 5th; tel: 01 43 26 79 23; www. hotel-grandes-ecoles.com; €; metro: Cardinal Lemoine; map p.155 C1

At first glance, you might think you were in the French countryside here, even though the hotel is only a short walk (uphill) from the metro. There are 50 large, prettily furnished rooms around a cobbled courtyard and garden of established trees and trellised roses. Handy for the rue Mouffetard market.

Hôtel Le Sainte-Beuve
9 rue Ste-Beuve, 6th; tel: 01 45 48 20 07; www.parishotel charme.com; €€; metro: Vavin; map p.154 A1

The stylish, middle-range Sainte-Beuve is set on a quiet

Breakfast is charged separately in the majority of Parisian hotels, so check before reaching for a *croissant*. It can be ridiculously expensive, and all too often served in a claustrophobic cellar breakfast room. It's usually far better value to plump for coffee and *croissants* in a local café.

An alternative to staying in a hotel is a bed and breakfast. Several companies organise home stays. Alcôve & Agapes, Le Bed & Breakfast à Paris (8 bis rue Coysevox, 18th; tel: 01 44 85 06 05; www.bedandbreak fastinparis.com) has more than 100 homes on its register. Good Morning Paris (43 rue Lacépède, 5th; tel: 01 47 07 28 29; www.goodmorning paris.fr) offers about 40 rooms through-out the city (prices from 40 euros for one person to about 80 euros for three).

street, steps from the excellent shops on rue d'Assas and a short walk from the Jardin du Luxembourg. The rooms are tastefully furnished, with air conditioning; those on the top floor have skylights in the bathrooms and romantic views over the rooftops.

The 7th

Amélie
5 rue Amélie, 7th; tel: 01 45 51 74 75; www.hotelamelie.fr; €; metro: Varennes, La Tour Maubourg; map p.157 C4
A short walk from the Eiffel Tower, this small and friendly family-run hotel has some of the lowest rates in the area. Renovated rooms have small refrigerators and private bathrooms. A narrow wooden staircase leads to the four levels of rooms; there is no lift. Breakfast is served in the small lobby.

Bourgogne et Montana
3 rue de Bourgogne, 7th; tel: 01 45 51 20 22; www.bourgogne-montana.com; €€; metro: Assemblée Nationale; map p.157 D4
A charming hotel in a building dating back to 1789, tucked behind the Assemblée Nationale: Palais Bourbon. The 32 renovated spacious rooms are good value for this

expensive neighbourhood. The large doubles are worth the extra splurge and come with double basins.

Hôtel Lenox
9 rue de l'Université, 7th; tel: 01 42 96 10 95; www.lenoxsaintgermain.com; €€; metro: St-Germain-des-Prés; map p.154 A3
This trendy hotel on a quiet road in the upmarket 7th *arrondissement* is decorated in Art Deco style and is very popular among style-conscious creative types. The rooms are spotless, and amenities include a bar, room service and wi-fi internet. Reserve well in advance.

Hôtel de Verneuil
8 rue de Verneuil, 7th; tel: 01 42 60 82 14; www.hotel verneuil.com; €€; metro: St-Germain; map p.154 A3
A cosy, characterful hotel in an elegant 17th-century building in the upmarket 7th *arrondissement*, with small but attractive rooms in the traditional style and discreet service. Singer Serge Gainsbourg lived just opposite, and the wall outside his old house is decorated with graffiti in

Price ranges, which are given as a guide only, are for a standard double room with bathroom, including service and tax but excluding breakfast (usually from around €5–20, depending on the rating of the hotel):

€	under €120
€€	€120–200
€€€	€200–350
€€€€	over €350

homage. Well placed for St-Germain. Wi-fi is available, if you purchase a card from reception.

Montparnasse

Hôtel Aviatic
105 rue de Vaugirard; tel: 01 53 63 25 50; www.aviatic.fr; €€; metro: St Placide; map p.154 A1
An unpretentious small hotel on a quiet, pleasant street not far from the Jardin du Luxembourg. The comfortable bedrooms have recently been refurbished, and there is a charming breakfast room decorated with posters, and an elegant Empire-style lounge. Worth upgrading to a superior room, if your budget allows.

Below: standards and ratings are governed by the tourism authority.

77

Language

Frerench is the native language of over 90 million people and the acquired language of 180 million. It is a Romance language, descended from Latin. Pronunciation is vital: as a rule, remember to emphasise each syllable but do not pronounce the last consonant of a word, unless it is followed by a vowel. Note that 'er', 'et' and 'ez' endings are pronounced 'ay' (this includes the plural 's') and that 'h's are silent. In general, if you attempt to communicate in French, the fact that you have made an effort is likely to break the ice and win favour with Parisians. For food vocabulary, see 'Food and Drink'.

The Alphabet

a = ah, b = bay, c = say, d = day, e = uh, f = ef, g = zhay, h = ash, i = ee, j = zhee, k = ka, l = el, m = em, n = en, o = oh, p = pay, q = kew, r = ehr, s = ess, t = tay, u = ew, v = vay, w = dooblah vay, x = eex, y = ee grek, z = zed.

Useful Words/ and Phrases

GENERAL

yes *oui*
no *non*
please *s'il vous plaît*
thank you (very much) *merci (beaucoup)*
you're welcome *de rien*
excuse me *excusez-moi*
hello *bonjour*
hi/bye *salut*
OK *d'accord*
goodbye *au revoir*
good evening *bonsoir*
How much is it? *C'est combien?*
What is your name? *Comment vous appelez-vous?*
My name is... *Je m'appelle...*
Do you speak English? *Parlez-vous anglais?*

I am English/American *Je suis anglais(e)/ américain(e)*
I don't understand *Je ne comprends pas*
Please speak more slowly *Parlez plus lentement, s'il vous plaît*
Can you help me? *Pouvez-vous m'aider?*
I'm looking for... *Je cherche...*
Where is...? *Où est...?*
I'm sorry *Excusez-moi/Pardon*
I don't know *Je ne sais pas*
Have a good day! *Bonne journée!*
That's it *C'est ça*
Here it is *Voici*
There it is *Voilà*
See you tomorrow *A demain*
See you soon *A bientôt*
When? *Quand?*
What time is it? *Quelle heure est-il?*
here *ici*
there *là*
left *gauche*
right *droite*
straight on *tout droit*
far *loin*
near *près d'ici*

opposite *en face*
beside *à côté de*
over there *là-bas*
today *aujourd'hui*
yesterday *hier*
tomorrow *demain*
now *maintenant*
later *plus tard*
this morning *ce matin*
this afternoon *cet après-midi*
this evening *ce soir*

bakery *la boulangerie*
bookshop *la librairie*
department store
le grand magasin
delicatessen
la charcuterie/le traiteur
fishmonger's *la poissonnerie*
grocery *l'épicerie*
tobacconist *tabac*
market *le marché*
supermarket *le supermarché*

SIGHTSEEING
tourist information office
*l'office du tourisme/
le syndicat d'initiative*
free *gratuit*
open *ouvert*
closed *fermé*
every day *tous les jours*
all year *toute l'année*
all day *toute la journée*
to book *réserver*
town map *le plan*
road map *la carte*

DINING OUT
breakfast *le petit-déjeuner*
lunch *le déjeuner*
dinner *le dîner*
meal *le repas*
first course *l'entrée*
main course *le plat principal*
drink included
boisson comprise
wine list *la carte des vins*
the bill *l'addition*
fork *la fourchette*
knife *le couteau*
spoon *la cuillère*
plate *l'assiette*
glass *le verre*
I am a vegetarian
Je suis végétarien(ne)
I'd like to order
Je voudrais commander
service included
service compris
Enjoy your meal
Bon appétit!

ON ARRIVAL
I want to get off at...
Je voudrais descendre à…
Is there a bus to…? *Est-ce
qui'il y a un bus pour…?*
Which line do I take for...?
*Quelle ligne dois-je prendre
pour...?*
How far is...? *A quelle
distance se trouve...?*
Validate your ticket
Compostez votre billet
airport *l'aéroport*
railway station *la gare*
bus station *la gare routière*
metro stop *la station
de Métro*
bus *l'autobus, le car*
bus stop *l'arrêt*
platform *le quai*
ticket *le billet*
return ticket *aller-retour*
toilets *les toilettes*
I'd like a (single/double)
room *Je voudrais une cham-
bre (pour une/deux personnes)*
...with shower *avec douche*
...with bath *avec salle de bain*
Is breakfast included?
*Le prix comprend-il le
petit-déjeuner?*
bed *le lit*
key *la clé*
elevator *l'ascenseur*
air conditioned *climatisé(e)*

EMERGENCIES
Help! *Au secours!*
Stop! *Arrêtez!*
Where is the nearest
telephone? *Où est le
téléphone le plus proche?*
Where is the nearest
hospital? *Où est l'hôpital
le plus proche?*
I am sick *Je suis malade*
I have lost my passport/
purse *J'ai perdu mon
passeport/porte-monnaie*

SHOPPING
I'd like to buy
Je voudrais acheter
How much is it?
C'est combien?
Do you take credit cards?
*Est-ce que vous acceptez les
cartes de crédit?*
I'm just looking
Je regarde seulement
size (clothes) *la taille*
size (shoes) *la pointure*
receipt *le reçu*
chemist *la pharmacie*

79

Literature and Theatre

François Villon's bawdy medieval poetry, the 19th-century realist novels of Victor Hugo or Honoré de Balzac, the Symbolist poetry of Charles Baudelaire and the Existentialist novels of Jean-Paul Sartre are just a few of the literary works that have taken inspiration from the city of Paris across the centuries. This section introduces some of the writers who have put the capital on the literary map, and gives a listing of book shops and theatres where you can browse, buy or see their works.

Writers and Dramatists

Over the centuries Paris has acted as a magnet for writers, a breeding ground for intellectual thought, and a source of inspiration in itself. Early written work depicting Parisian life includes the story of tragic 12th-century lovers, Abélard and Héloïse, in which the brutality of life in fiercely Catholic medieval Paris is vividly described.

The poetry of François Villon (1431–c.1463) takes an equally tough approach: in his bawdy poems the erstwhile vagabond Villon describes an unattractive city, rife with depravity and crime. Even in the later writings of the satirical François Rabelais (1483–1553), the capital fares poorly (he slates such eminent institutions as the Sorbonne).

17TH TO 19TH CENTURIES

The 17th century is considered the golden age of French drama. Corneille (1606–84) and Molière (1622–73), wrote plays with strong social commentaries, and Racine (1639–99), reinvented the Classical tragedies.

Above: Left Bank lit.

By the first half of the 19th century, the city took centre stage again, lifted to almost mythological status in the work of novelist Honoré de Balzac (1799–1850). His vast output of over 90 short stories and novels, including Paris-based *Le Père Goriot* and *Cousine Bette*, was slavishly produced to order from his Parisian garret. Victor Hugo (1802–85) had his first big success with *Notre-Dame de Paris* (1831), and such was its influence that it precipitated the cathedral's long-awaited restoration in the 19th century.

The poet Charles Baudelaire (1821–67) credits his explorations of the French capital as the inspiration for the prose poem form, first used in his *Spleen de Paris* of 1860; rugged and versatile, the new medium proved a worthy vehicle for expressing the angst of living in such a metropolis. Parisian-born Emile Zola (1840–1902) set his *Ventre de Paris* around Les Halles market district, the 'underbelly of Paris' of the title. His *L'Assomoir* reveals the poverty and squalor below the glamour of Second-Empire Paris, while in *Bel-Ami* Guy de Maupassant follows a provincial determined to succeed in corrupt Third Republic Paris.

20TH CENTURY AND BEYOND

In the 20th century, St-Germain and Montparnasse became known for their literary scenes. Paris continued to provide intellectual stimulus for French writers, from Surrealist André Breton and New Wave writers such as Raymond Queneau (*Zazie dans le Métro*) to the Existentialists Jean-Paul Sartre, Simone de

Left: browsing on the banks of the Seine.

This unusual shop, whose name is a combination of the words galerie (store) and brocante (second-hand goods) stocks old magazines and periodicals, from 1960s *Vogue* and *Elle* (English-language editions included) to humorous French magazines dating from World War I. They also sell 'birthday newspapers'.

Gibert Joseph
26 and 30 boulevard St-Michel, 6th; tel: 01 44 41 88 88; metro: St-Michel; map p.154 B2
A second home for Sorbonne students, who come here to buy and sell text and reference books. There is a small selection of books in English. Gibert also stocks stationery and music in its sprawling shops along the same street.

La Hune
170 boulevard St-Germain, 6th; tel: 01 45 48 35 85; metro: St-Germain-des-Prés; map p.154 A2
Sandwiched between Café de Flore and Les Deux Magots, this great bookshop is a home-from-home for intellectuals dedicated to keeping up the area's literary pretensions.

Below: one-stop bookshop.

Beauvoir and Albert Camus.

After World War I, an influx of writers from outside France also moved to Paris, and the influence of their time there is seen in novels such as *Down and Out in London and Paris* (George Orwell), *A Moveable Feast* (Ernest Hemingway) and *The Autobiography of Alice B. Toklas* (Gertrude Stein).

Later French authors writing on their capital include 'Paris noir' Léo Malet (1909–96), Georges Simenon (1903–89), creator of the detective Maigret, crime writer Daniel Pennac (1944–) and Patrick Modiano (1945–) who tackles the theme of identity in its social and ethnic dimensions.

Bookshops

Abbey Bookshop
29 rue Parcheminerie, 5th; tel: 01 46 33 16 24; metro: Cluny La Sorbonne; map p.154 B2
Fans of Mavis Gallant, Margaret Atwood and other Canadian literary lights will appreciate the large stock of second-hand books by their compatriots here. It is a good source of reference books too, and the service is amiable.

Brentano's
37 avenue de l'Opéra, 2nd; tel: 01 42 61 52 50; metro: Pyramides; map p.152 A1
Brentano's has a distinctly American flavour, with big sections on business and self-help, as well as all the usual novels, travel and children's lit.

fnac
Forum des Halles, 1 rue Pierre Lescot, 1st; tel: 01 40 41 40 00; metro: Les Halles; map p.154 C4
Books, music, high-fi and videos are all sold in this giant, long-established French chain. Concert tickets can also be bought here. Branches across the city. Late opening most nights.

La Galcante
52 rue de l'Arbre Sec, 1st; tel: 01 44 77 87 44; www.la galcante.com; metro: Louvre Rivoli; map p.154 B3

For an informal approach to book-buying, take a look at the second-hand books on sale at stalls along the Seine. These so-called *bouquinistes* won't be cheap but they do provide the romantic book-buying experience.

Right: evening at the theatre.

Downstairs you'll find a fine selection of French literature and theory; upstairs are densely packed shelves of art, photography, interior design, graphic art and fashion tomes.

Librairie 7L
7 rue de Lille, 7th; tel: 01 42 92 03 58; metro: Assemblée Nationale; map p.151 E1
Given the exemplary collection of decorative arts and photography books here, as well as all the latest design magazines, it's not surprising to learn that Karl Lagerfeld is behind 7L. Helpful staff.
SEE ALSO FASHION, P.57

San Francisco Book Co.
17 rue Monsieur le Prince, 6th; tel: 01 43 29 15 70; metro: Odéon; map p.154 B2
Although the staff can be gruff, this second-hand bookshop has an excellent range of English-language fiction. Flip through the paperbacks on its stalls on the street for a good read for €1.

Shakespeare & Co.
37 rue de la Bûcherie, 5th; tel: 01 43 25 40 93; metro: St-Michel; map p.154 B2
This shop follows in the footsteps of Paris's most famous English bookshop, founded in 1921 by Sylvia Beach in rue de l'Odéon, and frequented by Gertrude Stein, Hemingway

and Ezra Pound. It closed during World War II, and the present shop was founded in 1956 by American George Whitman. It contains a wide range of literature, from the Bard to the beatniks and has drawn in expatriate writers such as William Burroughs and James Baldwin for a browse. It still stays open until midnight, and there are lots of nooks upstairs where you can relax and read.

Village Voice
6 rue Princesse, 6th; tel: 01 46 33 36 47; metro: St-Germain des Prés; map p.154 A2
Unbeatable for its selection of the latest English-language fiction, nonfiction, poetry and literary magazines. The staff are very helpful, and the regular book readings are well run.

W.H. Smith
248 rue de Rivoli, 1st; tel: 01 44 77 88 99; metro: Concorde; map p.151 E2
This branch of the British chain has been here for over a century and is always awash with expats and tourists scouring the magazine racks. Open on Sunday afternoon.

Founded through the bequest of writer Edmond de Goncourt (1822–96), France's most prestigious literary gong, the Prix Goncourt, has been awarded annually since 1903 for the finest work of literary prose published in French that year. The judging committee, the 10-member Académie Goncourt, meets once a month at Drouant *(see p.128)*. The Goncourt has a symbolic prize of 10 euros but ensures literary acclaim.

Further Reading
The Eiffel Tower And Other Mythologies, by Roland Barthes. A collection of essays by this influential French social and literary critic, in which he considers Paris's most famous landmark.
The Oxford Companion to French Literature, by Sir Paul Harvey and J.E. Heseltine.
A Concise History of France, by Roger Price. Excellent overview of French history.
Wine Atlas of France, by Hugh Johnson and Hubrecht Duijker. Illustrated wine atlas.

CLASSIC LITERATURE
Villon, François, *Le Grand Testament* (1461–2).
Rabelais, François, *Gargantua and Pantagruel* (1532–52).
Prévost, Abbé, *Manon Lescaut* (1723–31).
Hugo, Victor, *The Hunchback of Notre-Dame* (1831), *Les Misérables* (1862).
Balzac, Honoré de, *Eugénie Grandet* (1833), *Old Goriot* (1834).

Dickens, Charles, *A Tale of Two Cities* (1859).
Zola, Emile, *Thérèse Raquin* (1867), *L'Assomoir* (1877), *The Belly of Paris* (1874), *Nana* (1880).
Baudelaire, Charles, *Le Spleen de Paris* (1869).
Maupassant, Guy de, *Bel-Ami* (1885).
Orwell, George, *Down and Out in Paris and London* (1933).
Stein, Gertrude, *The Autobiography of Alice B. Toklas* (1933).
Sartre, Jean-Paul, *Roads to Freedom* (1945–49).
De Beauvoir, Simone, *The Mandarins* (1954).

Theatres

Jean Cocteau once said, 'In Paris, everybody wants to be an actor'. Fortunately, as well as posing in streets and cafés, there are some fine performances in theatres too.

Comédie Française
1 place Colette, 1st; tel: 01 44 58 15 15; www.comedie-francaise.fr; metro: Palais-Royal
Since 1799 this neoclassical building adjacent to the Palais Royal (entrance on place Colette) has been the headquarters of the Comédie Française, France's national theatre. In 1680 several smaller theatre groups merged with the ensemble of the French playwright Molière to form this troupe, and less than a year later, Louis XIV designated the building his court theatre; Napoleon was later to make it his state theatre.

Most productions are of the classical repertoire, by playwrights including Molière, Racine and Corneille, although plays by more modern classic writers, such as Genet and Anouilh, are also staged.

Odéon – Théâtre de l'Europe
Place de l'Odéon, 5th; tel: 01 44 85 40 40; www.theatre-odeon.fr; metro: Odéon
First opened in 1782 as a venue for the Comédie Française, this grand Neoclassical building near the Jardins du Luxembourg stages classics, translations of foreign plays, and contemporary works.

Théâtre de la Huchette
23 rue de la Huchette, 5th; tel: 01 43 26 38 99; www.theatre-huchette.com; metro: St-Michel
This minuscule theatre has been playing Ionesco's *La Cantatrice Chauve* (The Bald Soprano) for more than 50 years. A fun evening, if your French is up to it, although the theatre can get very hot in summer. Tickets are generally available on the day.

Théâtre National du Chaillot
Palais du Chaillot, 1 place du Trocadéro, 16th; tel: 01 53 65 30 04; www.theatre-chaillot.fr; metro: Trocadéro; map p.150 A1
The palatial Art Deco complex has three auditoria of wildly varying sizes, which are mostly used for classics and global dance performances. There's also a bar with wonderful views of the Eiffel Tower.
SEE ALSO DANCE, P.52

Théâtre National de la Colline
15 rue Malte-Brun, 20th; tel: 01 44 62 52 52; www.colline.fr; metro: Gambetta
Modern theatre with a focus on contemporary playwrights.

Théâtre du Vieux Colombier
21 rue du Vieux-Colombier, 6th; tel: 01 44 39 87 00; www.theatreduvieuxcolombier.com; metro: St-Sulpice, Sèvres-Babylone
Small-scale productions of classical and modern drama from the Comédie Française troupe in this beautifully revamped theatre.

Right: Molière.

The foyer of the Comédie Française contains the chair in which Molière was sitting in 1673 during a performance of his play *Le Malade Imaginaire* (The Hypochondriac) when he collapsed. The audience believed that this was all part of the act – an old man feigns death in the play – and responded with enthusiasm; tragically, this was not the case, and the great dramatist died later the same day.

Monuments

The highlight of this chapter, the Eiffel Tower, is also the symbol of Paris and the most popular tourist attraction in the city, pulling in a whopping 6 million visitors per year. With this in mind, it is difficult to believe that the iron tower was once a highly controversial addition to the Paris skyline. Another of the city's top-ten attractions, the Arc de Triomphe (1.4 million visitors per year), is also featured here. In addition, we list statues commemorating revolutions, memorials honouring national heroines and monuments that stand proud as lasting symbols of international unity.

Arc de Triomphe de l'Etoile

Place Charles-de-Gaulle, 8th; tel: 01 55 37 73 77; www.monum.fr; Oct–Mar: daily 10am–10.30pm, Apr–Sept: daily 10am–11pm; entrance charge; metro: Charles de Gaulle Etoile; map p.150 B3

Officially renamed place Charles de Gaulle after the death of the president in 1969, the circular area at the top of the Champs-Elysées is popularly known to Parisians as l'Etoile ('the star'), after the 12 avenues branching out from its centre. It is dominated by one of the most enduring of Parisian icons and a memorial to megalomania, the Arc de Triomphe de l'Etoile (its full name distinguishes it from the smaller Arc de Triomphe du Carrousel, *see right*). Although commissioned by Napoleon in 1806, the ornately sculpted arch was not completed until after his death. All the great conqueror saw of it was a wood-and-canvas model. His chance to pass under the real thing finally came, however, when his body was triumphantly

Above: Napoleon's meglomanic Arc de Triomphe.

returned to Paris for reburial in Les Invalides in 1840.

The arch soon became a focal point for state occasions, for example the funeral of Victor Hugo in 1885, when the writer's coffin was placed underneath it, while most of Paris, it seemed, came to pay

their respects. At the liberation of Paris following World War II, this was the spot where General de Gaulle commenced his triumphal march down the Champs-Elysées. The arch has less auspicious connections, however: when Adolf Hitler arrived in Paris as conqueror in 1940, the Arc de Triomphe was the first sight in the city he wanted to see.

Beneath the arch, the Unknown Soldier was laid to rest in 1920 and, in 1923, the eternal flame was lit. It is rekindled each evening at 6.30pm, during a wreath-laying ceremony. The arch itself is decorated with elaborate friezes depicting battle scenes and sculptures, notably Burgundian sculptor François Rude's *La Marseillaise*, and is carved with the names of battles won by Napoleon. The platform above the arch can be reached via stairs (lift for visitors with disabilities or with pushchairs) and offers fabulous views over Paris. It is here that you can best appreciate the *tour de force* of geometric planning that the avenues represent.

Left: the statue of Jeanne d'Arc sits opposite the Tuileries.

St Mark's in Venice (brought to Paris as booty along with numerous other artistic treasures). The present four horses are the work of Bosio, and were placed here in 1828.

The view through the arch across place de la Concorde and all the way to the Arc de Triomphe de l'Etoile is superb, even though the arch looks somewhat forlorn, stuck in the middle of the large open space between the Louvre and the Tuileries. (It was less isolated in front of the Palais des Tuileries, but the latter was pulled down in 1882.)

SEE ALSO PARKS AND GARDENS, P.122

Chapelle Expiatoire

59 Boulevard Haussmann, 8th; Thur–Sat 1–5pm; entrance charge; metro: St-Lazare; map p.151 E3

This atmospheric chapel was built on the site of what was once the Madeleine Cemetery, and the burial ground of Louis XVI and Marie-Antoinette and 3,000 other

---

> The **Tombeau du Soldat Inconnu** (Tomb of the Unknown Soldier), below the Arc de Triomphe, was the first memorial of its type in the world. An unknown French soldier was laid to rest here in 1920, symbolising the 1,390,000 who fell in World War I.

The best time to visit is early morning or evening, when the arch is quietest. The arch can be accessed via an underpass, not via the road itself: under no circumstances attempt to cross the roundabout on foot, which is always crazy with fast-moving traffic.

Arc de Triomphe du Carrousel

Place du Carrousel, 1st; metro: Palais Royal-Musée du Louvre, Tuileries; map p.154 A4

This arch stands to the east of the Jardin des Tuileries. Work began on both it and its larger namesake, the Arc de Triomphe de l'Etoile (see left), in 1806, with both arches intended to glorify the victorious campaigns of Napoleon.

The Arc de Triomphe du Carrousel was designed by imperial architects La Fontaine and Percier, and was a Neoclassical copy of the triumphal arch of Emperor Septimus Severus in Rome. With its three gateways (20m/65ft wide and 15m/50ft high), it forms the entrance to the courtyard of the Jardin des Tuileries and was inaugurated in 1808. It was originally crowned by the four bronze horses from

Below: the smaller scale Arc de Triomphe du Carrousel gives a view all the way to La Défense.

series of French historical events. In 1792, during the Revolution, the statue of Louis XIV was destroyed, and Napoleon had the 45m (148ft) high Colonne de la Grande Armée (Triumphal Column), decorated with reliefs commemorating his glorious campaigns, placed here instead. The bronze used to make the column was taken from 1,200 pieces of enemy cannon captured during various battles. A statue of Napoleon stood at the top of the column, but Napoleon III found it too small and had it replaced by the Roman-style imperial one up there today.

In 1871 the column was pulled down by Communard insurrectionists. Since the painter Gustave Courbet was suspected of having had a hand in the deed, he paid for the monument's re-erection from his own pocket.

Colonne de Juillet

Place de la Bastille, 11th; metro: Bastille; map p.155 E2
The tall column in the middle of place de la Bastille commemorates the victims of the 1830 and 1848 revolutions, who are buried underneath it. Their names are engraved in gold on the side of the column. The monument is topped by a gilded statue of Liberty.

Eiffel Tower

Champs de Mars, 7th; tel: 01 44 11 23 45; www.tour-eiffel.fr; Jan–Jun, Sept–Dec: daily 9.30am–11.45pm, last lift 11pm,10.30pm for top floor,

The Eiffel Tower weighs 10,000 tonnes, and consists of around 18,000 individual steel sections. A hefty 60 tonnes of paint are needed to give it just one coat. Despite its massive dimensions, the weight of the Eiffel Tower is distributed in such a way that each square centimetre of ground area is only subjected to 4.5kg (10lb) of pressure (roughly equivalent to the weight of an average person sitting on a chair). Even during the fiercest storms, the top of the tower never moves more than 7cm (3in).

victims of the French Revolution. On the restoration of the monarchy in 1815, Louis XVIII had the bodies of the former king and queen removed to the royal Basilica of St-Denis, and this Greco-Roman-style chapel built in forgiveness for the crimes of the Revolution. The last service to be held here was in 1882.

Colonne de la Grande Armée

Place Vendôme, 1st; metro: Opéra, Tuileries; map p.151 E2
The monument in the middle of place Vendôme reflects a

9.30am–6.30pm steps only, Jun–Sept: daily 9am–12.45am, last elevator midnight, 11pm for top floor, 9am–12.30am steps only; entrance charge; metro: Bir-Hakeim, RER: Champ de Mars Tour Eiffel; map p.156 B4
The 300-m high Tour Eiffel (Eiffel Tower, *see left*) was built according to plans by architect Gustave Eiffel between 28 January 1887 and 31 March 1889 for the Paris Universal Exhibition of 1889. Initially, the reception to the tower was frosty, with the Opéra architect Charles Garnier and the novelist Guy de Maupassant among its most vocal opponents. Maupassant organised a protest picnic under the tower's legs: 'the only place out of sight of the wretched construction'.

However, public support grew, and in 1916 the tower was granted a practical purpose: the first transoceanic radio contact was made from here in that year; radio programmes have been broadcast from the tower ever since. The 21-m high television antenna was

Above: more meglomania documented on the Colonne de la Grande Armée.

erected in 1957. The uppermost platform contains a meteorological station as well as electronic equipment used for air-traffic control.

The first platform is 57m up, while the second level (home to the upmarket **Jules Verne** restaurant) is at 115m. In total, there are 1,652 steps.

From the second platform, the only access upwards is by lift, which means further queuing. This takes visitors to the third level, 300m up, from which there are views for approximately 65km (40 miles) on a clear day. The platform on the third level is glazed, and there are signs indicating which sights are which. Also on this level is Gustave Eiffel's salon, modelled as it would have been in his day, and the more recent addition of a gift shop.
SEE ALSO RESTAURANTS, P.138

Flamme de la Liberté
Place de l'Alma, 8th; metro: Alma Marceau; map p.150 C2
In 1987, the Flame, a replica of the one held by Lady Liberty in New York, was erected on the northern side of the Pont de l'Alma. The golden statue was a gift from the *International Herald Tribune* to celebrate Franco-American friendship. For several

years, it was covered with posters commemorating Diana, Princess of Wales, who died after a car crash in the nearby Pont de l'Alma tunnel on 31 August 1997.

Jeanne d'Arc
Place des Pyramides, 1st; metro: Tuileries; map p.154 A4
In the middle of the small place des Pyramides, on the site where, according to legend, the Maid of Orléans was wounded in 1429 during the Paris siege, is a gleaming golden equestrian statue of Joan of Arc. There is a procession to this statue on All Saints' Day *(Toussaint)* every 1 November. Joan is a cult figure for the right wing and the National Front.

Obelisk
Place de la Concorde, 8th; metro: Concorde; map p.151 E2
The c.23-m high pink granite monolith on place de la Concorde is nearly 3,300 years old, and was presented to Louis-Philippe (1830–48) by the Ottoman governor of Egypt (Mehmed Ali) in 1831. It weighs around 230 tonnes and formerly stood in front of the Temple of Luxor. Hieroglyphs proudly recount the deeds of Rameses II.

Below: the Colonne de Juillet at Bastille.

Museums and Galleries

The acquisitiveness of French monarchs, the victory spoils of Napoleon and the taste of countless collectors have combined to assemble in Paris some of the world's greatest cultural masterpieces. In this listing, the three big venues, the Louvre, Centre Pompidou and Musée d'Orsay, are covered first, followed by the city's other museums and galleries. Note that most museums close either on Monday or Tuesday, and that ticket offices usually shut at least 30 minutes prior to the offical closing time.

Musée du Louvre

Palais du Louvre, rue de Rivoli, 1st; tel: 01 40 20 50 50; www.louvre.fr; Mon–Sat 9am–6pm, Wed and Fri until 9.45pm; entrance charge under 18s free, under 26s free on Fri 6–9.45pm, free for everyone on first Sun of month, tickets valid all day and allow re-entry; metro: Palais Royal-Musée du Louvre; map p.154 B3–4

The Musée du Louvre is

Below: the *Winged Victory*.

divided into three wings: **Richelieu** in the north, **Sully** in the east and **Denon** in the south. The collections are spread over seven different sections, each assigned its own colour to facilitate orientation. The following is a selection of the highlights from the various sections.

THE MEDIEVAL LOUVRE

A good place to start is the exhibition on the Medieval Louvre, en route to the Crypte Sully under the Cour Carrée, where the remains of Philippe-Auguste's fort and keep, and some of the artefacts discovered in excavations in the 1980s, can be seen.

On the ground floor of the Sully and Richelieu wings are the Oriental A   ties, which include Mesopotamian   statuette of Ebih-il   C), with striking la   yes, and the black l   y-lonian *Code of   bi* (1792–1750BC)   the world's first lega   ents.

On the south s   ne Sully Wing is the g   Hellenic statue *Venus   Milo*

If you plan to visit several museums during your stay, buying a Paris Museum Card means you avoid the queues to visit 60 museums or monuments in Paris and the Ile de France region and you also save money on entrance prices. Tickets are available for two, four or six days (30, 45 and 60 euros, respectively) and can be purchased from tourist offices and museum/gallery ticket offices. For more details, see www.parismuseumpass.fr.

(2nd century BC), bought by the French Government for 6,000 francs in 1820 from the Greek island of Milos.

From here, head to the Denon Wing to see the Etruscan sarcophagus of the reclining couple. Continuing along the ground-floor level, you will reach the Italian sculpture section and Michelangelo's *Slaves* (1513–20), sculpted in marble for Pope Julius II's tomb but never finished, and Canova's beautiful neoclassical *Psyche Revived by the Kiss of Cupid* (1793).

Left: crowds at the Louvre.

Mode et du Textile covers Paris fashions and textiles from the 16th century to the present day. Each year it mounts a large display focusing on a different aspect of its collection, from the earliest existing dresses to the ground-breaking designs of the big-name couturiers of the 20th and 21st centuries, such as Christian Dior, Yves Saint-Laurent, Gucci and Versace.

Upstairs, the **Musée de la Publicité**, designed by architect Jean Nouvel, is home to a rich collection of around 100,000 posters from the Middle Ages to the present day. Only a fraction of the vast collection can ever be exhibited at one time.

Below: from the Musée des Arts Décoratifs.

Mona Lisa

The Louvre's first, and most famous, resident, the *Mona Lisa* (1503) hangs in a specially designed room in the Denon Wing. Leonardo's enigmatic Florentine noble-woman hangs on its own wall in the Salle des Etats, with masterpieces from the Venetian Renaissance, including Veronese's vast *Wedding at Cana*, on the other walls.

Grande Galerie

On the same floor is the Grande Galerie, which starts at the top of the Escalier Daru opposite the *Winged Victory of Samothrace* (2nd century BC), the Hellenistic figurehead commemorating a victory at sea. Here hang large 19th-century French paintings, including Delacroix's iconic *Liberty Leading the People*, Géricault's *Raft of the Medusa* and David's *Sabine Women*. The Spanish School, with masterpieces by El Greco and Goya, is nearby.

Richelieu Wing

The Richelieu Wing houses a vast collection of French sculpture on the ground floor and is focused around two splendid sculpture courts, home to Guillaume Coustou's two giant *Marly Horses*. The second floor of the Richelieu and Sully wings are dedicated to paintings and include Rembrandt's *Bathsheba Bathing* (1654).

Galerie d'Apollon

After a 5.2-million euro restoration and three years under wraps, the Galerie d'Apollon (Apollo's Gallery), commissioned by Louis XIV in 1661, reopened in November 2004. The glittering gallery showcases paintings, tapestries and sculptures from the 17th–19th centuries, and houses the crown jewels.

ADDITIONAL MUSEUMS

In a separate wing are three other collections (107 rue de Rivoli; all Tue–Fri 11am–6pm, Sat–Sun 10am–6pm). The **Musée des Arts Décoratifs** presents a survey of interior design, from medieval tapestries to 21st-century design.

In the same wing, the **Musée des Arts de la**

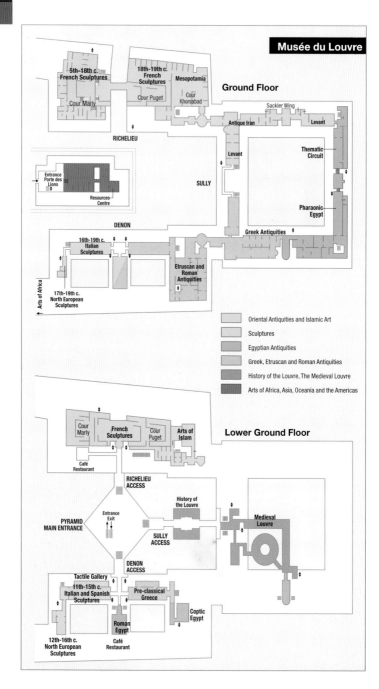

Musée du Louvre

Ground Floor

5th-18th c. French Sculptures

18th-19th c. French Sculptures

Mesopotamia

Cour Marly

Cour Puget

Cour Khorsabad

Sackler Wing

Antique Iran

Levant

RICHELIEU

Levant

Thematic Circuit

Entrance Porte des Lions

Resources Centre

SULLY

Pharaonic Egypt

DENON

Greek Antiquities

16th-19th c. Italian Sculptures

Etruscan and Roman Antiquities

Arts of Africa

17th-19th c. North European Sculptures

- Oriental Antiquities and Islamic Art
- Sculptures
- Egyptian Antiquities
- Greek, Etruscan and Roman Antiquities
- History of the Louvre, The Medieval Louvre
- Arts of Africa, Asia, Oceania and the Americas

Lower Ground Floor

Cour Marly

French Sculptures

Cour Puget

Arts of Islam

Café Restaurant

RICHELIEU ACCESS

History of the Louvre

Medieval Louvre

PYRAMID MAIN ENTRANCE

Entrance Exit

SULLY ACCESS

DENON ACCESS

Tactile Gallery

11th-15th c. Italian and Spanish Sculptures

Pre-classical Greece

Coptic Egypt

Roman Egypt

12th-16th c. North European Sculptures

Café Restaurant

90

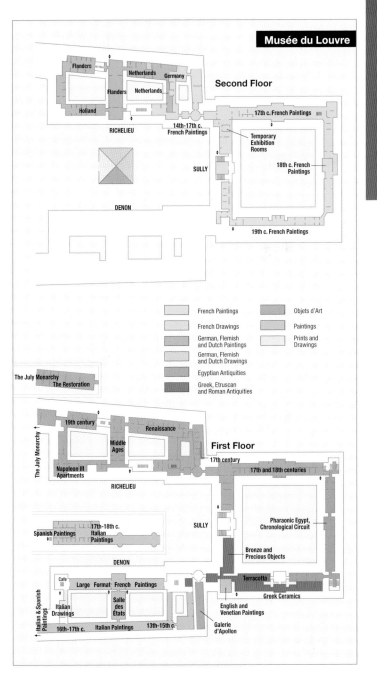

Musée du Louvre

Second Floor

Flanders

Netherlands

Germany

Flanders

Netherlands

Holland

RICHELIEU

14th-17th c. French Paintings

17th c. French Paintings

Temporary Exhibition Rooms

18th c. French Paintings

SULLY

DENON

19th c. French Paintings

French Paintings

French Drawings

German, Flemish and Dutch Paintings

German, Flemish and Dutch Drawings

Egyptian Antiquities

Greek, Etruscan and Roman Antiquities

Objets d'Art

Paintings

Prints and Drawings

The July Monarchy
The Restoration

19th century

Renaissance

Middle Ages

First Floor

17th century

17th and 18th centuries

Napoleon III Apartments

RICHELIEU

The July Monarchy

Spanish Paintings

17th-18th c. Italian Paintings

SULLY

Pharaonic Egypt, Chronological Circuit

Bronze and Precious Objects

DENON

Cafe

Large Format French Paintings

Terracotta

Greek Ceramics

Italian & Spanish Paintings

Italian Drawings

Salle des États

English and Venetian Paintings

16th-17th c. Italian Paintings

13th-15th c.

Galerie d'Apollon

Above: part of the colourful Stravinsky Fountain.

Above: the Centre Pompidou, with its external escalators and bold design.

To the south of the Centre Pompidou is Nikki de Saint-Phalle's *Fontaine de Stravinsky*, with colourful, spouting and spinning forms, each named after music by the Russian composer.

Centre Pompidou – Musée National d'Art Moderne

Rue St-Martin, 4th; tel: 01 44 78 12 33; www.centrepompidou.fr; Mon, Wed, Sun 11am–10pm, ticket desks close 9pm, Atelier Brancusi: daily except Tue 2–6pm; entrance charge, under 18s free, free first Sun of month; metro: Rambuteau, Hôtel de Ville, map p.155 C3–4

Often dubbed 'Beaubourg', after the area in which it stands, this is Paris's main showcase for modern and contemporary art and a dynamic arts venue. It was designed by architects Richard Rogers, Renzo Piano and Gianfranco Franchini at the request of ex-president Pompidou, hence the name, and its inside-out design, dominated by external pipes, tubes, scaffolds and escalators, caused extreme controversy when it was unveiled in 1977. However, the pipes are not just for show: the blue ones convey air, the green ones carry water, the yellow ones contain the electrics, and the red ones conduct heating. The slightly sunken forecourt provides a perfect stage for street entertainment.

The centre underwent extensive renovation for the millennium: the entrance hall and ticket office were extended, an educational area was created, and the **Bibliothèque Publique d'Information** (a large public library) was housed within the centre. Also incorporated into the complex are a performance space, auditorium and cinema, a space for children and, adjacent, the avant-garde music institute **IRCAM**.
SEE ALSO CHILDREN, P.40; MUSIC, P.107

MUSÉE NATIONAL D'ART MODERNE

The main attraction for visitors, however, is the **Musée National de l'Art Moderne**, situated on the fourth and fifth floors. Start on level five, which covers the modern period, from 1905–1960. Level four features contemporary art, from the 1960s to the present day. Regular rehangs are intended to allow visitors to see as much of the vast collection (roughly 50,000 works by 5,000 artists) as possible.

Highlights of the modern period on level five include works by Picasso, Matisse, Kandinsky, Klee, Klein and Pollock, and sections on Dadaism and surrealism, while the excellent contemporary collection includes pieces by Andy Warhol, Xavier Veilhan, Claude Viallat, Verner Panton, Joseph Beuys, Gerhard Richter and Jean Dubuffet. Displays of 20th-century design and architecture, as well as installations, are interspersed among the paintings. Temporary exhibitions are shown on level six. Also on the sixth floor is the fashionable, minimalist and expensive **Georges** restaurant.

Included within the price of the museum ticket is a visit to a reconstruction of sculptor Constantin Brancusi's studio, the Atelier Brancusi, which was moved wholesale to the square in front of the centre.
SEE ALSO RESTAURANTS, P.130

Musée d'Orsay

1 rue de la Légion d'Honneur, quai Anatole France, 7th; tel: 01 40 49 48 14; www.musee-orsay. fr; Tue–Sun 9.30am–6pm, ticket desks close 5pm, Thur until 9.45pm, ticket desks close 9pm; entrance charge, under 18s free, free first Sun of month; metro Solférino, map p.151 E1

France's national museum of 19th-century art is housed in the former Gare d'Orsay, an ornate Beaux-Arts railway station designed by Victor Laloux. Opened in 1900 to serve passengers to the World Fair, the station was built around a metal frame with a long, glass-roofed nave hidden behind a grand stone facade: a triumph of modernity at that time, rivalling Gustave Eiffel's tower. In 1939, however, it ceased to serve main-line trains, as the platforms were too short for modern expresses.

In 1977 President Giscard d'Estaing saved the building from demolition and declared that it would be converted into a new national museum, thus fulfilling the prophesy of the painter Edouard Detaille, who said at the opening ceremony in 1900 that the station would be better suited as a museum.

Italian architect Gae Aulenti came up with the design for a skylit central sculpture aisle along the line of the old tracks, inserting large internal partitions to create a series of rooms on either side. The Musée d'Orsay was finally opened to the public by François Mitterrand in 1986.

THE COLLECTION

The museum's collection covers the period from 1848 to 1914. Although best known for its Impressionist works, it covers all key movements in later 19th-century French art, beginning with the late Romantics and official salon painters, through Realism, Impressionism and Symbolism to Post-Impressionism and the Nabis. Although overwhelmingly dominated by French painting, over the past few years those in charge at the Musée d'Orsay have been making an effort to acquire works by key European and American artists from the same period.

The collection also covers photography, presented in temporary exhibitions from the work of pioneers, such as Fox Talbot, Daguerre and Niepce, to portraits by Nadar, Muybridge's experiments with movement, and photos by artistic amateurs such as Zola and Lewis Carroll.

The works are arranged on several levels around a vast central aisle, which makes a grand setting for sculpture by artists including David, Rodin and Maillol. Other artworks are shown chronologically, starting on the ground floor.

In room 1 are works by Ingres (notably *La Source*), while in room 2 are the Romantic paintings of Delacroix including the tumultuous *Lion Hunt*, striking for its bold use of colour. Much of the rest of the ground floor covers the Academic School and its regimented work, or *art pompier*, dominated by historical and mythological subjects. Cabanel's *Birth of Venus*, bought by Napoléon III in 1863, is a fine example of this. In contrast is Edouard Manet's nude *Olympia* (1863), which was pronounced pornographic at the 1865 Paris salon and is considered one of the first 'modern' paintings.

On the upper floor are the museum's biggest draw, the Impressionist paintings, which hang bathed in soft light from the station's glass-vaulted roof. Pass through galleries full of paintings by Monet, Manet, Renoir, Pissarro, Degas, Cézanne and Van Gogh.

> Most national museums charge an entrance fee, but municipal museums are all free. Entrance is often cheaper on Sunday, and reductions are usually given for children, senior citizens and those with a valid student card. Entry for under 18s is generally free. Some museums charge less on Sunday, and entrance is always free on the first Sunday of the month for the following: the Louvre, Musée d'Orsay, Centre Pompidou, Orangerie, Musée Rodin, Musée Picasso and Musée du Moyen Age.

Below: Camille Pissarro's *Femme dans un clos*.

Centre Nationale de la Photographie

The Centre Nationale de la Photographie is split over two sites: the **Jeu de Paume** (its main venue) and a small sister site in the Marais's **Hôtel de Sully**.

HÔTEL DE SULLY

62 rue St-Antoine, 4th; tel: 01 42 74 47 75; Tue–Fri noon–7pm, Sat, Sun 10am–7pm; entrance charge; metro St-Paul; map p.155 D2–3

This grand 17th-century mansion, built by architect Jean Androuet Du Cerceau in 1625 and bought in 1635 by Sully (minister under Henri IV) is a magnificent second

venue for changing exhibitions mounted by the Centre Nationale de la Photographie.

JEU DE PAUME

Jeu de Paume, Jardin des Tuileries, place de la Concorde, 8th; tel: 01 47 03 12 50; www.jeudepaume.org; Tue noon–9pm, Wed–Fri noon–7pm, Sat, Sun 10am–7pm, last admission 30 mins before closing; entrance charge; metro Concorde; map p.151 E2

Napoléon III had the Jeu de Paume built as an indoor court for real tennis, but since then it has been used mostly as a showcase for artworks, first (until the mid-1980s) as the home of the Impressionist collection now at the Musée d'Orsay *(see p.92)*, and since 2005 as the main site of the Centre Nationale de la Photographie, which specialises in changing exhibitions on all photographic disciplines, including major fashion-photo retrospectives and contemporary video exhibits.

Cité des Sciences

Parc de la Villette, 19th; tel: 01 40 05 70 00; www.cite-sciences.fr; Tue–Sat 10am– 6pm, Sun 10am–7pm; entrance charge; metro: Porte de la Villette

This museum within the vast Parc de la Villette is not one for academics: its exhibits are interactive, with buttons, levers, keyboards and screens to keep mind and body alert. It is a wonderful place to bring children.

Begin at **L'Univers** with a spectacular planetarium and explanation of the big bang. **La Vie** is an eclectic mix of medicine, agriculture and economics. **La Matière** reproduces a nuclear explosion and permits you to land an Airbus

Left: aspects of the Cité des Sciences.

Apparently, there is one rat below for every human inhabitant above ground. They reduce solid waste by 50 per cent but are a real hazard to the sewer workers.

320, and **La Communication** has displays of artificial intelligence, three-dimensional graphics and virtual reality. There's more fun for kids at the **Cité des Enfants**.

Dalí Paris – Espace Montmartre

11 rue Poulbot, 18th; tel: 01 42 64 40 10; www.daliparis.com; daily 10am–6pm; entrance charge; metro: Abbesses; map p.152 B4

This Montmartre museum houses a collection of around 330 sculptures and drawings by the surrealist artist, including his clocks, intended to represent 'the fluidity of time'.

Les Egouts de Paris

Quai d'Orsay, 7th; tel: 01 53 68 27 81; May–Sept: Sat–Wed 11am–5pm, Oct–Apr: 11am–4pm, closed last three weeks of Jan; entrance charge; metro: Alma Marceau; map p.151 C1

Described by Victor Hugo in *Les Misérables* as the 'other Paris', the sewer network follows the better-known streets above ground. Accompanied by a film and, unsurprisingly, a rather strong odour, this is the alternative tour of Paris.

Galeries Nationales du Grand Palais

3 avenue du Général Eisenhower, 8th; tel: 08 92 68 46 94; www.rmn.fr; Wed–Mon 10am–10pm, Thur until 8pm: 10am–1pm to visitors with advance tickets, 1–10pm to those without reservations, ticket desks shut 30 mins before closing; entrance charge; metro: Champs Elysées-Clemenceau; map p.151 D2

Above: the beautifully designed Institute du Monde Arabe.

With its 5,000 sq. m (53,820 sq ft) of space, the Grand Palais, built for the World Fair in 1900, is one of the capital's most important exhibition centres and hosts not only several major (often blockbuster) art exhibitions but also the Paris Motor Show every spring. Recent blockbuster shows include The New Realists, Titian, and Turner, Whistler, Monet. Note that it is strongly advisable to book in advance, as queues can be extremely long.

Institut du Monde Arabe

1 rue des Fossés St-Bernard, 5th; tel: 01 40 51 38 38; www.imarabe.org; Tue–Sun 10am–6pm; tours at 3pm; entrance charge; metro: Jussieu; map p.155 D2

One of the most striking buildings on the Seine, this high-tech institute is a blend of modern Western and traditional Arab styles, symbolic of the institute's *raison d'être*: to create links and establish a deeper cultural understanding between the Western and Islamic worlds. It houses a cultural centre and museum of Arab-Islamic art and artefacts.

The nine-storey palace of glass, aluminium and concrete was designed by architect Jean Nouvel as one of François Mitterrand's grands projets *(see p.31).* The southern facade is a flat patterned wall of gleaming symmetry that recalls traditional Arab latticework. The light-sensitive prisms open and close according to the movement of the sun. Views from the rooftop terrace (which has a restaurant) are breathtaking.

The chronological tour (which can be difficult to follow, as the information panels are in French only) starts on the 7th floor, which is devoted to 4,000 years of pre-Islamic objects.

The first centuries of Islam are the focus of the second section, on the 6th floor, which is also partly dedicated to the institute's temporary exhibitions. An excellent collection of mathematical and scientific instruments reminds us of the Arab world's dominance in maths and science during the Middle Ages. The 6th-floor circuit ends with a display of rare textile fragments, mostly from the 9th and 10th centuries.

The third section, on the 4th floor, gives you access to the peaceful, plant-filled interior courtyard that Nouvel designed in the tradition of the ryad, or patio. This part of the collection covers the dynasties in the Arab-Islamic world from the 9th to the 19th centuries, when the search for the aesthetic was present in all things, whether in crafts, book illustrations or carpets.

Much of the floor features an excellent and, if you understand French, highly informative display of rugs and carpets. Also on the 4th floor is the institute's small jewellery collection.

Maison de l'Air et l'Espace

27 rue Piat, 20th; tel: 01 43 28 47 63; Mar–Oct: Tue–Fri 1.30–5.30pm, Nov–Feb: 1.30–5pm; entrance charge; metro: Pyrénées

This Belleville museum is an air-measuring station hooked up to a weather satellite, with great views over the city. A permanent exhibition demonstrates the alarming levels of air pollution in Paris.

95

The Jewish Museum has an archive of more than 3,000 documents relating to the Dreyfus case, in which Jewish army officer Alfred Dreyfus was wrongly accused and condemned for spying. Those chosen for display show how the case polarised French society: there is a copy of *J'Accuse*, Emile Zola's impassioned defence of Dreyfus that hit the headlines of *L'Aurore* in January 1898.

Maison de Balzac

47 rue Raynouard, 16th; tel: 01 55 74 41 80; www.paris.fr/ musees; Tue–Sun 10am–6pm; free; metro: Passy; map p.156 A4

This house in the villagey Passy district is where the writer Honoré de Balzac (1799–1850) penned much of his massive opus *La Comédie Humaine*. The atmospheric museum is furnished as at the time and houses a rich collection of Balzacian manuscripts and memorabilia, such as first editions, love letters, portraits and Balzac's desk, where he used to sit up all night writing.

Musée de l'Armée

Les Invalides, 7th; tel: 08 10 11 33 99; www.invalides.org; Apr–Sept: daily 10am–6pm, Oct–Mar: daily 10am–5pm, closed first Mon of month; entrance charge; metro: Invalides, La Tour Maubourg; map p.157 D4

Spread across either side of the Cour d'Honneur at the Invalides complex, this large museum offers an extensive view of people's capacity for inhumanity to others, and skill at warfare, from the Stone Age to Hiroshima, with a terrifying selection of weapons, armour and poignant displays of the two world wars.

In a separate wing, the **Musée de l'Ordre de la Libération** commemorates the Resistance fighters who received the Order of Liberation, France's highest honour created by Charles de Gaulle in 1940.
SEE ALSO CHURCHES, P.49

Musée d'Art et d'Histoire du Judaïsme

71 rue du Temple, 3rd; tel: 01 53 01 86 60; www.mahj.org; Mon–Fri 11am–6pm, Sun 10am–6pm, closed Jewish holidays; entrance charge; metro: Rambuteau; map p.155 C4

Since 1998 Paris's Jewish museum has been housed in the Hôtel de St-Aignan, built in 1650 for the Comte d'Avaux by the architect Pierre Le Muet. After the French Revolution, it became the town hall, then from 1842 was converted into a warren of workshops. By the end of the 19th century, many of the inhabitants were Jewish refugees from the pogroms in eastern Europe. The building was acquired by the city of Paris in 1962 and has been beautifully restored. The museum places a rich array of art, artefacts and documents in the context of Jewish communities and religious celebrations.

Musée d'Art Moderne de la Ville de Paris

Palais de Tokyo, 11 avenue du Président Wilson, 16th; tel: 01 53 67 40 00; www.paris.fr/ musees; Tue–Sun 10am–6pm; entrance charge; metro: Iéna, Alma Marceau; map p.150 B1

The municipal collection of modern art is housed in the Palais de Tokyo, built, along with the nearby Palais de Chaillot, for the 1937 World Fair. The museum gives a coherent survey of 20th-century art, in particular relating to the city of Paris, with strong holdings of the Fauves, the Ecole de Paris (Modigliani, Soutine and Van Dongen, for example) and conceptual art from the 1970s. Highlights include Matisse's *La Danse* (1932) and Raoul Dufy's huge *Fée de l'Electricité* ('Electricity Fairy') mural, a celebration of light and energy, commissioned for the 1937 World Fair. The museum also holds excellent temporary exhibitions.

Musée des Arts Forains

53 avenue des Terroirs de France, 12th; tel: 01 43 40 16 22; open by appointment only; entrance charge; metro: Cour St-Emilion

The items here were amassed by Jean-Paul Favand, an antiques dealer, who, in 1996,

Below: Zola skewers the army with his J'accuse.

Above: inside the
Musée de la Chasse.

cier Henri Cernuschi, who
acquired the collection on a
tour of China and Japan in
1871–3 and then built himself
this residence beside Parc
Monceau to house it.

Renovated and extended,
the museum reopened in June
2005, bringing extra space
and natural daylight to the
army of terracotta tomb figures, bronze vessels, Buddhist
statues and fine ceramics.

Musée de la Chasse

Hôtel Guénégaud, 60 rue des
Archives, 3rd; tel: 01 53 01 92
40; www.chassenature.org;
Tue–Sun 11am–6pm; entrance
charge; metro: Rambuteau; map
p.155 D4

The private mansion in which
the Museum of Hunting and
Nature is housed is the only
building in Paris that can be
proven to be entirely the work
of the architect François
Mansart (1598–1666). The
museum holds a collection of
paintings, engravings, antique
hunting weapons and masks.

Musée Cognacq-Jay

Hôtel Donon, 8 rue Elzévir, 3rd;
tel: 01 40 27 07 21;
www.cognacq-jay.paris.fr;
Tue–Sun 10am–5.40pm; free;
metro: St-Paul; map p.155 D3

Another of the Marais's grand
private mansions, the Hôtel
Donon houses the splendid
collection of 18th-century
paintings, furniture and objets
d'art bequeathed to the city
by Ernest Cognacq and his
wife Marie-Louise Jay,
founders of La Samaritaine
department store, which sadly
closed in 2005 for health and

Above: Parisian legend,
Edith Piaf.

safety reasons. The collection,
which includes works by
Rembrandt and Canaletto, is
displayed over a succession
of salons and small rooms,
which are furnished to give
the feel of a private house.

Musée Edith Piaf

5 rue Crespin-du-Gast, 11th; tel
01 43 55 53 72; Oct–May, July,
Aug: Mon–Thur 1–6pm by
appointment only; entrance
charge; metro: Ménilmontant

This tiny museum, run by Les
Amis d'Edith Piaf, is a touch-
ing tribute to the diminutive
queen of French chanson.
Memorabilia on show include
the tiny black dress and shoes
worn by 'The Little Sparrow'.

Musée Grevin

10 boulevard Montmartre, 9th;
tel: 01 47 70 85 05; www.
grevin.com; Mon–Fri 10am–
5.30pm, Sat, Sun 10am–7pm,
last entry 1 hour before closing;
entrance charge; metro: Grands
Boulevards; map p.152 B2

This waxworks gallery, a lavish confection of Venetian
rococo, rosewood and mar-
ble, with a grandiose staircase
by Rives, is full of amusingly
incompatible figures from
Marie-Antoinette and Gandhi
to virtual heroine Lara Croft
and French goalkeeper Fabien
Barthez. There's also a spectacular hall of mirrors.

---

was able to acquire the Pavil-
lons de Bercy (an 18th-century
wine depot) to house his collection. His desire to re-create
a fairground as a poetic, rather
than technological universe,
has resulted in a gorgeous
museum, with 19th-century
carousels, organs, amusement
stalls, stage sets and other
attractions that not only function, but are also works of art.

Musée Bourdelle

16–18 rue Antoine-Bourdelle,
15th; tel: 01 49 54 73 73; www.
bourdelle.paris.fr; Tue–Sun
10am–6pm; free; metro: Montparnasse; map p.157 D2

One of several museums in
Montparnasse dedicated to
artists, this is the showcase
for the work of the sculptor
Antoine Bourdelle (1861–
1929), a pupil of Rodin. Bourdelle is especially known for
his huge Modernist friezes,
inspired by dancer Isadora
Duncan *(see p.53)*, on the
Théâtre des Champs-Elysées.

Musée Cernuschi

7 avenue Vélasquez, 8th; tel: 01
53 96 21 50; www.cernuschi.
paris.fr; Tue–Sun 10am–
5.45pm; free; metro: Monceau,
Villiers; map p.151 D4

The Musée Cernuschi houses
one of the most important collections of Asian art in Europe,
thanks to 19th-century finan-

The Musée Bourdelle is housed
within the artist's former studio
and apartments. A new wing,
designed by architect Christian
de Portzamparc, showcases the
artist's bronzes.

97

Right: an ornate ceiling at the Musée Carnavalet.

Musée de l'Histoire de Paris

Hôtel Carnavalet, 23 rue de Sévigné, 3rd; tel: 01 44 59 58 58; www.carnavalet.paris.fr; Tue–Sun 10am–6pm, ticket desks close 5.30pm; free; metro: St-Paul; map p.155 D3

The Musée Carnavalet traces the history of Paris from its origins from the Gallo-Roman Lutetia to the present day, as seen through the eyes of contemporary artists. It is spread across a network of intimate rooms in two adjoining city mansions: the **Hôtel Carnavalet** (16th and 17th centuries), home of Madame de Sévigné from 1677 to 1696, and the **Hôtel Le Peletier de St-Fargeau** (17th century).

There are over 100 rooms, home to paintings, *objets d'art*, sculpture, furniture, costumes and other items documenting centuries of Parisian art and decor, misery and grandeur. If you have plenty of time follow the floor plan supplied at the entrance and tour the museum chronologically. Otherwise target a particular theme, such as Parisian life under Louis XIV, the French Revolution, Napoléon, the Belle Epoque or 20th century.

Musée Jacquemart-André

158 boulevard Haussmann, 8th; tel: 01 45 62 11 59; www.

> The Carnavalet was the home for 20 years of Madame de Sévigné (1626–96), salon hostess and prolific letter-writer, whose writings reveal so much about the life of 17th-century French aristocrats. The Sévigné rooms, which retain the original wood panelling, are devoted to her life.

musee-jacquemart-andre.com; daily 10am–6pm; entrance charge; metro: Miromesnil; map p.151 D3

The Hôtel André was built by Henri Parent in 1869–75 for the collector Edouard André (son of a wealthy banking family) at a time when this area of smart western Paris was first being developed. In 1881, André married society portrait painter Nélie Jacquemart, who hung up her paintbrushes to accompany him as he travelled Italy and Asia or scoured salerooms.

The grand colonnaded entrance, spacious reception rooms, lavish painted ceilings and chic gentleman's smoking room, plus a set of smaller apartments for daily use, give a vision of the affluent lifestyle of the *haute-bourgeoisie* under the Second Empire.

Perhaps the most unexpected room in the house is the *Jardin d'Hiver*, or Winter Garden, with its lush plants and spectacular double-revolution marble staircase. Highlights in the collection downstairs include works by Chardin, Boucher, Nattier, Prud'hon, David, Franz Hals and Rembrandt.

Upstairs, the area that was originally intended to be Nélie's studio became the Jaquemart-Andrés's 'Italian museum', a fine collection of Renaissance paintings, with highlights by Botticelli, Botticini and Mantegna. Perhaps the most adorable painting is the dinky *St George and the Dragon* by Paolo Uccello.

Musée Maillol – Fondation Dina Vierny

6 rue de Grenelle, 7th; tel: 01 42 22 59 58; www.museemaillol. com; Wed–Mon 11am–6pm, last admission 5.15pm; entrance charge; metro: Rue du Bac; map p.157 E3

Dina Vierny was introduced to French sculptor Aristide Maillol in 1934, when she was 15 and he was 73; for the next 10 years (until Maillol's death) she was his principal model. In 1995, she opened this museum in the 18th-century **Hôtel Bouchardon** (named after Edmé Bouchardon, who sculpted the *Four Seasons* fountain at the entrance).

The museum showcases Maillol's work, along with art by contemporaries Cézanne

Cézanne, Degas, Sisley, Morisot, Renoir and Boudin. The painting was rejected by the official salon, and a scathing critic coined the term 'Impressionism'.

Above all, however, it is the set of square canvases of *Nymphéas* ('Water Lilies'), of 1916–19, that attract visitors. The paintings are almost luminous, viridian green and electric blue exercises in colour, inspired by the water lilies, watery reflections and weeping willows of Monet's Japanese garden at Giverny. Other paintings in the series are showcased in the Orangerie (*see p.102*).

Thanks to donations, Marmottan has a representative collection of Monet's fellow Impressionists and Realist contemporaries, including works by Pissarro, Renoir, Manet and Gauguin, as well as superb First Empire furniture.
SEE ALSO OUTSIDE THE PÉRIPHÉRIQUE, P.29

Musée de la Mode – Musée Galliera

10 avenue Pierre-1er-de-Serbie, 16th; tel: 01 56 52 86 00; www.galliera.paris.fr; Tue–Sun 10am–6pm; entrance charge; metro: Iéna; map p.150 B2
The Parisian fashion museum, housed in an

imposing palace built by Gustave Eiffel, has 12,000 outfits and 60,000 accessories from the 18th century to the present day. To rotate this rich collection, only a fraction of which can be displayed at one time, two exhibitions are held each year focusing on a historic period, a theme or a designer.

Musée de Montmartre

12 rue Cortot, 18th; tel: 01 49 25 89 37; www.museedemontmartre.fr; Tue–Sun 11am–6pm; entrance charge; metro: Anvers, Lamarck Caulaincourt, Abbesses; map p.152 B4
This museum chronicles the life and times of Montmartre and its artists' quarter, and is housed in a 17th-century manor. The area's oldest house, it was once home to studios rented by artists including Renoir, Dufy and Utrillo. The museum is an evocation of past simplicity, gaiety and bohemian living, with Toulouse-Lautrec posters, notably *Le Moulin Rouge*, in which Louise Weber dances the can-can, plus reconstructions of Utrillo's favourite café, complete with zinc counter and absinthe bottles, and an artist's studio, with yellowing photographs and a wonderful view over Paris.

Musée du Montparnasse

21 avenue du Maine, 15th; tel: 01 42 22 91 96; www.museedumontparnasse.net; Tue–Sun 12.30–7pm; entrance charge; metro: Montparnasse Bienvenüe; map p.157 E2
Tucked away down one of

and Degas, drawings by Matisse, multiples by Duchamp and works by Russian and naïve artists. More of Maillol's work is on display in the Jardin des Tuileries.
SEE ALSO PARKS AND GARDENS, P.122

Musée Marmottan

2 rue Louis-Boilly, 16th; tel: 01 42 24 07 02; www.marmottan.com; Tue–Sun 11am–6pm; entrance charge; metro: La Muette
The Musée Marmottan, in a mansion in smart western Paris, gives an unrivalled overview of the career of Claude Monet (1840–1926). Major paintings are accompanied by sketchbooks, palettes and personal effects. Among the fine collection of Monet's paintings at the Musée Marmottan is *Impression, Soleil Levant* ('Impression, Sunrise'), the canvas that gave the Impressionist movement its name. The piece, painted *c.*1873, was shown at an exhibition held in 1874 in the studio of the photographer Nadar on boulevard des Capucines, alongside works in the same style by

Below: one of Maillol's sculptures in the Tuileries.

the small alleys of artists' studios that previously littered Montparnasse, this museum was once a studio and art school run by Russian *avant-garde* artist Marie Vassilieff. Exhibitions here focus on different aspects of the area's artistic heritage, including its connections with artists such as Jean Cocteau, Henri Matisse and Pablo Picasso, through photos and archive material as well as paintings.

Musée de la Musique

221 avenue Jean-Jaurès, 19th; tel: 01 44 84 45 00; www.cite-musique.fr; Tue–Sat noon–6pm, Sun 10am–6pm; metro: Porte de Pantin

One of the largest collections of instruments in the world, with items from the 17th century to the present day. The museum was planned as far back as 1795 but the collection did not open to the public until 1860. In 1993 it moved to the Cité de la Musique.

As well as fine collections of 18th–century lutes and harpsichords, there are some splendid examples of violins and cellos by the makers Stradivarius, Guarneri and Amati. It also has accordians, electric guitars and over 600 instruments from Africa and Asia. A regular series of concerts is held here.

SEE ALSO MUSIC, P.107

A brilliant colourist and meticulous draughtsman, Moreau reworked themes from mythology and the Bible in a highly personal pantheon. He often combined areas of sweeping, broadly painted colour with obsessively rendered detail in bejewelled costumes, imaginary architecture and exotic bestiaries, inspired by medieval and Renaissance paintings, and by the Mogul miniatures and Hindu sculpture he saw in Paris museums.

Musée National des Arts Asiatiques – Musée Guimet

6 place d'léna, 16th; tel: 01 56 52 53 00; www.museeguimet.fr; Wed–Mon 10am–6pm; entrance charge; metro: léna; map p.150 B2

The national museum of Asian art, which has around 45,000 items, was originally based around the collection of Emile Guimet, a wealthy 19th-century industrialist, whose museum of world religions first opened in this classical-revival building in 1889.

His collection was later augmented by the Oriental collections from the Louvre and by subsequent acquisitions and donations. These often reflect both France's colonial history and the work of French archaeologists,

most notably in their findings of Cambodian sculpture, Chinese paintings from Dunhuang and the Treasure of Begram from Afghanistan.

The downstairs galleries focus on India and Southeast Asia, while the upper floors feature the art of China, Japan, Korea, Nepal, Tibet and central Asia. Highlights include the Giant's Way, part of the temple complex from Angkor Wat, Cambodia.

Musée National Eugène Delacroix

6 place Furstenberg, 6th; tel: 01 44 41 86 50; www.musee-delacroix.fr; Wed–Mon 9.30am–5pm; entrance charge; metro: St-Germain-des-Prés; map p.154 B3

Hidden in a courtyard just off place Furstenberg is this little gem of a museum where the Romantic artist Eugène Delacroix (1798–1863) spent his last years. Delacroix moved here to be near the church of St-Sulpice, where he wrestled for ten years with the subject of good and evil in a series of large frescoes.

Although there are no major works in the museum (these are housed in the Louvre and Musée d'Orsay, *see p.88, 92*), there are several fine small paintings, notably of the novelist George Sand, plus self-portraits and sketches from his formative journey to North Africa. Per-

Above: unenlightened specimen collection in the Galerie de Zoologie.

sonal effects, such as letters from friends, including the poet Charles Baudelaire, and, in the studio, brushes and a palette with neatly arranged teardrops of paint, add to the sense of intimacy. There is also a gorgeous garden.

Musée National Gustave-Moreau

14 rue de La Rochefoucauld, 9th; tel: 01 48 74 38 50; www. musee-moreau.fr; Wed–Mon 10am–12.45pm, 2–5.15pm; entrance charge; metro: Trinité; map p.152 A3

The Symbolist artist (1825–98) conceived this museum himself, having the double-storey studio built on top of the partially demolished family home. He left it to the state, along with the hundreds of oil paintings and thousands of drawings and goauches that now fill the space. On the first floor you can see the cramped apartment where Moreau lived with his parents; the second floor, the lower level of the studio, is hung with large, mostly unfinished canvases; and, on the upper level, is his *Jupiter et Semélé*, which dramatically juxtaposes the tiny figure of Semélé with the giant figure of Jupiter.

Left: harps, harpsichords and viols at the Musée de la Musique.

Muséum National d'Histoire Naturelle

Jardin des Plantes, 36 rue Geoffroy St-Hilaire, 5th; tel: 01 40 79 54 79; www.mnhn.fr; Wed–Mon 10am–6pm; entrance charge; metro: Gare d'Austerlitz, Jussieu; map p.155 D1

The Jardin des Plantes (botanical garden) was established in 1636 by Louis XIII as a source of medicinal herbs to treat the royal family. In the 1700s, a maze, an amphitheatre and exhibition galleries were added. The revolutionaries added a small zoo and renamed the complex the Muséum National d'Histoire Naturelle.

In 1889, the **Galerie de Zoologie** was opened, for the display, conservation and study of millions of specimens brought back by European naturalists and explorers travelling the world. After World War II, the gallery fell into disrepair, and in 1965 it was closed. Twenty years later the majority of the

The distinctive style of Delacroix is marked by his use of vivid colour (Cézanne called him 'the palette of France') and exotic, often violent subject matter. He is best known for his monumental works, his animal compositions and watercolours.

museum's 7 million skeletons, insects, stuffed birds and mammals were transferred to an underground research centre, and work began on renovating the old building and transforming it into an exhibition space.

The **Grande Galerie de l'Evolution** finally opened in 1994, with the objective of illustrating principles of evolution and dramatising the impact of human behaviour on the environment. The hall has retained elements of a 19th-century museum, such as parquet floors, iron columns, display cases, etc, but the interior space has been completely modernised and equipped with interactive displays (mostly in French) examining everything from micro-organisms to the global ecosystem.
SEE ALSO PARKS AND GARDENS, P.122

Musée National du Luxembourg

19 rue de Vaugirard, 6th; tel: 01 42 34 25 95; www.museedulux embourg.fr; Wed–Mon 9am–6pm; entrance charge; metro: St-Sulpice, RER: Luxembourg; map p.154 A2

The Musée du Luxembourg, next to the Palais du Luxembourg, was the first public gallery in France when, from 1750–80, paintings from the

101

royal collection were put on view to the public two days a week. In the 19th century, the gallery was used to display works by living artists acquired by the state, until it was superseded by the creation of the Musée National d'Art Moderne in 1945. Now run by the Senate and national museums, it is used for temporary art exhibitions, most of which cover historical topics.
SEE ALSO PARKS AND GARDENS, P.121

Musée National de la Marine

Palais de Chaillot, 17 place du Trocadéro, 7th; tel: 01 53 65 69 69; www.musee-marine.fr; Wed–Mon 10am–6pm, ticket desks close 5.15pm; entrance charge; metro: Trocadéro; map p.150 A1

Battleships, cannon barrels and carved figureheads of forbidding mythological women are a useful reminder to Parisians of France's long maritime tradition. While naval warfare, Texel, Trafalgar *et al* loom large, the museum, located in the west wing of the Art Deco Palais de Chaillot, also addresses navigation and seafaring in general.

The focus is on models and paintings. Highlights include the ornate *Canot de l'Empereur* (imperial barge) and

Joseph Vernet's 13 panoramic canvases of the ports of France, commissioned in 1750 by the Marquis de Marigny, Director of the Buildings of France under Louis XV.

The development of modern marine warfare is traced from the first torpedoes, invented in the 18th century, to the rapid transformation of the navy at the end of the 19th century: from sailing fleet to battleships of World War I, to nuclear submarines.
SEE ALSO ARCHITECTURE, P.32

Musée National du Moyen Âge – Thermes de Cluny

6 place Paul-Pinlevé, 5th; tel: 01 53 73 78 00; www.musee-moyenage.fr; Wed–Mon 9.15am–5.45pm; entrance charge; metro: Cluny La Sorbonne; map p.154 B2

Once the residence of the Abbots of Cluny, the Gothic **Hôtel de Cluny** houses one of the world's finest collections of medieval artefacts. Many of the treasures reflect life in the religious communities, such as illuminated manuscripts, embroideries, stained glass, liturgical vestments and various church furnishings.

Among the tapestries is the exquisite 15th-century *La Dame à la Licorne* ('The Lady and the Unicorn') in a first-

floor rotunda. The six panels are beautifully worked in the *millefleurs* style of design, using rich, harmonious colours. The museum also holds 21 of the original heads of the *Kings of Judah*, sculpted in 1220 for Notre-Dame cathedral but vandalised in the Revolution.

The Hôtel de Cluny was constructed on the remains of a huge Gallo-Roman bathhouse complex, believed to have been built in 200AD by the guild of *nautes* (boatmen): ships' prows are carved on the arch supports of the *frigidarium* (cold bathhouse). As elsewhere in their empire, the Romans living in Lutetia (their name for Paris) regarded bathing as the essence of civilisation.

Cluny's medieval garden is not a reproduction of a medieval garden but an imaginative modern representation of the Middle Ages, taking its inspiration from objects in the collection and evoking the two spheres of the spiritual and the profane that governed the medieval world.

Musée National de l'Orangerie

Orangerie, Jardin des Tuileries, 1st; tel: 01 44 77 80 07; www.musee-orangerie.fr; Mon, Wed, Thur–Sun 12.30–7pm, Fri until 9pm; entrance charge; metro: Concorde; map p.151 E1

Below: medieval patridges in the Musée du Moyen Âge.

The Orangerie was built as a hothouse by Napoleon III, but since the 1920s has been the showcase for eight of Claude Monet's water-lily paintings, in which the Impressionist painter captured the play of colour on the pond in his Japanese garden at Giverny at different times of day. Recently renovated, the two vast oval rooms upstairs show off the paintings as specified by Monet.

In the space downstairs is the Jean Walter and Paul Guillaume collection, an array of works by artists including Cézanne, Renoir, Matisse, Picasso, Soutine, Modigliani, Utrillo and Rousseau.
SEE ALSO OUTSIDE THE PÉRIPHÉRIQUE, P.29

Musée National Picasso

Hôtel Salé, 5 rue de Thorigny, 3rd; tel: 01 42 71 25 21; www.musee-picasso.fr; Oct–Mar: Wed–Mon 9.30am–5.30pm, Apr–Sept: Wed–Mon 9.30am–6pm; metro: St-Paul, Chemin Vert; map p.155 D3
One of the finest buildings in the Marais, the **Hôtel Salé** was constructed with the booty of a 17th-century tax collector. Three centuries later, the French tax authorities scored another coup. Following the death of Pablo Picasso in 1973, his family was faced with an enormous inheritance tax bill, so, in lieu

> Born in Málaga in Spain, Pablo Picasso (1881–1973) settled in Paris at the age of 23, having studied art in Barcelona and Madrid.

of payment, they donated to the French nation a large collection of his works. These included 200 paintings, more than 3,000 drawings and 88 ceramics, along with sculptures, collages and manuscripts, as well as Picasso's own private collection of works by Cézanne, Matisse, Modigliani and others.

The museum shows all Picasso's different periods, in chronological order (the blue, pink, Cubist, Classical and post-Cubist phases). The famous beach pictures of the 1920s and 1930s are here, as well as remarkable portraits of his model-mistresses, Marie-Thérèse and Dora Maar.

Musée National Rodin

Hôtel Biron, 77 rue de Varenne, 7th; tel: 01 44 18 61 10; www.musee-rodin.fr; Apr–Sept: Tue–Sun, museum 9.30am–5.45pm, park closes 6.45pm, last admission 5.15pm, Oct–Mar: Tue–Sun, museum 9.30am–4.45pm, park closes 5pm, last entry 4.15pm; entrance charge; metro: Varenne; map p.157 D4
Auguste Rodin's first critically acclaimed sculpture was The Age of Bronze (1877), depict-

ing a naked youth caressing his hair, modelled by a Belgian soldier. The establishment was shocked, maintaining that the statue was too lifelike to be regarded as art. A card stuck to the work at the Paris salon read, 'Beware – moulded from the body of the model.' Eventually, the French Government bought the statue, and Rodin's reputation was confirmed.

The artist came to live in the Hôtel Biron in 1908 and stayed until his death in 1917. He paid rent with his best works, which form the basis of the museum's collection. Here you can admire The Kiss (removed from the Chicago World Fair of 1893 for being too shocking), The Thinker (reputedly Dante contemplating the Inferno), The Burghers of Calais, The Hand of God, Balzac and many other works.

Bronze casts of many of his major works are displayed amid the large lawns, hedged enclosures, pools, mature trees and topiaried yews, with studies and smaller works dotted around the house.

Also included in the exhibition are works by Camille Claudel, the most famous of Rodin's mistresses and a gifted artist in her own right.

Below: a burgher of Calais.

Above: perfume bottles in the Fragonard museum.

Above: in the Musée Zadkine.

Musée Nissim de Camondo

63 rue de Monceau, 8th; tel: 01 53 89 06 40; www.ucad.fr; Wed–Sun 10am–5.30pm; entrance charge; metro: Monceau; map p.151 D4

The Camondos, a wealthy Jewish banking family from Istanbul, settled in Paris in the late 19th century. In 1910, Comte Moïse de Camondo inherited two houses overlooking the Parc Monceau. He knocked them down and built this mansion modelled on the Petit Trianon at Versailles. The family moved in during 1914.

In 1935 he bequeathed both the mansion and the collection to the state, his purpose being to preserve 'the finest examples I have been able to assemble of this decorative art which was one of the glories of France.' He also requested that the museum be named after his son Nissim, who had died in aerial combat in World War I. Preserved much as Moïse left it, the house reveals a connoisseur's taste for the 18th century in all its refinement: Aubusson tapestries, Savonnerie carpets, Sèvres porcelain and fine marquetry furniture from the century's best cabinetmakers, including Oeben and Reisener.
SEE ALSO PARKS AND GARDENS, P.125

Musée du Parfum Fragonard

9 rue Scribe, 8th; tel: 01 47 42 04 56; www.fragonard.com; Mon–Sat 9am–6pm, Sun 9am–5pm; free; metro: Opéra; map p.152 A2

Across the street from the Opéra is this small museum tracing 5,000 years of perfumery. A heady fragrance permeates the air in this finely restored 19th-century town house.
SEE ALSO PAMPERING, P.119

Musée du Quai Branly

29–55 quai Branly, 7th; tel: 01 56 61 70 00; www.quaibranly.fr; Tue–Sun 11am–7pm, Thur–Sat until 9pm; entrance charge; metro: Pont de l'Alma; map p.150 B1

Located just northeast of the Eiffel Tower is Jacques Chirac's cultural legacy – his *grand projet* – the Musée du Quai Branly, opened in 2006. The museum houses a collection of around 300,000 objects of art from Africa, Asia, the Americas and Oceania, with over 3,600 items on display. With its colonial overtones, the collection has sparked some controversy, but the building itself – a striking foliage-covered maroon edifice by architect Jean Nouvel – has been more warmly received.

Musée Vivant du Cheval

Grandes Ecuries, Chantilly; tel: 03 44 57 40 40; www.musee vivantducheval.fr; stables, rotunda and gallery: Wed–Mon 2–5pm; museum exhibition closed for restoration until 2011; entrance charge; train: Paris Gare du Nord–Chantilly Gouvieux

Chantilly's Equestrian Museum is set in the former royal stables, within 10 minutes' walk of the Château de Chantilly. The stables are impressive – according to popular belief their instigator, Louis-Henri, Duke of Bourbon (1692–1740), was convinced that he would be reincarnated as a horse and built a future home fit for an equestrian king. Equestrian memorabilia and art is on display, but the main attraction is the horses, which give spectacular dressage displays in the stables' central rotunda three times a

> The shop **Paris Musées** (29 bis rue des Francs-Bourgeois, 4th; tel: 01 42 74 13 02; Mon 2–7pm, Tue–Fri 11am–1pm, 2–7pm, Sat 11am–7pm, Sun noon–7.30pm; metro: St-Paul) has reproductions from the city-run museums and galleries (such as the Petit Palais), as well as works from contemporary artists.

day (11.30am, 3.30pm, 5.15pm).
SEE ALSO PALACES, P.114

Musée Zadkine

100 bis rue d'Assas, 6th; tel: 01 55 42 77 20; www.zadkine. paris.fr; Tue–Sun 10am–6pm; free; metro: Notre-Dame-des-Champs; map p.154 A1

The Russian cubist sculptor Ossip Zadkine (1890–1967) spent much of his artistic career working in the garden atelier of this, his former house. Now a museum of his work, showcasing over 100 sculptures and numerous sketches, it still retains the feeling of an oasis.

Arranged chronologically, the works represent the materials he fashioned (wood, clay, stone and bronze) and his creative periods: Primitivism, Cubism, Abstraction. Some of his most celebrated figures are here, along with models for his masterpiece, the *Monument à la Ville Détruite*, erected in the Dutch port of Rotterdam in 1947.

Palais de la Découverte

Avenue Franklin-D.-Roosevelt, 8th; tel: 01 56 43 20 21; www.palais-decouverte.fr; Tue–Sat 9.30am–6pm, Sun 10am–7pm; entrance charge; metro: Champs-Elysées Clemenceau, Franklin D. Roosevelt; map p.151 D2

Situated next to the Grand Palais *(see p.94),* this museum on elementary and contemporary science is organised as a series of interactive experiments, with a commentary by exhibition curators. Areas covered include astronomy (the **planetarium** is a highlight), biology, chemistry, mathematics, physics and earth sciences. There is also an electrostatics room, a space devoted to the

sun, a room on the evolution of the earth and living species, and an area that explains acoustics.

Palais de Tokyo: Site de Création Contemporaine

13 avenue du Président Wilson; 16th; tel: 01 47 23 54 01; www. palaisdetokyo.com; Tue–Sun noon–midnight; entrance charge; metro: Iéna, Alma Marceau; map p.150 B1

In the opposite wing of the Palais de Tokyo from the Musée d'Art Moderne de la Ville de Paris *(see p.96)* is the **Site de Création Contemporaine**, described as a 'laboratory for contemporary art'. An adventurous, multidisciplinary programme focuses on the work of young artists, through exhibitions, performances and workshops. There's also a trendy and popular restaurant.

Petit Palais

Avenue Winston Churchill; tel: 01 53 43 40 00; www.petit palais.paris.fr; Tue–Sun 10am–6pm, Thur until 8pm; entrance charge; metro: Champs Elysées Clemenceau; map p.151 D2

The rococo-style Petit Palais, built, along with nearby Grand Palais *(see p.94)* on the occasion of the 1900 World Fair, houses the collection of the **Musée des Beaux-Arts de la Ville de Paris**. The building, inspired by the Grand Trianon at Versailles with its polychrome marble, magnificent long gallery and arcaded garden, houses the municipal fine and decorative arts collection. This includes some fine examples of Greek and Roman antiquities, icons, 17th–19th-century paintings, sculpture, tapestries and fabulous Art Nouveau furniture.

Below: the ornate façade of the Petit Palais.

Music

Music in Paris is not all accordions and maudlin songs of lost love: there are distinctive musical traditions in a wide variety of genres. From church-organ music to Edith Piaf, from saucy operetta to Gypsy jazz, from authentic Arab to poet-rock, there is something to cater for every taste and occasion. Many of the venues listed below are also worth visiting in their own right, with the grand opulence of the historic Palais Garnier opera house, the bohemian atmosphere of La Cigale and the intimate charm of jazz cellars and *chanson* cafés. Listed below are some of the best.

Classical Music

Paris has a long and distinguished classical-musical history. Among composers in the early period working in and around the city were Josquin Desprez (1440–1521); the bass-viol virtuoso Augustin Saint-Colombe (1630–1701); his pupil Marin Marais (1656–1728); and Marc-Antoine Charpentier (c.1640s–1704).

Notable baroque composers based in Paris included Louis Couperin (1626–61), Jean-Baptiste Lully (1632–87), court composer to Louis XIV, and the composer and great theorist Jean-Philippe Rameau (1683–1764).

After the death of Rameau, music in France underwent a hiatus until the appearance of Hector Berlioz (1803–69). Embodying the Romantic ideal in both his music and personal life, Berlioz was revolutionary in his approach to form and orchestration. Following in his wake came the grand opera composers Gounod, Bizet, Massenet and Meyer-

Above: the modern facade of the Bastille Opéra.

beer, all closely associated with either the Paris Opéra or Opéra Comique.

The ground work for a further musical revolution was laid by the late-19th century composers, Saint-Saëns, Fauré and Dukas. The final iteration of this cycle of innovation came with *L'apres midi d'un faune* (1894), by Claude Debussy (1862–1918). A new freedom of harmony, rhythm and form was introduced to music, with the clear influence of Impressionism and

Symbolism. This achievement was consolidated in the early works of Maurice Ravel (1875–1937).

The watershed for French music in the 20th century is marked by two events: the first performance of Igor Stravinsky's *Rite of Spring* in Paris in 1913, and World War I. The violence and iconoclasm of Stravinsky's work almost seem to have presaged the destruction that was to come.

Following the lead of Stravinsky, Ravel, and the eccentric Erik Satie (1866–1925), the group of composers known as *Les Six* (Auric, Durey, Honegger, Milhaud, Poulenc and Tailleferre) produced works that might broadly be described as 'neoclassical', by imposing Modernist techniques on to Classical forms.

Later composers of the 20th century include Olivier Messaien (1908–1992), influenced by mystical Catholicism as well as birdsong, and his pupil Pierre Boulez (1925–), a seminal figure in the postwar *avant-garde*.

Left: the wonderfully ornate Palais Garnier.

Opéra Comique – Théâtre National
Place Boieldieu, 2nd; tel: 01 42 44 45 40; www.opera-comique. com; charge; metro: Richelieu Drouot; map p.152 B2
Indulge in the spirit of the naughty 90s at the Salle Favart, where every surface is covered in either gold or a coy mural, and where operetta is still performed in grand style: huge casts, lavish costumes, and music by Offenbach *et al*.

Opéra Nationale de Paris, Bastille
120 rue de Lyon, 12th; tel: 08 92 89 90 90; www.operadeparis.fr; metro: Bastille, RER: Gare de Lyon; map p.155 E2
Ever since it was opened by Mitterrand as one of his *grands projets (see p.31)* in 1989, the 'new' opera, where ballet and opera perform-ances are staged, in conjunc-tion with the Palais Garnier *(see below)*, has been the object of much polemic from politicians, art critics and public alike. The building, designed by architect Carlos Ott, is coming apart, and nets are in place to keep stone tiles from falling on people's heads; the acoustics, too, have been widely criticised.
SEE ALSO DANCE, P.52

Some museums host worth-while concerts. Watch out for the programmes offered by the Louvre, the Musée National du Moyen Age and the Musée d'Orsay.

Classical Venues
Châtelet – Théâtre Musical de Paris
1 place du Châtelet, 1st; tel: 01 40 28 28 40; www.chatelet-theatre.com; box office closed July and Aug; metro: Châtelet; map p.154 C3
Smart venue, all burgundy velvet and gold leaf. Presents a varied programme of opera (concert versions), ballet, orchestral and chamber music, jazz and variétés. Regular concerts on Sunday mornings as well.

Cité de la Musique
221 avenue Jean-Jaurès, 19th; tel: 01 44 84 45 00; www.cite-musique.fr; metro: Porte de Pantin
Opened in 1995, this complex at La Villette includes a con-cert venue, a museum of musical instruments, and a book shop. Its Conservatoire, plays host to world-class per-formers and features many free concerts. Free buses back into the centre are pro-vided for concert-goers.
SEE ALSO MUSEUMS AND GALLERIES, P.100

IRCAM
1 place Igor-Stravinsky, 4th; tel: 01 44 78 48 43; www.ircam.fr; metro: Hôtel de Ville; map p.155 C3
Set up in 1969 by Pierre Boulez as a centre for *avant-garde* music. Hosts concerts, festivals and courses.

Maison de Radio France
116 avenue du Président-Kennedy, 16th; tel: 01 56 40 15 16, information: 01 42 30 15 16; www.radiofrance.fr; metro: Passy; map p.156 A3
This vast complex is home to state-owned radio station France Musique as well as the **Orchestre National de France** under Kurt Masur and the **Orchestre Philhar-monique de Radio France** under Myung-Whun Chung. Although a somewhat imper-sonal venue, it does offer a large and varied programme of events including the **Présences** contemporary music festival in February.

Below: Satie lived here.

> The Palais Garnier's ornate five-storey horseshoe-shaped auditorium contains nearly 2,000 seats, though of these 258 provide only a limited view of the stage.

Above: the modern Cité de la Musique at the Parc de la Villette.

Opéra National de Paris, Palais Garnier

Place de l'Opéra, 9th; tel: 08 36 69 78 68; www.operadeparis.fr; metro: Opéra, RER: Auber; map p.152 A2

Soaring over place de l'Opéra is the city's historic opera house, the Palais-Garnier, which puts on opera and ballet alongside the newer Opéra Bastille (see p.107).

In 1860 architect Charles Garnier was commissioned by Napoleon III to build an opera house reflecting the pomp and opulence of the Second Empire. The auditorium, decked out in velvet and gilt, is dominated by a vast chandelier, which crashed down on the audience during a performance in 1896. The auditorium ceiling was painted by Marc Chagall in 1964. Tours also take in the library and museum, showcasing scores, costumes and sets.

SEE ALSO DANCE, P.52

Salle Cortot

78 rue Cardinet, 17th; tel: 01 47 63 85 72; metro: Malesherbes

Part of France's elite music school, the Ecole Normale de Musique de Paris, this concert hall has exceptional acoustics – the great French pianist Cortot claimed it 'sounds like a Stradivarius'. It offers free student concerts.

Salle Gaveau

45 rue La Boétie, 8th; tel: 01 49 53 05 07; www.sallegaveau.com; metro: Miromesnil; map p.151 D3

Gorgeous venue built in 1906–7 and the scene of legendary performances by Casals, Cortot, Ysaye and other great names. After a long restoration, the hall once again offers a programme of piano recitals, chamber music, and **Les Grandes Voix** series.

Salle Pleyel

252 rue du Faubourg St-Honoré, 8th; tel: 01 42 56 13 13; www.sallepleyel.fr; metro: Ternes; map p.150 C4

Originally built in 1927 by piano-makers Pleyel, this concert hall burnt down after just nine months. The reconstruction in 1929, at a time of economic difficulties, was ruined by poor design and acoustics. In 2006 the venue finally reopened, having been rebuilt properly, retaining the Art Deco facade outside while providing a sleek white space with 2,000 seats and crystal-clear acoustics inside. The hall is home to the **Orchestre de Paris** under Christoph Eschenbach (who gives 50 concerts a year here) and hosts visits from top-class international orchestras.

Théâtre de la Ville

2 place du Châtelet, 4th; tel: 01 42 74 22 77; www.theatredelaville-paris.com; metro: Châtelet; map p.154 C3

Large concrete theatre that hosts classical concerts as well as world music, dance and theatre. Sister venue **Les Abbesses** (18th) shares the same box office.

Théâtre des Champs-Elysées

15 avenue Montaigne, 8th; tel: 01 49 52 50 50; www.theatrechampselysees.fr; metro: Alma Marceau; map p.150 C2

Lovely Art Nouveau theatre, with bas-reliefs by Bourdelle, and notorious as the scene of the première of Stravinsky's *Rite of Spring* in 1913. Although unsubsidised, it still hosts many of the world's greatest classical performers.

Contemporary and Jazz

Caveau de la Huchette

5 rue de la Huchette, 5th; tel: 01 43 26 65 05; www.caveaudelahuchette.fr; concerts daily 10.15pm; metro: St-Michel, RER: St-Michel Notre-Dame; map p.154 B2–C2

Jazz cellar frequented by GIs in World War II and now frequented by Left Bank students and arty types.

The Cavern

21 rue Dauphine, 6th; tel: 01 43 54 53 82; metro: Odéon; map p.154 B3

Check out the latest bands and drink the bar dry if the music's somewhat lacking.

La Chapelle des Lombards

19 rue de Lappe, 11th; tel: 01 43 57 24 24; www.la-chapelle-des-lombards.com; Thur–Sat 11pm–dawn; metro: Bastille; map p.155 E2

Afro-Caribbean jazz and Brazilian samba.

Chez Adel

10 rue de la Grange-aux-Belles, 10th; tel: 01 42 08 24 61; Tue–Sun noon–midnight; metro: Jacques Bonsergent; map p.153 D2

Neighbourhood café serving a daily diet of *chanson*.

La Cigale

120 boulevard de Rochechouart, 18th; tel: 01 49 25 81 75; www.lacigale.fr; metro: Anvers; map p.152 B3–4

Gorgeous old theatre, once host to crooner Maurice Chevalier, now featuring big names in rock and pop.

Le Divan du Monde

75 rue des Martyrs, 18th; tel: 01 42 52 02 46; www.divandumonde.com; metro: Anvers, Pigalle; map p.152 B3

Old Montmartre nightspot, now a venue for indie, hip-hop, and crossover acts.

Le Limonaire

18 cité Bergère, 9th; tel: 01 45 23 33 33; http://limonaire.free.fr; concerts Mon–Sat 10pm, Sun 7pm; metro: Grands Boulevards; map p.152 B2

Bistrot à vins for *chanson*, cabarets and silent films with piano accompaniment.

New Morning

7–9 rue des Petites-Ecuries, 10th; tel: 01 45 23 51 41; www.newmorning.com; concerts daily 9pm; metro: Château d'Eau; map p.152 C2

Aficionado's destination for modern jazz, blues, hip-hop, and cutting-edge pop.

Le Sunset/Le Sunside

60 rue des Lombards, 1st; tel: 01 40 26 46 60; www.sunset-sunside.com; metro: Châtelet; map p.153 C2

Well-established club with electric jazz and world music on the ground floor and acoustic jazz in the cellar.

La Vieille Grille

1 rue du Puits-de-l'Ermite, 5th; tel: 01 47 07 22 11; concerts Mon–Sat 8pm, Sun 3pm, 5pm; metro: Place Monge; map p.155 C1

One-of-a-kind artist-run venue for tango, *chanson*, klezmer and children's shows.

Listings and Tickets

The listings magazines *L'Officiel des Spectacles* and *Pariscope* appear every Wednesday at newspaper kiosks across the city. *Figaroscope*, the Wednesday supplement of *Le Figaro* newspaper is a useful source

> Paris is renowned for its *chansons*: cabaret-style songs with an emphasis on storytelling. Famous exponents include Maurice Chevalier, Charles Trenet, Georges Brassens, Charles Aznavour, and the legendary Edith Piaf, the 1.4-m 'Little Sparrow', who belted out *La Vie en Rose* and other classics.

for listings. In addition, the tourist office website has up-to-date information in several languages (www.paris-info.com). Parisvoice.com is a good source of information in English for what's on.

MAIN TICKET AGENCIES

CROUS

39 avenue Georges-Bernanos, 5th; tel: 01 40 51 36 00; www.crous-paris.fr; metro: Port Royal

Reduced-price seats for students (with student cards).

fnac Billeterie

fnac stores: 136 rue de Rennes, 6th; 1–7 Forum des Halles, rue Pierre Lescot, 1st; 74 avenue des Champs-Elysées, 8th; www.fnacspectacles.com

Huge book and music chain (also DVDs) through which tickets can be reserved. Bookings can also be made online at www.fnac.fr.

Kiosque

15 place de la Madeleine, 8th; no tel; Tue–Fri 12.30–8pm, Sat from 12.30pm for matinees, from 2pm for evening performances, Sun 12.30–4pm; metro: Madeleine; map p.151 E2

Half-price tickets on the day.

Virgin Megastore

52 avenue des Champs-Elysées, 8th; tel: 01 49 53 50 00, 01 44 68 44 08; Mon–Sat 10am–midnight, Sun noon–midnight; metro: Franklin D. Roosevelt; map p.151 C2–3

Tickets via this vast store that sells music and DVDs.

Below: a band in action at Le Divan du Monde in Pigalle.

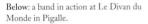

Nightlife

There's no shortage of after-dark revelry, and even early-morning revelry, in Paris, if you know where to look. In general, exclusive places are clustered around the Champs-Elysées, while cooler venues tend to come and go in the Bastille and Oberkampf areas. The Marais is the focal point of the Parisian gay scene *(see 'Gay and Lesbian', p.66)*. For information on what's on, keep your ears to the ground and look out for flyers and free listings booklets in bars. This chapter covers cabarets, DJ bars, bars/clubs and larger nightclubs. For jazz venues, consult 'Music' *(see p.106)*.

Cabarets

Lavish floor shows, geared mainly towards coach-loads of tourists and businessmen, hark back to the 'naughty' image of Paris of yesteryear. Prices are high (around €100 for a show, dinner and champagne package). The most established places are:

Crazy Horse Saloon
12 avenue George V, 8th; tel: 01 47 23 32 32; www.crazyhorse.fr; Tue–Sat; entrance charge; metro: George V; map p.150 C2
The Horse puts on two slickly choreographed shows a night from Tuesday to Friday, and three on Saturday. It pretends to promote 'the art of nudity'. It's probably the most erotic of the carabet shows, although still comparatively tasteful.

Le Lido
116 bis avenue des Champs-Elysées, 8th; tel: 01 40 76 56 10; www.lido.fr; nightly; entrance charge; metro: Franklin D. Roosevelt, George V; map p.150 C3
The 'Bluebell Girls' high-kick and jiggle their way through two shows a night, with countless costume changes and special effects.

Moulin Rouge
82 boulevard de Clichy, 18th; tel: 01 53 09 82 82; www.moulin rouge.fr; daily, dinner 7pm; entrance charge; metro: Blanche; map p.152 A4
There are two shows a night (and some matinees) at this legendary venue. Sixty 'Doris Girls' parade in 1,000 spectacular costumes, all feathers, sequins and rhinestones, with their show entitled *Féerie* ('enchantment'). Also featuring a giant aquarium.

DJ Bars and Bar/Clubs

L' Alcazar (Mezzanine)
62 rue Mazarine, 6th; tel: 01 53 10 19 99; www.alcazar.fr; daily 7pm–2am; free; metro: Odéon; map p.154 B3
A cool bar and even hipper DJs pull in a mixed crowd of Parisians and tourists at this Terence Conran-owned venue. Big-name French DJs and live acts Wednesday to Saturday.

Andy Whaloo
69 rue des Gravilliers, 3rd; tel: 01 42 71 20 38; Tue–Sun 5pm–2am; entrance charge; metro: Arts et Métiers; map p.155 C4

Left: Paris is known for its cabaret.

Left: a night out in the Marais.

bar in the basement, which is sometimes used for open-mic sessions. Upstairs is just for drinking – ideal for sampling the excellent cocktails. Popular with tourists and young professionals.

Wax
15 rue Daval, 11th; tel: 01 40 21 16 16; Tue–Thur until 2am, Fri–Sat until 5am; free; metro: Bastille; map p.155 E3
Close to place de la Bastille, Wax attracts a good-looking but unpretentious crowd, who delight in its bright 1960s-style decor (very Austin Powers). There are boothes, a bar and central dance floor.

Le World Place
32–4 rue Marbeuf, 8th; tel: 01 56 88 36 36; www.worldplace.fr; Mon–Thur, Sun 7pm–2am, Fri–Sat 7pm–5am; metro: Franklin D Roosevelt; map p.151 C2
This super-chic bar-cum-restaurant, founded by Johnny Depp, Sean Penn, John Malkovich and Mick Hucknall, does music nights and some record launches. Fashion code to match.

Created by the same team as London's Sketch and Momo, this is a laid-back place, with a Moroccan feel. Decor is cool: paint cans are used as stools, with lots of comfy cushions; hookahs complete the picture. DJs play a range of music from hip-hop to techno.

La Fabrique
53 rue du Faubourg St-Antoine, 11th; tel: 01 43 07 67 07; daily 11am–5am; entrance charge Fri–Sat only; metro: Bastille; map p.155 E2
A microbrewery, brasserie and DJ bar (some star names) attracting a fashionable crowd. Music is mostly cool electro, with laid-back jazz on Sunday afternoon.

Favela Chic
18 rue du Faubourg du Temple, 11th; tel: 01 40 03 02 66; www.favelachic.com; Tue–Thur 7.30pm–2am, Fri, Sat 7.30pm–4am; entrance charge Sat; metro: République; map p.153 D1
Favela aims to create the eponymous shabby look, albeit with a glamorous veneer. A fashionable crowd come for Brazilian food, after which the refectory tables are pushed out of the way, and

dancing to hot Latin tunes begins. Excellent *caipirinhas*.

La Fourmi
74 rue des Martyrs, 18th; tel: 01 42 64 70 35; Mon–Thur, Sun 8.30am–2am, Fri, Sat 8am–4am; free; metro: Pigalle; map p.152 B4
A laid-back DJ bar in Montmartre that attracts a trendy arts and media crowd. Nice to hang out in by day, and with a smooth crossover into an evening venue. Good place to pick up club flyers.

L'Ile Enchântée
65 boulevard de la Villette, 10th; tel: 01 42 01 67 99; http://lileenchantee.free.fr; Mon–Fri 8am–2am, Sat–Sun 5pm–2am; free; metro: Colonel Fabien; map p.153 E3
Fashionable venue that combines a bar, restaurant and club. The restaurant has the feel of a gastropub. Intimate area for dancing.

Lizard Lounge
18 rue Bourg Tibourg, 4th; tel: 01 42 72 81 34; www.cheapblonde.com/lizard; daily until 2am; free; metro: St-Paul; map p.155 C3–D3
This urban/industrial-style place in the Marais has a DJ

Regular buses in Paris run Mon–Sat 6.30am–8.30pm, with some continuing until 12.30am. The metro runs daily 5.40am–12.40am. After this, there is a limited night-bus service, the Noctambus, between place de Châtelet and various suburbs. These buses run Mon–Fri every hour from 1.30–5.35am and Sat–Sun every half hour 1–5.35am. Bus stops are marked by an owl sign. Routes A–H, P, T and V run in the Right Bank and the suburbs in the north, while I–M, R and S serve the Left Bank and south. Travel passes are valid on these buses; alternatively, buy a ticket on the bus.

Above: the stage at Le Bus Palladium.

Clubs

Les Bains Douches
7 rue du Bourg-l'Abbé, 3rd; tel: 01 48 87 01 80; www.lesbains douches.net; Wed–Sun 11pm–6am; entrance charge: metro: Etienne Marcel; map p.155 C4
These former Turkish baths are frequented by the smart set, some of whom are there more for rubbernecking than dancing. Also popular with a gay clientele.

Le Baron
6 avenue Marceau, 8th; tel: 01 47 20 04 01; www.clublebaron. com; daily 11.30pm–5am; free; metro: Alma-Marceau; map p.150 C2
Graffiti artist Monsieur André and partner tranformed this place from seedy hostess bar to VIP nightclub – hence the boudoir-style decor. Popular with a jet-set, designer-clad crowd and famously hard to get into. Live bands, and DJs and, surprisingly, there is karaoke on Sunday.

Batofar
11 quai François-Mauriac, 13th; tel: 01 53 14 76 59; www.bato far.org; daily 8.30pm–dawn; entrance charge; metro: Bibliothèque François Mitterrand
Live music and clubbing events on a renovated, bright-red lighthouse ship on the Seine. Restarant and bar on deck, club and chill-out spaces below. A plus in summer is the laid-back terrace.

Le Bus Palladium
6 rue Pierre Fontaine, 9th; tel: 01 45 26 80 35; www.lebuspalla dium.com; times vary; entrance charge; metro: Blanche, St Georges; map p.152 A3
An iconic disco in the 1960s, this place is cool all over again. See the website for the varied programme and for times. Free drinks for women on Tuesday.

Le Cab
2 place du Palais-Royal, 1st; tel: 01 58 62 56 25; www.cabaret.fr; Tue–Sat 11.30pm–5am; metro: Palais, Royal Musée du Louvre; map p.154 B4
Heavily designed basement club and lounge attracting showbiz people, models and associated crowd for cocktails and club music. Strict door policy; dress to impress.

Les Etoiles
61 rue du Château-d'Eau, 10th tel: 01 42 47 16 49; Thur–Sat 9pm–3am; free; metro: Château d'Eau; map p.153 C2–D2
A stylish Latino club in an old cinema. Attracts excellent musicians and a hip crowd, and is fun for beginners, who can partake in salsa classes.

La Flèche d'Or
102 bis rue de Bagnolet, 20th; tel: 01 44 64 01 02; www. flechedor.fr; Mon, Sun 8pm–2am, Wed–Sat 8pm–5am; free; metro: Alexander Dumas
This place is an enjoyable anarchic music and clubbing venue set in an old train sta-

tion. New management has transformed the place with a varied music programme. Popular with creatives types.

Folies Pigalle
11 place Pigalle, 9th; tel: 01 48 78 25 26; www.folies-pigalle. com; Tue–Sat midnight– dawn, Sun 6pm–midnight; entrance charge Fri–Sun only; metro: Pigalle; map p.152 B3
Resident DJs serve up house to a crowd of mixed ages and sexual proclivities. After-parties particularly popular.

La Java
105 rue du Faubourg-du-Temple, 10th; tel: 01 42 02 20 52; www. la-java.fr; Wed, Thur 9pm–3am, Fri–Sat 11pm–6am, Sun 2pm– 2am; entrance charge; metro: Belleville, Goncourt; map p.153 E2
Mainly Latin American music in an historic Belleville dancehall, once the pride of Paris – Edith Piaf and Maurice Chevalier made their names here.

Limelight
162 avenue de France, 13th; tel: 01 56 61 44 04; Wed–Sun until 2am; entrance charge; metro: Bibliothèque François Mitterrand
Within the futuristic mk2 Bibliothèque cinema complex on the so-called 'New Left Bank'. It is exclusive, vast, minimalist – and many, very cool.
SEE ALSO CINEMA, P.51

La Loco
90 boulevard de Clichy, 18th; tel: 01 53 41 88 88; www.laloco. com; daily 11pm–6am; entrance charge; metro: Blanche; map p.152 A4
Right next door to the Moulin

> Looking good is important in fashionable Parisian clubs. Dress up if you want to make your way past notoriously pernickety bouncers.

Rouge, this vast mainstream club has three dance floors, each playing a different kind of music. Popular with an international crowd. Informal dress code.

Le Milliardaire
68 rue Pierre-Charron, 8th; tel: 01 42 89 44 14; Thur–Sat 11.30pm–5am; free; metro: Franklin D. Roosevelt; map p.150 C2
Like name, like nature: 'Billionaire' is popular with a jet-set crowd. DJs and live acts provide the varied music, but it's mainly a backdrop to designer posing. Ladies night (free bar for girls) on Thursday.

Nouveau Casino
109 rue Oberkampf, 11th; tel: 01 43 57 57 40; www.nouveau casino.net; entrance charge; times vary; metro: Parmentier; map p.155 E4
This club in the heart of hip Oberkampf hosts good live music and club nights in a range of styles including house, techno, soul, jazz and electronic. For times and the programme, see the website.

Le Paris, Paris
5 avenue de l'Opera, 8th; tel: 01 42 60 64 45; www.leparisparis. com; entrance charge; metro: Opéra, Concorde; map p.152 A1
A very hip subterranean club attracting what the French dub a 'plugged-in jet-set crowd'. Dress in your finest if you want to get past the tough doormen.

Point Ephémère
200 quai de Valmy, 10th; tel: 01 40 34 02 48; www.point ephemere.org; daily 10am–2am; free; metro: Jaurès; map p.153 E3
By the Canal St-Martin, the Point Ephémère is an early-to-late feast of art, food (in its café-restaurant), experimental music and club nights. Popular with local *bobos*.

Le Rex Club
5 boulevard Poissonnière, 2nd; tel: 01 42 36 10 96; www.rexclub. com; entrance charge; metro: Bonne Nouvelle; map p.152 B2
A techno, house and drum 'n' bass stalwart with megastar djs, aimed at hard-core clubbers. The relaxed door policy is refreshing: you are unlikely to get turned away just because your face doesn't fit.

Le Showcase
Pont Alexandre III, Port des Champs-Élysées, 8th; tel: 01 45 61 25 43; www.showcase.fr; Fri, Sat, Sun; metro: Invalides, Champs-Elysées Clemenceau; map p.151 D1
In 2007, former hangars underneath the Pont Alexandre III were opened as this huge, seriously glam riverside club, courtesy of film producer Albert Cohen. Concerts are also staged here. Hip-hop, live pop/rock and electronic sounds attract a beautiful crowd. If a late night does not appeal, try 'Brunch Musical', every Sunday, from 11.30am.

WAGG
62 rue Mazarine, 6th; tel: 01 55 42 22 00; www.wagg.fr; Fri, Sat 11.30pm–6am, Sun 5pm–midnight; entrance charge; metro: Odéon; map p.154 B3
Supposedly Jim Morrison's last haunt, this club now plays house and disco music to an enthusiastic crowd. 1970s Carwash is popular on Friday nights, as is salsa on Sunday afternoon.

Below: posing and rubber-necking at Les Bains Douches.

Palaces

Most of the châteaux covered here are set outside the Péripherique ring road, but all are accessible by public transport as well as by car. Imperial Malmaison, favourite home of Joséphine Bonaparte, can be visited in half a day. Day trips include the moated French Renaissance palace at Chantilly; Fontainebleau, seat of sovereigns from Louis IX to Napoleon III and a glittering example of French Mannerism; Vaux-le-Vicomte, notable for its fabulous Classical French garden and its intriguing history; and, last but not least, Versailles, premier former royal residence and France's third most-visited site.

Château de Chantilly

Chantilly; tel: 03 44 27 31 80; www.chateaudechantilly.com; Nov–Mar: Wed–Mon 10.30am–5pm, Apr–early Nov: Wed–Mon 10am–6pm, park open later; entrance charge; train: Paris Gare du Nord–Chantilly Gouvieux, then 20 mins walk

The Château de Chantilly was built between the 16th and 19th centuries for a succession of French dynasties. In 1875–85 new buildings were erected to house the art collections of Henri d'Orléans, Duke of Aumale and his son Louis-Philippe.

The latter donated Chantilly to the Institut de France in 1886, stipulating that the original hang of the artworks be maintained; the paintings, classed as the Musée Condé, are thus arranged according to dimension, regardless of school or period, and the effect is neat and eccentric. Included are masterpieces by Poussin, Watteau, Nattier, Delacroix, Corot, Raphael, Van Dyck and Ingres.

The park includes a formal French garden by André Le Nôtre, a rambling English gar-

Above: one of the opulent bedrooms of the Château de Chantilly.

den and an Anglo-Chinese garden set around a *hameau* ('hamlet'), which served as a model for the one at Versailles. The **Hameau** is around 20 mins on foot from the main château and can be reached by motorised boat, which costs extra but enables you to tour the château's moat and Grand Canal.

Chantilly is world-renowned for its racecourse, and horse-lovers (and youngsters) should enjoy the nearby Musée Vivant du Cheval (Equestrian Museum). SEE ALSO MUSEUMS AND GALLERIES, P.104–5

Château de Fontainebleau

Place Général-de-Gaulle; Fontainebleau; tel: 01 60 71 50 70; www.musee-chateau-fontainebleau.fr; Apr–Sept: Wed–Mon 9.30am–6pm, Oct–Mar 9.30am–5pm; gardens open daily May–Sept: 9am–7pm, Mar, Apr, Oct: 9am–6pm; Nov–Feb 9am–5pm; entrance charge; train: Gare de Lyon–Fontainebleau-Avon

Although a castle stood on the site of the present *château* at Fontainebleau as early as the 12th century, it was not until the reign of François I (1494–1547) that

Joséphine Bonaparte, first wife of Napoleon I.

The estate passed through various hands until 1799, when it caught the eye of Joséphine; she reputedly borrowed money for the down-payment from the previous owner's steward – a sum that Napoleon repaid on his return from conquering Egypt. She engaged the services of architects Percier and Fontaine to renovate the existing building in her favoured neoclassical style: simple, geometric forms and minimal decoration.

While Malmaison was initially used by the consular couple purely as a country retreat, by 1800 Napoleon was spending an increasing amount of time here, even holding official meetings on the estate. In 1809, since Joséphine could not give her husband his much-needed heir (despite having two children by her first marriage to Viscount Alexandre de Beauharnais), Napoleon nullified the marriage. He gave his former wife the Malmaison estate and it was here that she spent most of her time until her death in 1814.

Below: a portrait of Napoleon at Chantilly.

the estate evolved. Keen to make the most of the forest in the area for hunting, François transformed the existing buildings into a grand Mannerist palace. Henri IV (1553–1610) added the wing housing the Deer Gallery, Diana Gallery, the Dauphin's entrance and the buildings around the kitchen courtyard.

Renovation and additions continued under monarchs from Louis XIV (1638–1715) to Louis XVI (1754–93), but with the latter came the Revolution and a bleak period for the palace; it was stripped of its contents and left to ruin.

Napoleon then rescued it. In 1803 he founded a military school here and in 1804 he began full refurbishment, mostly in the then-fashionable Empire style. Napoleon also converted the Small Apartments for his personal use. In 1814, however, he signed his first act of abdication.

After the Restoration, Louis Philippe (1773–1850) refurbished much of the interior, Napoléon III (1808–73) carried on Louis Philippe's work, and Empress Eugénie (1826–1920)

Malmaison's gardens are landscaped in the rustic style typical of English country gardens. Look out for the huge cedar tree on your right as you stand with your back to the house; it was planted in 1800 to celebrate Napoleon's victory at Marengo.

had new salons installed and opened a Chinese Museum in the Great Pavilion.

In the 20th century, the palace was used for different purposes: from 1945–65 it was the headquarters of the military branch of Nato.

Château de Malmaison

Avenue du Château de Malmaison, Rueil-Malmaison; tel: 01 41 29 05 55; www.chateau-malmaison.fr; summer: Wed–Mon 10am–12.30pm, 1.30–5.45pm, winter: till 5.15pm; entrance charge, combined with Bois-Préau; RER A to La Défense, then bus 258, or RER to Rueil plus a 20-min walk
In the quiet suburb of Rueil-Malmaison, 15km (9 miles) southwest of central Paris, is Malmaison, former home of

Château de Vaux-le-Vicomte

Maincy; tel: 01 64 14 41 90; www.vaux-le-vicomte.com; end Mar–mid-Nov: daily 10am–6pm, mid-Nov–end Mar: by prior arrangement only; entrance charge; train: Paris Gare de Lyon–Melun, then taxi 7km (4 miles)

This *château*, 60km (37 miles) from Paris, was built for Louis XIV's Superintendent of Finances, Nicolas Fouquet, by architect Louis Le Vau, painter Charles Lebrun and garden designer André Le Nôtre. On 17 August 1661, he hosted a house-warming party, with Louis XIV as guest of honour. Fouquet, however, had not reckoned on kingly jealousy, nor the double-dealing (if you believe the Vaux spin) of Colbert, another of Louis's ministers and Fouquet's rival. In September 1661, the master of Vaux was thrown into jail on charges of embezzling state funds; he died in prison 19 years later.

Meanwhile, Louis XIV engaged the services of Fouquet's design trio to transform the hunting lodge at Versailles into a palace fit for a king. Vaux was stripped of its furnishings and returned to Fouquet's wife only in 1673. In 1705 it passed into the hands of the Maréchal de Villars, and in 1764 was sold to the Duc de Choiseul-Praslin, Louis XV's Naval Minister. In 1875, the *château* was bought by the French industrialist Alfred Sommier, who restored it. It opened to the public in 1968.

Surrounded by an artificial moat, the building is a fine example of the harmonious traditional French style, lavishly decorated with gilding and elaborate wainscoting. Its crowning glory, however, is its **garden**, the first to be laid out in what is known as the French style, with geometric lines, intricate parterres, optical illusions and clever water management. If you don't have the energy to hike around the gardens, you could hire a golf buggy, which can even be driven through the 1,000-m long **Grand Canal**. Novelty boats can also be hired.

Château de Versailles

Versailles; tel: 01 30 83 76 20; www.chateauversailles.fr; palace: Apr–Oct: Tue–Sun 9am–6.30pm, Nov–Mar: Tue–Sun 9am–5.30pm, Petit Trianon and Hameau, Grand Trianon: Apr–Oct: daily noon–6.30pm, Nov– Mar: daily noon–5.30pm, most parts of *château* last admission 30 mins before closing, Gardens: Apr–Oct: daily 7am–sunset, Nov–Mar:

8am–sunset, Grandes Eaux Musicales shows: Apr–Sept Sat–Sun; entrance charge except gardens in winter; RER Versailles-Rive Gauche

THE PALACE

The main part of the palace includes the lavish State Apartments of the king and queen, notably the King's State Bedroom, in which the monarch's every move was scrutinised by his courtiers. Also here is the vast **Salle des Glaces** (Hall of Mirrors), the ultimate glass corridor, where the Treaty of Versailles was signed. The best time to visit the gallery is the afternoon, when the sun streams in.

Other highlights include, in the Hercules Room, the ceiling painting *The Apotheosis of Hercules* (1733–6), by François Lemoyne, and, in the Battle Gallery, a copy of the imposing *Crowning of the Empress Joséphine at Notre-Dame* (1804) by Jacques-Louis David.

For a supplement – beware, there are charges for most 'extras' at Versailles – access is granted to Louis XIV's private bedroom and the apartments of the *dauphin*

Below: the immense formal gardens at the Château de Versailles.

and *dauphine*. There are also tours of the private apartments of Louis XV, Louis XVI and the Opéra; the Opéra and Royal Chapel; the apartments of Madame de Pompadour and Madame du Barry; and Marie-Antoinette's suite.

THE TRIANONS AND HAMEAU

The two other main buildings on the estate are the **Grand and Petit Trianon**, both located to the northwest of the main house. If you don't fancy the 30-minute walk, take the mini train that runs regularly from the *château*, along the Grand Canal and across to the Trianons and back. Bicycles and horse-drawn carriages may also be hired. Marie-Antoinette's **Hameau** (classed, along with the Petit Trianon, as 'Marie-Antoinette's Estate'), a cluster of thatched cottages, is a 10-minute walk to the northeast.

THE GARDENS AND PARK

These are the work of André Le Nôtre, who grappled with hillocks and marshland to create the ultimate French outdoor playground for Louis XIV. A main feature is the

Left: the suite of Marie-Antoinette, Versailles.

Grand Canal, an artificial stretch of water that covers 45 hectares (111 acres) and can be explored by boat. Around the canal is a network of pathways, fountain basins, hidden groves studded with statues, and sculpted bushes.

Château de Vincennes

Avenue de Paris, Vincennes; tel: 01 43 28 15 48; http://en. chateau-vincennes.fr; daily, May– Aug: 10am–6pm, Sept– Apr: daily 10am–5pm; entrance charge; metro: Château de Vincennes

In 1370 Charles V completed this medieval *château*, which, over the centuries, has had many uses: from a palace to a prison, a porcelain factory and, under Napoleon I, an arsenal. Henry V died here in 1422. Napoleon III started a restoration programme but the *château* was heavily damaged in World War II. The restoration is now complete, and there is a museum in the 14th-century keep.

SEE ALSO PARKS AND GARDENS, P.120

Palais-Royal

Place du Palais-Royal, 1st; gardens open daily 7.30am– 8.30pm; free; metro: Palais Royal Musée du Louvre; map p.154 B4

Cardinal Richelieu, appointed prime minister in 1624, commissioned Jacques Lemercier to build a mansion near the Louvre. A few years later, after the adjacent city wall had been pulled down, the cardinal had the building converted into a large residence (1634–9), known as the Palais Cardinal. On his death in 1642, Richelieu left the palace to the crown, and it became the childhood home of Louis XIV, and renamed the Palais-Royal.

Artist Jean Cocteau lived for years in an apartment in the Galerie Montpensier. The novelist Colette died in the Galerie Beaujolais in 1954.

At the beginning of the 18th century the dukes of Orléans took up residence. The palace was turned into a den of debauchery through infamous 'libertine dinners' held by Philippe d'Orléans. Gambling and prostitution were rife, as the police were banned from entering.

In 1780, to compensate for his family's free spending, Louis-Philippe built shops in the galleries around the palace and let them at exorbitant prices. After the Revolution, the complex became the focal point of Parisian life, until the Palais fell to the Orléans once again after the demise of Napoleon.

The Palais-Royal was damaged in the Paris Commune (1871), but then faithfully rebuilt. The galleries now house bookshops, art shops and a number of fashionable boutiques. In the main courtyard are artist Daniel Buren's striking black-and-white columns, unveiled in 1986.

SEE ALSO PARKS AND GARDENS, P.122

Below: the courtyard of the Palais-Royal.

Pampering

Stereotypically style- and image-conscious, the Parisians take servicing the body beautiful and the business of ageing very seriously. The city thus has a growing number of spas, all purporting to provide an antidote to hectic urban life, and the ones listed below are just the tip of the iceberg. If you are looking to be pampered, there are venues where you can be suitably scrubbed and pummelled, boutiques where you can be beautified and delicately scented, and, failing all else, a host of shops where you can purchase any number of products promising to mask bits that might politely be described as less than perfect.

Cosmetics and Skincare

Galerie Noémie
92 avenue des Champs-Elysées, 8th; tel: 01 44 76 06 26; Mon–Thur 11am–7pm, Fri–Sat 11am–9pm; www.galerie noemie.com; metro: George V; map p.150 C3
Cute make-up, quirkily packaged in palettes, gives away the fact that owner Noémie is also a painter.

Séphora
70 avenue des Champs-Elysées, 8th; tel: 01 53 93 22 50; www.sephora.fr; Sun–Thur 10am–midnight, Fri–Sat 10am–1am; metro: Franklin D. Roosevelt; map p.151 C2
The flagship store of the popular French beauty-products chain, which stocks everything from its excellently priced own-brand cosmetics to designer perfume.

Perfume

Détaille 1905
10 rue St-Lazare, 9th: tel: 01 48 78 68 50; www.detaille.com; Tue–Sat 11am–2pm, 3–7pm; metro: St Lazare; map p.152 A2
Opened in 1905 by the war artist Edouard Détaille, this lovely old shop offers just six

Above: posh perfume.

fragrances: three for women; three for men.

Diptyque
34 boulevard St-Germain, 5th; tel: 01 43 26 77 44; www.diptyueparis.com; Mon–Sat 10am–7pm; metro: Maubert Mutualité; map p.155 C2
Although Diptyque's scented candles and eau de toilettes are available abroad, there is nothing like a visit to the founders' glorious boutique. Close your eyes as you inhale a field of jasmine, mimosa, honeysuckle, broom or freshly mown hay.

Editions de Parfums Frédéric Malle
37 rue de Grenelle, 7th; tel: 01 42 22 76 40; www.editionsde parfums.com; metro: Sèvres Babylone; map p.157 E3
The grandson of Parfums Christian Dior's founder, Frédéric Malle gave seven of the world's leading 'noses' carte blanche to create a fragrance under their own names. Sniff the results in his elegant boutique.

Guerlain
68 avenue des Champs-Elysées, 8th; tel: 01 45 62 52 57; www.guerlain.com; Mon–Sat 10.30am–8pm, Sun: 3–7pm; metro: Franklin D. Roosevelt; map p.151 C2
This store harks back to the glory of yesteryear, with its spectacular, romantic Belle-Epoque interior. The classic perfumes are also gorgeous.

Maître Parfumeur et Gantier
84 bis rue de Grenelle, 7th; tel: 01 45 44 61 57; www.maitre-parfumeur-et-gantier.com; Mon–Sat 10am–7pm; metro: Rue du Bac, Sèvres Babylone; map p.157 E3
In the 18th century there were 250 parfumeurs et gantiers in Paris, the salons where ladies went to have their gloves perfumed, buy powder for their

Left: Sephora, Champs-Elysées.

This 1920s Paris mosque includes a tiled *hammam* where you can be scrubbed, steamed and massaged, all at great prices. Swimwear must be worn. Towels and gowns may be hired. The complex has a Moorish tearoom, for mint tea and sticky pastries to undo all the good work.

SEE ALSO CHURCHES, MOSQUES AND SYNAGOGUES, P.48

Hammam Medina Center
43–5 rue Petit, 19th; tel: 01 42 02 31 05; www.hammam-medina. com; women: Mon–Fri 11am–10pm, Sun 9am–7pm, mixed: Sat 10am–9pm; metro: Ourcq
A lovely spot for steaming, scrubbing and massage, in a spa designed as a *hammam*. Nice pool.

Spa Nuxe 32 Montorgueil
32 rue Montorgueil, 1st, tel: 01 55 80 71 40; www.nuxe.com; Mon, Tue, Fri, Sat 9am–7.30pm, Wed, Thur 9am–9pm; metro: Éti-enne Marcel; map p.154 C4
A fabulously renovated 17th-century wine storehouse. A calm-inducing stream runs through the whole place. Treatments include pedi-cures, manicures, over 10 types of massage (also avail-able for two), aromatic baths, wraps, exfoliation and facials. Men can be buffed here too.

hair and scent for their body. Today, perfumer Jean Laporte keeps the spirit of the tradi-tion alive. Alongside nostalgic scents such as *Eau de Camellia*, there is Laporte's celery-based *Grain de Plaisir eau de toilette*: irresistible.

Parfumeries Fragonard
51 rue des Francs-Bourgeois, 4th; tel: 01 44 78 01 32; www.fragonard.com; Mon–Sat 10.30am–7.30pm, Sun noon–7pm; metro: St-Paul; map p.152 A2
Perfumes and scented soaps from one of the best known perfumers in France.
SEE ALSO MUSEUMS AND GALLERIES, P.104

Spas

Les Bains du Marais
31–3 rue des Blancs-Manteaux, 4th; tel: 01 44 61 02 02; www. lesbainsdumarais.com; Mon, Fri–Sat 10am–8pm, Tue–Thur, Sun 10am–11pm; metro: St-Paul; map p.155 C3–D3
A modern take on the tradi-tional *hammam*, complete with steam room, massage and facial treatments, and a restaurant/café. Booking essential.

L'Espace Payot
62 rue Pierre-Charon, 8th; tel: 01 45 61 42 08; www.espacepayot.com; Mon–Fri 7am–10pm, Sat 9am–7pm, Sun 10am–5pm; metro: George V; map p.150 C2
French skincare guru Dr Nadia Payot's institute is one of the biggest spas in the capital, with great facilities including a gym and pool.

Hammam de la Mosquée
1 place du Puits de l'Ermite, 5th; tel: 01 43 31 18 14; Mon, Wed–Thur, Sat 10am–9pm, Fri 2–9pm; men: Tue 2–9pm, Sun 10am–9pm; metro: Monge; map p.155 C1

Below: ready for a good scrub and soak.

Parks and Gardens

In 1759 the Enlightenment writer Voltaire declared 'We must cultivate our garden', but it was not until the 19th century that parks became a touchstone for the health of the capital. While the 1980s were the decade of monumental building, the 1990s and early 21st century have seen the city's gardens flourish. Derelict sites are being converted into parks with a fervour not seen since town planner Baron Haussmann's day, and Parisians are looking to green spaces as an escape from the stress of urban living.

Bois de Boulogne

16th; metro: Porte Dauphine, Les Sablons, Porte Maillot; map p.150 A3–4

Past the necklace of the Périphérique ring road to the west of Paris, the Bois de Boulogne is one of the reasons that the adjacent 16th *arrondissement* is preferred by the wealthy as a place to live. Embraced by an elbow of the Seine, this 860-hectare (2,125 acre) expanse of woods and gardens has been the Sunday-afternoon playground for generations of Parisian families.

Above: old masters enjoying the fresh air

In 1852, Napoléon III demolished the perimeter wall of the royal hunting ground, originally built by

A good place to start exploring the Bois de Boulogne is from the beautiful Art Nouveau metro stop at Porte Dauphine and the best way is by bicycle, which can be rented near the Pavillon Royal, off the Route de Suresnes. A network of cycle paths and nature trails intersect the woods, enabling easy access to the vast park and its scenic lakes and waterfall.

Henri II, and the park was remodelled on Hyde Park in London. It now offers gardens; wild woods; horse racing at two of France's most famous racecourses, Longchamps and Auteuil; a sports stadium; boating; and restaurants (including **Le Pré Catalan**). On the northern edge is the **Jardin d'Acclimatation**, an amusement park for children. Outdoor theatre is performed at the **Jardin Shakespeare** during the summer.

Be advised that walking around the park at night, when it becomes a popular spot for prostitutes, is not recommended.

SEE ALSO CHILDREN, P.41; RESTAURANTS, P.133; SPORT, P.145

Bois de Vincennes

12th; Château: tel: 01 43 28 15 48; www.monum.fr; daily, May–Aug 10am–6pm, Sept–Apr 10am–5pm; entrance charge; Parc Floral: tel: 01 43 28 41 59; daily 9.30am–dusk; entrance charge; metro: Château de Vincennes, Porte Dorée

On the southeast edge of Paris lies the Bois de Vincennes, the city's largest park, renowned for its *château*, racecourse and zoo. There is also a Buddhist tem-

Left: a restful afternoon in the park.

Kahn called the gardens 'the vegetal expression of my thoughts concerning a reconciled world', an idea complemented by 72,000 photographs of world landscapes taken between 1910 and 1931 and exhibited in perpetual rotation.

Jardin du Luxembourg

Place Auguste-Comte, place Edmond Rostand, rue de Vaugirard, 6th; tel: 01 42 34 23 89; www.senat.fr/visite; free; metro: Odéon, RER: Luxembourg; map p.154 B1

The quintessential Parisian park, the beautifully landscaped Jardin du Luxembourg is a haven of manicured greenery where young couples rendezvous under the plane trees by the romantic baroque *Fontaine de Médicis*, old men play *boules*, and children sail boats across the carp-filled lake in the middle. Statues of the queens of France gaze down from the terrace, while the thwack of tennis balls disturbs the reverie of sunbathers and smart nannies pushing babies in designer prams.

On Wednesdays and weekends, the *Guignol* pup-

Below: children sail boats in the Luxembourg gardens.

ple, baseball field and miniature farm within the park's boundaries.

Like the Bois de Boulogne, the Bois de Vincennes developed from what was originally a royal hunting ground, enclosed in the 12th century by Philippe-Auguste with a 12-km (7-mile) wall.

PARC FLORAL

Within the Bois de Vincennes, **Le Parc Floral de Paris** is a favourite with families who wander the **Vallée des Fleurs**, in bloom all year round, the pine wood and the water garden and take advantage of the adventure playground. On summer weekends it puts on an excellent season of jazz and classical concerts by the lake.

OTHER SIGHTS

A highlight of the park is the **Château de Vincennes**, completed by Charles V in 1370 and used variously as a palace, prison, factory, arsenal and museum. Another notable building is **La Cartoucherie**, once an arsenal,

Look out for the *boulodrome* in the Jardin du Luxembourg, where an increasingly aged group of enthusiasts play this most typically French of games.

now a complex of theatres where plays are staged by some of France's most *avant-garde* companies, including the **Théâtre du Soleil**. SEE ALSO PALACES, P.117

Jardin Albert Kahn

14 rue du Port, Boulogne; Tue–Sun 11am–6pm, summer: 11am–7pm; free; metro: Boulogne-Porte de St-Cloud

More traditional horticulture is found beyond the southeast tip of the Bois de Boulogne, where the legacy of financier Albert Kahn (1860–1940) takes the form of an extraordinary park, created between 1895 and 1910.

Japanese, English and French gardens lie alongside an Alpine forest and North American prairie. The grass is cut at different levels, from 'beatnik' style to 'sailorboy'.

121

There are 300 varieties of apple and pear trees in the Jardin du Luxembourg, and an apiary, which produces several hundred kilos of honey a year.

Above: pots, bins and trolleys in the Jardin des Plantes.

pet show is performed in the **Théâtre des Marionettes**. More serious entertainment is located at the corner with rue de Vaugirard, where people play chess under the fragrant orange trees. Other attractions within the park include the Musée du Luxembourg, showcase for changing art exhibitions, and the **Palais du Luxembourg**. This palace was built for Marie de Médici on the former site of a mansion belonging to Duke François of Luxembourg, following the murder of her husband, Henri IV. It is now the seat of the Sénat (the Upper House of Parliament) and open for guided visits only

The palace's Italianate style, modelled on the Pitti Palace in Florence, was intended to remind Marie of home. The widowed queen moved into the building in 1625, but was forced into exile by Richelieu before its completion, and died, lonely and embittered, in Cologne.

During the Revolution, the palace was used as a prison, and in World War II the Germans made it their headquarters. The adjacent Petit Luxembourg is the official home of the president of the Senate.

SEE ALSO CHILDREN, P.41; MUSEUMS AND GALLERIES, P.101; SPORT, P.144

Jardin du Palais-Royal

Rue du Valois, 1st; daily 7.30am–8.30pm; free; metro: Palais Royal Musée du Louvre; map p.154 B4
The garden adjacent to the Palais-Royal was once a

meeting point for agitators during the French Revolution: two days before the storming of the Bastille, the journalist Desmoulins issued his call to arms to the citizens here. Nowadays, it is something of an oasis in the middle of the big-city bustle.
SEE ALSO PALACES, P.117

Jardin des Plantes

36 rue Geoffroy-St-Hilaire, 2 rue Bouffon, place Vallubert, 57 rue Cuvier, 5th; tel: 01 40 79 56 01; www.mnhn.fr; main garden daily 7.30am–7.30pm; free; *ménagerie*, Apr–Sept: daily 9am–6pm; entrance charge; metro: Gare d'Austerlitz, Place Monge, Jussieu; map p.155 D1
This botanical garden was opened in 1640 as a medicinal herb farm for Louis XIII. The oldest tree in Paris is located here, a false acacia planted in 1635. The garden expanded during the 1700s, with the addition of a maze, amphitheatre and exhibition galleries. In 1889, the **Galerie**

One of the earliest hot-air balloon flights was launched from the Jardin des Tuileries in 1783.

de Zoologie was opened in the grounds, its object to display, conserve and study the millions of specimens brought back by globetrotting European naturalists and explorers.

Opened in 1794, the **Ménagerie** is a small zoo that is popular with children, with its panthers, monkeys, orang-utan, flamingoes, reptile house and farm.

Also within the park is the lavishly restored **Grande Galerie de l'Evolution**, part of the **Muséum National d'Histoire Naturelle**.
SEE ALSO CHILDREN, P.40–1; MUSEUMS AND GALLERIES, P.101

Jardin des Tuileries

Rue de Rivoli, 1st; daily 7.30am–7pm; free; metro: Tuileries, Concorde; map p.151 E1
Once a rubbish tip and a clay quarry for tiles (*tuiles*, hence the name), this garden, now one of the city centre's two main parks, was initially created, in 1564, for Catherine de Médici in front of her palace, to remind her of her native Tuscany.

In 1664, André Le Nôtre, redesigned the park with his predilection for straight lines and clipped trees, a grand addition to the royal axis on which it stands. At that time the axis included the Louvre and Arc de Triomphe; now the Grande Arche de La Défense continues the line. The park was then opened to the public and quickly became the first fashionable outdoor area in which to see and be seen, with the unexpected spin-offs of the first deckchairs and public toilets.

In the 1990s the Tuileries were renovated, restoring Le Nôtre's original design and incorporating a new sloping terrace and enclosed garden. New sculptures were added, while fragile old ones were moved to better-protected or alternative sites. Coysevox's winged horses are now in the Louvre, and several works by Aristide Maillol are now in the Jardins du Carrousel.

The eastern end of the garden is marked by the **Arc du Triomphe du Carrousel**, while at the western end are the twin museums of the **Galerie Nationale du Jeu de Paume** (Site Concorde) and the **Musée de l'Orangerie**. These buildings are all that remain of the Palais des Tuileries, burnt down during the Paris Commune of 1871. Also at the western end of the park, right by **place de la Concorde**, is a bookshop dedicated solely to volumes on gardening.

A focal point of the park is the hexagonal pool, a favourite spot of children with sailing boats, and of ducks with attitude. There are plenty of metal seats dotted around this area – and the park in general – for those wishing to sit for a while. It may seem slightly antisocial, but the Parisian

Above: catching a ride on the carousel.

custom is to claim two chairs: one to sit on, the second as a foot rest.

An amusing way of exploring the Tuileries is to hire a Segway, a kind of electric scooter. After some initial instruction, you are left to your own devices to explore the park. It may look more than slightly ridiculous, especially when Segway users are moving in a group, but it is a fun and speedy way to check out the park.

Note that the Passerelle de Solférino, a footbridge across the Seine, opened in 1999, links the gardens to the Left Bank and the Musée d'Orsay.

SEE ALSO MONUMENTS, P.85; MUSEUMS AND GALLERIES, P.102

Parc André-Citroën

Rue Balard, rue St-Charles, quai Citroën, 15th; Mon–Fri 8am–dusk, Sat–Sun 9am–dusk; free; metro: Balard, Javel
On the western side of the city, on the banks of the Seine, the once-derelict site of a former Citroën car factory has been turned into the Parc André-Citroën. Now a stunning modern park, where futuristic formal gardens mix

Below: reading by the Tuileries' lake, near place de la Concorde.

123

with spacious lawns and a wild garden; two huge glasshouses glisten next to the esplanade; and children leap in and out of the fountain's jets.

Beyond the glasshouses lie two gardens, one 'black' and one 'white'. On the northeastern side of the park a series of six more colourful gardens have been planted, each to a different colour scheme: gold, silver, red, orange, green and blue.

Below: a fine display in the Parc de Bercy.

Around 700 vines grow by the Parc Georges-Brassens, along rue des Morillons. They produce the annual Clos des Morillons wine, which is full bodied, with a fine bouquet.

Each garden is linked to a metal, a planet, a day of the week, and a sense: thus gold is linked to the sun, Sunday and the intangible sixth sense.

The tethered **Eutelsat balloon** climbs 135m (443ft) into the air at weekends to give visitors a panoramic aerial view over the capital.

Parc de Bercy

Rue de Bercy, 12th; summer: Mon–Fri 8am–9pm, Sat–Sun 9am–9pm, winter: Mon–Fri 8am–5.30pm, Sat–Sun 9am–5.30pm; free; metro: Bercy, Cour St-Emilion

A new park was created in the 1990s for this regenerated area of the city, now increasingly agreeable and fashionable. A highlight is the lake, filled with water from the Seine. Green areas within the park include an orchard, gardens representing the four seasons, the lovely rose and herb gardens, and a peaceful patch of lawn.

The park is also the attractive setting for the **Palais Omnisports de Paris-Bercy**, a vast stadium where a range of sporting events are staged. On its northern side, a cubist building (the former American Center) by American architect Frank Gehry, is the new headquarters of French cinema and home to the French national film archive, the **Cinémathèque Française**.

SEE ALSO CINEMA, P.51; SPORT, P.144

Parc des Buttes-Chaumont

Rue Botzaris, rue Manin, rue de Crimée, 19th; Oct–Apr: daily 7am–8.15pm, May, mid-Aug–Sept: daily 7am–9.15pm, Jun–mid-Aug: daily 7am–10.15pm; free; metro: Botzaris, Buttes-Chaumont

To the south of La Villette and on the city side of the Périphérique ring road, the Parc des Buttes-Chaumont was designed by Adolphe Alphand for town planner Baron Haussmann in the 1860s on the initially unpromising site of a rubbish dump, gypsum quarry and gibbet.

However, the uneven ground provided a perfect setting for a wooded, rocky terrain, and a lake has been created around an artificial 50-m 'mountain', capped by a Roman-style temple, with a waterfall and a cave containing artificial stalactites. Ice-skating, boating and donkey rides are also on offer, and the puppet show in the open-air theatre has been a popular attraction for over 140 years.

SEE ALSO CHILDREN, P.41

Parc Georges-Brassens

Rue des Morillons, 15th; Mon–Fri 8am–dusk, Sat–Sun 9am–dusk; free; metro: Porte de Vanves, Porte de Versailles

The far-flung southwest of Paris is the capital's most populated district and home to one of its newest parks, the Parc Georges-Brassens. Opened in 1982 on the site of an old abattoir, the park is now a child's playground paradise, with playhouses, rock

The views across Paris are magnificent from the top of the cascade of steps in the Parc des Buttes-Chaumont.

piles, rivers and mini lakes. The park includes a garden designed for the blind: close your eyes, follow the trickling of fountains and smell the fragrant foliage. Braille signs give relevant information on herbs and shrubs. At weekends, the old market halls host a giant antiquarian book market.

Parc Monceau

Boulevard de Courcelles, avenue Hoche, rue Monceau, 17th; Nov–Mar: daily 7am–8pm, Apr–Oct: daily 7am–10pm; free; metro: Monceau; map p.151 C4

As part of his extensive restructuring of Paris in the mid-19th century, town planner Baron Haussmann built city parks such as this one, where the 8th and the upmarket 17th *arrondissements* meet. The green space could be described as a 19th-century version of a theme park with an English-style garden and lake, a fake Egyptian pyramid, Venetian bridge, Greek colonnade, ancient tombs and various follies. Nowadays, it is particularly popular with the local yummy mummies and their offspring.

Two fine museums, the **Musée Nissim de Camondo** and the **Musée Cernuschi**, overlook the park, set in the grand private mansions that are typical of this area. The former has an impressive collection of 18th-century decorative arts, housed in a grand Belle-Époque mansion, while the latter exhibits Chinese art.
SEE ALSO MUSEUMS AND GALLERIES, P.104

A canal cuts through the Parc de la Villette, and a pleasant way to arrive or leave is by barge. Visit www.canauxrama.com or tel: 01 42 39 15 00 for details.

Above: sketching by the Géode in the Parc de la Villette.

Parc de la Villette

Avenue Corentin-Cariou, avenue Jean-Jaurès, 19th; tel: 01 40 03 75 75; www.villette.com; daily 10am–7pm; entrance charge; metro: Porte de la Villette, Porte de Pantin

In northeast Paris, nestling against the Périphérique, is Parc de la Villette. Built on the site of a huge abattoir, which was rendered obsolete by improved refrigeration techniques and poor design (the cows could not even get up the steps), are 55 hectares (136 acres) of futuristic gardens around a colossal science museum, the **Cité des Sciences**.

Other attractions in the park include **La Géode**, a giant silver ball housing a wraparound cinema; plus **L'Argonaute**, a retired naval submarine; and **Cinaxe** (entrance charge), a flight-simulator-cum-cinema (not for the queasy).

The former slaughterhouse now houses a cultural and conference centre in the immense 19th-century Grande Halle. Next door, the **Cité de la Musique**, one of Mitterrand's last projects, is an ultramodern complex designed by architect Christian de Portzamparc. It includes the **Musée de la Musique**, charting the development of classical, jazz and folk music and houses an impressive collection of over 4,500 musical instruments. Portzamparc also designed the music and dance conservatory nearby.
SEE ALSO MUSEUMS AND GALLERIES, P.94, 100; MUSIC, P.107

GARDEN HIGHLIGHTS

The Parc de la Villette's gardens are the largest to be built in Paris since Haussmann's time. Designed by Bernard Tschumi and opened in 1993, they comprise several thematic areas such as the **Jardin des Frayeurs Enfantines** ('Garden of Childhood Fears'), with a huge dragon slide, and the **Jardin des Vents** ('Garden of Winds'), home to multi-coloured bamboo plants. Abstraction continues in the form of Tschumi's Folies: red, angular tree houses minus the trees, each with a specific function: play area, workshop, daycare centre or café.

125

Restaurants

There are bistros, brasseries, glamorous starred restaurants where waiting staff outnumber the diners, Breton crêperies, Moroccan couscouseries, railway-station buffets and workers' canteens. Wherever you dine, however, you'll find the same respect for food, preferably eaten in the company of friends, and usually accompanied by a glass of red wine. With France's legendary dedication to the gastronomic arts still going strong, good food can be found at all prices, in all kinds of establishments, and in all parts of the city, so there's plenty of opportunity in Paris to sample life as a true *bon vivant*.

The Islands

Brasserie de l'Ile St Louis
55 quai de Bourbon, 4th; tel: 01 43 54 02 59; €€; Mon–Tue, Fri–Sun noon–1am, Thur 6pm–1am, closed Aug; metro: Pont Marie; map p.155 C2
Lively brasserie with a beautiful terrace overlooking Notre-Dame. A good place to watch the sun set over the Seine.

L'Escale
1 rue des Deux-Ponts, 4th; tel: 01 43 54 94 23; €€; Mon–Sat nonstop; metro: Pont-Marie; map p.155 C2–D2
This old-fashioned, pleasantly bustling brasserie-cum-wine bar serves good, heartening dishes such as leek quiches, *chou farci* (stuffed cabbage) and *clafoutis* (fruit-and-batter pudding). The wines are well sourced and affordable, and

Approximate prices for an average three-course dinner per person, including half a bottle of house wine, service and tax:
€   under €25
€€   €25–40
€€€   €40–60
€€€€   over €60

Above: salmon and caviar at Le Meurice.

the chips are far better than the average brasserie frites.

Le Flore en l'Ile
42 quai d'Orléans, 4th; tel: 01 43 29 88 27; www.lefloreenlile.com €/€€; daily nonstop; metro: Pont-Marie; map p.155 C2
The views from this café of the river and Notre-Dame are the main draw – that and, in summer, the ice cream it serves from nearby gélaterie Berthillon. They also do a range of brunch dishes based on eggs and seafood. The *gratin aux poires* (leek gratin) is excellent.

Taverne Henri IV
13 place du Pont-Neuf, 1st; tel: 01 43 54 27 90; €; Mon–Fri nonstop, Sat L; metro: Pont Neuf; map p.B3
This diminutive spot on the Ile de la Cité is a good bet for some straightforward French cuisine and wines. Try the excellent eggs baked with blue cheese and ham, washed down with a glass of white Beaujolais. Prices are reasonable, especially given the location.

Louvre, Tuileries and Concorde

Costes
Hôtel Costes, 239 rue St-Honoré, 1st; tel: 01 42 44 50 25; €€€€; daily 7am–1am; métro: Concorde or Tuileries; map p.151 E2
This restaurant in the chic Hôtel Costes is one of the most popular upmarket venues in Paris. Beautiful courtyard and a baroque interior with crystal chandeliers. Eclectic menu. Reserve.
SEE ALSO HOTELS, P.71

Le Fumoir
6 rue de l'Amiral-de-Coligny, 1st; tel: 01 42 92 00 24; www.lefumoir.com; €€; daily 11am–2am, closed two weeks in Aug; metro: Louvre-Rivoli;

Left: L'Atelier de Joël
Robuchon, in the 7th.

Yannick Alléno. Some of the
finest cooking in Paris.

Opéra and
Grands Boulevards

**Alain Ducasse au
Plaza Athénée**
25 avenue Montaigne, 8th;
tel: 01 53 67 65 00; www.alain-
ducasse.com; €€€€; Mon–Fri
7.45–10pm, Thur–Fri 12.45–
2.15pm; closed last 2 weeks in
Dec and mid-July to mid-Aug;
metro: Alma-Marceau; map
p.151 C2
Cooking elevated to an art
form from globetrotting chef
Alain Ducasse, France's first
recipient of six Michelin stars
(three apiece for two restaurants), with the help of his
acolyte Christophe Moret.
According to Ducasse, his
meals are not about fancy
presentation but purity and
essence of flavour. Expect
truffles in abundance, but
also superb vegetables from
Provence, where he first
made his name. The listed
neo-rococo decor has been
rejuvenated with a shower of

Below: a palatial venue for
French haute cuisine.

Haute cuisine is a costly affair,
and not just for the customers.
Running a first-class restaurant
in France costs, on average,
about 60 euros per customer,
and even the best establishments have profit margins of
only between 2 and 5 per cent.
Little wonder, therefore, that so
many chefs look to endorse-
ments of everything from
saucepans to fish kettles to
supplement their income.

map p.154 B3
With an admirable location
facing the Louvre, spacious,
sophisticated Le Fumoir is
renowned for shaking some
of the best cocktails in town.
It serves light pan-European
dishes, such as monkfish
with peas and asparagus
and sea bass with ginger.
Le Grand Véfour
17 rue de Beaujolais, 1st;
tel: 01 42 96 56 27; www.grand-
vefour.com; €€€€; Mon–Thur
12.30–1.30pm, 8–9.30pm, Fri
12.30–2pm, closed Aug; metro:
Palais-Royal; map p.152 B1
Hiding under the arches of
the Palais-Royal is one of the
most beautiful restaurants in

Paris. Le Grand Véfour
opened its doors in 1784 and
has fed the likes of Emperor
Napoleon and writers
Alphonse Lamartine, Colette,
and Victor Hugo. Today it
serves haute cuisine under
the aegis of chef Guy Martin.
Kinugawa
9 rue du Mont-Thabor, 1st; tel: 01
42 60 65 07; €€€€; Mon–Sat
noon–2.30pm, 7–10pm; metro:
Tuileries; map p.151 E2
Paris has some seriously
good Japanese restaurants,
and this is one of the best
and longest established; it is
a firm favourite with film
stars, too. Each of the set
menus is a good introduction
to its prowess: faultless quality and presentation in dishes
like turbot sashimi and egg
custard studded with gingko
nuts and chunks of whitebait.
Le Meurice
Hôtel Meurice, 228 rue de Rivoli,
1st; tel: 01 44 58 10 10; www.
meuricehotel.com; €€€€;
Tue–Fri noon–2pm, 7.30–10pm,
Sat 7.30–10pm, closed Aug;
metro: Tuileries; map p.154 A4
The very best ingredients
cooked in a subtle and
understated way by chef

127

Above: Art Nouveau stained glass at romantic brasserie Gallopin.

ethereal glittery crystals. Reserve well ahead.

Angl'Opéra

39 avenue de l'Opéra, 2nd; tel: 01 42 61 56 90; www.anglopera. com; €€€; Mon–Fri noon– 2.30pm and 7.30– 11.30pm; metro: Opéra; map p.152 A1

Gilles Choukroun turns out daring but yummy creations in the contemporary styling of the restaurant of the Hôtel Edouard VII. Unusual combinations of ingredients. A good choice if you've overdosed on classic French fare.

SEE ALSO HOTELS, P.72

Aux Lyonnais

32 rue St-Marc, 2nd; tel: 01 42 96 65 04; www.auxlyonnais. com; €€€€; Tue–Fri noon– 2pm, 7.30–11pm, Sat 7.30– 11pm, closed Aug; metro: Grands Boulevards; map p.152 B2

Founded in 1892, this bistro still retains its original decor, but has been beautifully revamped under Alain Ducasse. The menu pays tribute to Lyonnaise specialities, with renditions of pike, perch and crayfish quenelles. Dombes frog's legs, charcuterie, excellent cuts of beef and regional wines. Reserve well ahead.

Chartier

7 rue du Faubourg Montmartre, 9th; tel: 01 47 70 86 29; €; daily noon–11.30pm; metro: Grands Boulevards; map p.152 B2

Chartier is the best-known low-price eaterie in town. The atmosphere is an experience in itself, with Belle-Epoque decor and snappy waiters, although there has been controversy recently about the replacement of the checked tableclothes with white paper ones. Expect shared tables and plenty of bonhomie. Arrive early if you want to stand a chance of getting a seat.

Les Coulisses

20 Galerie des Variétés, Passage des Panoramas, 2nd; tel: 01 44 82 09 52; €€; Mon–Fri noon– 2pm, 7–11pm, Sat 7–11pm; metro: Grands Boulevards; map p.152 B2

Appropriately named 'Backstage', this reliable bistro is a second home to Parisian actors from the nearby Théâtre de Variétés. It offers authentic French dishes such as terrine de foie gras and hearty beef bourguignon plus a range of excellent home-made pastries.

Drouant

16–18 place Gaillon, 2nd; tel: 01 42 65 15 16; www.drouant.com €€€–€€€€; daily noon–2pm, 6–11pm; metro: Opéra; map p.152 A1

This old stalwart has had a big makeover, and it's now one of the most talked-about places in town. Star Alsace chef Antoine Westermann has revived the humble *hors d'oeuvre* tradition here, so you can eat the food in more or less any order you feel like, and friendly sharing is encouraged. Dishes include Thai beef salad and a modish deconstructed version of eggs in mayonnaise.

SEE ALSO LITERATURE AND THEATRE, P.82

Gallopin

40 rue Notre-Dame-des-Victoires, 2nd; tel: 01 42 36 45 38; www.brasseriegallopin.com; €€/€€€; daily noon–midnight; metro: Bourse; map p.152 B2

This brasserie opposite the Stock Exchange opened in 1876 and is still decorated in elegant Belle-Epoque style. The chef prepares refined versions of traditional dishes, including pâté maison, steak tartare and flambéed crêpes. The fish is a star attraction, with specialities such as haddock poached in milk with spinach, and deliciously fresh seafood platters. Excellent food in a distinguished setting.

Le Grand Colbert

4 rue Vivienne, 2nd; tel: 01 42 86 87 88; www.legrandcolbert. fr; €€€; daily noon–1am; metro: Bourse; map p.152 B1

Approximate prices for an average three-course dinner per person, including half a bottle of house wine, service and tax:

€	under €25
€€	€25–40
€€€	€40–60
€€€€	over €60

Michelin stars are taken very seriously in France. At the time of printing, Paris had 10 restaurants with three stars (London, for example, had only one). Losing a star can mean a sharp decline in the number of customers as well as a dent in the chef's pride.

In 2003, just the fear of dropping a star after a less-than-perfect score from a critic led chef Bernard Loiseau to commit suicide.

This large, beautiful brasserie, which opened in 1830, offers the sort of traditional dishes that the French have always demanded from their brasseries. Choose from beef carpaccio, goat's cheese in pastry, *sole meunière*, Burgundian snails or frogs' legs in garlic, ripe cheeses, and creamy chocolate mousse and feathery light *îles flottantes* (soft meringues in custard).

Maxim's

3 rue Royale, 8th; tel: 01 42 65 27 94; www.maxims-de-paris. com; €€€; Tue–Fri 12.30–2pm, 7.30–10pm, Sat 7.30–10.30pm; metro: Madeleine; map p.151 E2

Despite all the hype and tradition, Maxim's is no longer a popular evening out, but the food is pleasantly free of fashionable fripperies, and the 1900 decoration remains a gem. Service belongs to another more courteous age. A restaurant in a delightful time warp.

Le Roi du Pot-au-Feu

34 rue Vignon, 9th; tel: 01 47 42 37 10; €€; Mon–Sat noon–2.30pm, 7–10.30pm, closed mid-July– mid-Aug; metro: Madeleine; map p.152 A2

This traditional bistro, with its red-and-white tablecloths, specialises, as you might guess from the name, in *pot-au-feu*. Once a rural stew eaten by peasant farm-

ers, the dish is now fashionable among Parisian gourmets. The best part is the bone marrow. Although *pot-au-feu* dominates the menu, pâté de campagne, tarte tatin and other such French classics are creditably executed.

Spoon

14 rue de Marignan, 8th; tel: 01 40 76 34 44; www.spoon.tm.fr; €€€€; Mon–Fri noon–2pm, 7–11pm, closed last week in July, first three weeks in Aug and two weeks at Christmas; metro: Franklin D. Roosevelt; map p.151 C2

The prototype of top chef Alain Ducasse's mix-and-match global kitchens draws a hot mix of media, fashion and showbiz types. The restaurant has two personalities: the white-linen shades on the dining room walls are raised in the evening to reveal purple upholstered walls. Desserts are often of American inspiration and include chewing-gum ice cream. Book well ahead.

Taillevent

15 rue Lammenais, 8th; tel: 01 44 95 15 01; €€€€; Mon–Fri 12.15–10.30pm; metro: George V; map p.150 C3

One of the most illustrious haute-cuisine restaurants in town, but surprisingly unstuffy. The food is magnificent: the earthy signature, spelt, cooked 'like risotto' with bone marrow, black truffle, whipped cream and parmesan, is heavenly. Booking ahead is essential.

Beaubourg and Les Halles

Au Chien qui Fume

33 rue du Pont-Neuf, 1st; tel: 01 42 36 07 42; www.auchienqui fume.com €€; daily noon–2am; metro: Les Halles; map p.154 B4

The 'smoking dog' has an extensive brasserie menu,

including shrimp and langoustine salad, or duck *à l'orange*. All the classic desserts are on offer too, including iced nougat and chocolate mousse. Not a bad place to lap up the late-night atmosphere in Les Halles.

Au Pied de Cochon

6 rue Coquillière, 1st; tel: 01 40 13 77 00; €€€; daily nonstop; metro: Les Halles; map p.154 B4

In its heyday, the legendary all-night brasserie catered for the market workers; now it's rather more upmarket. The house speciality remains the

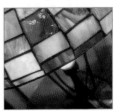

Right: from Le Roi du Pot-au-Feu to Drouant.

129

Above: typically French: oysters at a brasserie and dishes of the day chalked up on the ubiquitous blackboard.

---

same, however: grilled pig's trotter with Béarnaise sauce. If that lacks appeal, there are oysters and seafood, and a restorative onion soup.

Benoît
20 rue St-Martin, 4th; tel: 01 42 72 25 76; www.benoit-paris. com; €€€€; noon–2pm, 7–11pm; metro: Hôtel de Ville, Chatelet; map p.155 C4

This celebrated vintage bistro, long renowned for its excellent cooking and very high prices, fell into the Alain Ducasse fold in 2004, but the master chef promised not to change its style. Expect timeless terrines and casseroles,

highly professional service, and an elegant crowd playing at bistros in what is actually a very chic establishment.

La Fresque
100 rue Rambuteau, 1st; tel: 01 42 33 17 56; €–€€; daily noon–3pm, 7pm–midnight; metro: Les Halles; map p.155 C3–4

Sitting elbow to elbow at one of the big wooden tables is part of the charm here, as is the decor (white faïence tiles, frescoes, etc). The bistro fare, such as beef stew and duck, is excellent, and the staff are friendly, if sometimes harrassed. Always one vegetarian main course.

Georges
6th floor, Centre Georges-Pompidou, place Beaubourg, 4th; tel: 01 44 78 47 99; €€€€; Wed–Mon 11am–2am; metro: Rambuteau, Hôtel de Ville; map p.155 C3–4

The chic clientele do not go to Georges for the food but to see and be seen at the top of the Centre Pompidou. Excellent views.

Le Hangar
12 impasse Berthaud, 4th; tel: 01 42 74 55 44; €€; Tue–Sat noon–3pm, 6.30pm–midnight, closed Aug; metro: Rambuteau; map p.155 C4

Minimalist yet cosy, this modern bistro is just steps from the Centre Pompidou, tucked away in an alley. Pan-fried foie gras with puréed potatoes is always on the menu, as well as a towering chocolate soufflé. No credit cards.

Le Petit Marcel
65 rue Rambuteau, 4th; tel: 01 48 87 10 20; €; Mon–Thur 7am–midnight, Fri, Sat noon–midnight; metro: Rambuteau; map p.155 C3–4

A useful pit stop near the Centre Pompidou, this characterful bistro has walls lined with Art Nouveau tiles and a painted ceiling on the inside, and on the outside, seating on the terrace. Generous salads, omelettes, steak frites, tarte tatin: simple French fare, but decent, cheap and scrumptious. No credit cards.

La Tour de Montlhéry
5 rue des Prouvaires, 1st; tel: 01 42 36 21 82; €€€; daily noon–3pm, 7.30pm–5.30am; RER: Chatelet-les-Halles;

Approximate prices for an average three-course dinner per person, including half a bottle of house wine, service and tax:

€	under €25
€€	€25–40
€€€	€40–60
€€€€	over €60

R

130

'Le fooding' has become a watchword of modern French cooking. A contraction of the words 'food' and 'feeling', it was invented by journalist Alexandre Cammas in 1999 as a creed for re-energising French cuisine. Among its central tenets are being open-minded, a desire for sincerity, fun and an appetite for innovation. Its attempt to blow away the old conservatism seems to have met with some success.

map p.154 B4

This long-standing, late-opening purveyor of solid French food, also known as Chez Denise, is great fun. Portions are copious, the dining room cosy, and the atmosphere friendly. The menu runs to steaks, chips, game, offal and a few fish dishes.

Marais and Bastille

404

69 rue des Gravilliers, 3rd; tel: 01 42 74 57 81; €€; Mon–Fri noon–2.3pm, 8pm–midnight, Sat, Sun noon–4pm, 8pm–midnight; metro: Arts et Métiers; map p.155 C4

Packed, hip, and atmospheric, with low seating and iron grilles on the windows casting lacy patterns through the dim interior on to the tables. The Moroccan menu features filo-pastry pies, lamb brochettes, an exotic selection of couscous and tagines, as well as fragrant Berber desserts. Respectably good food at this price. Booking essential.

L'Ambassade d'Auvergne

22 rue du Grenier-St-Lazare, 3rd; tel: 01 42 72 31 22; €€€; daily noon–2pm, 7.30–10.30pm, mid-July–mid-Aug closed Sun; metro: Rambuteau; map p.155 C4

Auvergne fare is famously hearty, so make sure you come here with an appetite. One of this cheerful, almost rustic restaurant's signature dishes is the lentil salad, made with Puy lentils, bacon and shallots. End with a regional eau-de-vie, available to buy to take home if you like.

L'As du Fallafel

34 rue des Rosiers, 4th; tel: 01 48 87 63 60; €; Mon–Thur and Sun 11am–midnight, Fri 11am–mid-evening; metro: St-Paul; map p.155 D3

The best falafel in Paris is a meal in itself. There are also shawarma kebabs in pitta bread. Crowded but fun.

Auberge Pyrénées-Cévennes

106 rue de la Folie-Méricourt, 11th; tel: 01 43 57 33 78; €€/€€€; Mon–Fri noon–2pm, 7–11pm, Sat 7–11pm; closed mid-July–mid-Aug and first week in Jan; metro: République; map p.153 E1

There's a reason why this classy spot won a best bistro award recently: the waiters are friendly, the decor is unique (purple-and-white cloths, terracotta floors, and, oddly, a few stuffed animal heads on the wall), and the hearty food is top-notch. Try lentil caviar or frisée aux lardons (salad with bacon) to start, followed by cassoulet, pigs' feet, sausage and potatoes, fish quenelles, rum Babas or profiteroles.

Au Petit Fer à Cheval

30 rue Vieille-du-Temple, 4th; tel: 01 42 72 47 47; €€; daily 9am–2am; metro: St-Paul; map p.155 D3

People watching is as much a full-time occupation here as it is anywhere else along the Marais's trendy rue Vieille-du-Temple. With its tiny horse-shoe-shaped bar and cosy back room, this café is atmospheric and a great favourite with the bourgeois-bohemian crowd. Decent food and really friendly service.

Brasserie Bofinger

5–7 rue de la Bastille, 4th; tel: 01 42 72 87 82; www.bofingerparis.com; €€€; Mon–Fri noon–3pm, 6.30pm–1am, Sat, Sun noon–1am; metro: Bastille; map p.155 E2

Close to Opéra-Bastille, the huge (300-seater) Bofinger is the archetypal Belle-Epoque brasserie, complete with lush red-and-gold decor and a grand glass ceiling. This is a great place to experience true brasserie fare: delicious

Below: taking a break at the delightful Au Petit Fer à Cheval.

Above: Ladurée is famed for its macaroons.

oysters and seafood and specialities from Alsace such as choucroute and sausages. The sole meunière is also to be recommended. Jolly, old-fashioned waiters.

Guillaume
32 rue de Picardie, 3rd; tel: 01 44 54 20 60; €€/€€€; Mon–Fri nonstop, Sat D; metro: Temple; map p.155 D4

If the terrace is full at this trendy bar-restaurant, fear not: it has a large back room (with a huge peacock-feather chandelier). Cocktails cost a reasonable €8 each, and the champagne is discounted during the evening happy hour. The food is of the light variety: crostini with red tuna or guacamole, for example.

Le Pamphlet
38 rue Debelleyme, 3rd; tel: 01 42 72 39 24; €€; Tue–Sat 7.30–11pm, closed for two weeks in Aug and two weeks in Jan; metro: Filles du Calvaire; map p.155 D4

Whereas most restaurants in this part of town are low-key, local affairs, chef Alain Carrère offers a much more exciting French experience, and flawless quality. Squid-ink risotto with *escargot beignets* (snail fritters), and baked banana with spice-bread ice cream are just two

examples on a menu that changes daily. The tables are nicely spaced out, and the decor is warmly provincial. The dinner menue is superb-value at €30.

Paris Main d'Or
133 rue du Faubourg-St-Antoine, 11th; €€; tel: 01 44 68 04 68; Mon–Sat noon–3pm, 8–11pm, closed Aug; metro: Ledru-Rollin; map p.155 E2

This is an easy place to miss, since the dusky interior is viewed with difficulty from the outside and looks absolutely unextraordinary. However, do not be deceived, because you have just found one of the best Corsican restaurants in the city, with superb charcuterie, fish soup and cumin-roasted pork. Book ahead.

Le Petit Marché
9 rue de Béarn, 3rd; tel: 01 42 72 06 67; €; daily noon–3pm, 8pm–midnight; metro: Chemin Vert; map p.155 D3

The 'little market' is one of the hip bistros of the Marais's, and it pulls a matching fashion-conscious clientele without losing its friendly feel. The short, modern menu has a pronounced Asian slant: tuna flash-fried in sesame seeds and served with Thai sauce, or pan-fried scallops with

lime. From the similarly laconic wine list, the house red is a good bet.

Champs-Elysées and Trocadéro

L'Appart'
9–11 rue du Colisée, 8th; tel: 01 53 75 42 00; www.l-appart. com; €€/€€€; daily noon–2pm, 7–11pm; metro: Franklin D. Roosevelt; map p.151 D2

Close to the Champs-Elysées, this modern yet cosy bistro looks more like someone's apartment (hence the name), with shelves of books lining the walls. The cooking is creative but not fussy: colourful salads, candied aubergine, veal with mustard seeds, and fresh cod with mashed potatoes. Reasonably priced wines.

Guy Savoy
18 rue Troyon, 17th; tel: 01 43 80 40 61; www.guysavoy.com; €€€€; Tue–Fri noon–2pm, 7–10.30pm, Sat 7–10.30pm, closed mid-July–mid-Aug; metro: Charles de Gaulle-Etoile; map p.150 B3

It took some time for Savoy's imaginative haute cuisine to finally earn the highest Michelin rating, belated recognition for one of the most inventive chefs in Paris. The son of a gardener, Savoy has an obsession with vegetables that anticipated the current trend by more than a decade. He happily pairs truffles with lentils or artichokes, for example. He also regularly makes the rounds to greet his guests.

Approximate prices for an average three-course dinner per person, including half a bottle of house wine, service and tax:
€   under €25
€€   €25–40
€€€   €40–60
€€€€ over €60

France is constantly vying with Italy for the title of world's biggest wine producer. As in many European countries, the French are drinking less wine, but of better quality. France has over 8,000 sq km (3,000 sq miles) devoted to grape vines, producing more than 600 million cases of wine each year, a third of which are exported.

Ladurée

75 avenue des Champs-Elysées, 8th; tel: 01 40 75 08 75; www.laduree.fr; €€€; daily 7.30am–12.30am; metro: George V; map p.150 C3

Renowned in Paris for generations for its exquisite macaroons in an array of flavours, this café/patisserie/restaurant is always busy and very chic. An army of 45 pastry chefs and 40 cooks produce a range of delicious dishes from puff pastry filled with veal and mushrooms to baked cod with candied lemon. Desserts are a particular strength. There's also a branch at 16 rue Royale.

Market

15 avenue Matignon, 8th; tel: 01 56 43 40 90; www.jean-georges.com; €€€; Mon–Fri noon–3pm, 7–10pm, Sat, Sun noon–4.30pm, 7–10.30pm; metro: Charles de Gaulle-Etoile, Franklin D. Roosevelt; map p.151 D2

After a rocky debut, globe-trotting Alsatian-born, New York-based chef Jean-Georges Vongerichten has succeeded in creating a very popular contemporary table next to the glamorous new Parisian headquarters of Christie's auctioneers. The slick decor of polished grey stone and bleached wood accented by African art is signed by the Parisian decorator Christian Liagre, but the crowd is distinctly international, with a penchant for dishes such as a salad of mixed leaves, Japanese mushrooms, avocado and asparagus in a saké vinaigrette, scallops sautéed with citrus in sesame oil, and other East-meets-West-style preparations. Book ahead.

Pierre Gagnaire

Hôtel Balzac, 6 rue Balzac, 8th; tel: 01 58 36 12 50; www.pierre-gagnaire.com; €€€€; Mon– Fri noon–2pm, 7.30–10pm, Sun 7.30–10pm, closed one week in Feb and last two weeks of July; metro: Charles de Gaulle-Etoile, George V; map p.150 C3

Pierre Gagnaire is one of the most original and artistic chefs in the world today. The elaborate composition of his dishes verges on the baroque – think suckling lamb rubbed in ewe's-milk curd and capers served with roasted rice, Chinese cabbage with toasted rice, and snails with fennel shoots. A visit to this sedate grey dining room is essential for intrepid gastronomes. Book weeks, if not months, ahead.

Le Pré Catalan

Route de Suresnes, Bois de Boulogne, 16th; tel: 01 44 14 41 14; www.lenotre.fr; €€€€; Tue–Sat noon–1.45pm, 7.30–9.30pm, Sun noon–1.45pm; metro: Porte Maillot

Set in the heart of the Bois de Boulogne, this is one of the most romantic spots in Paris. Haute cuisine centring on fresh truffles, lobster, lamb and fresh seafood. The pastry chef is considered one of the best in France. Reserve.

SEE ALSO PARKS AND GARDENS, P.120

Tokyo Eat

Palais de Tokyo, 13 avenue du Président Wilson, 16th; tel: 01 47 20 00 29; €€; Tue–Sat noon–3pm, 7.30–11.30pm, Sun 5.30pm, 7.30–10.30pm; metro: Alma Marceau; map p.150 B1–2

An airy space with open kitchen and groovy lighting. The menu skips from global satays and unusual carpaccios to roast chicken. The terrace is open in summer.

Montmartre and Pigalle

Au Grain de Folie

24 rue de la Vieuville, 18th; tel:

Below: upmarket dining at Jean-Georges Vongerichten's Market.

01 42 58 15 57; €; Mon–Sat noon–11pm, Sun 12.30–2.30pm, 7.30–10.30pm; metro: Abbesses; map p.152 A4

A self-styled 'vegetarian place for non-vegetarians', this is a quaint spot for a healthy bite on your way to the Butte. Sit at a check-cloth-covered table, among the cooking implements and pot plants, and enjoy a bowl of home-made soup, a crispy vegetable platter, or a slice of savoury tart. A bit of a tight squeeze but that all adds to the friendly atmosphere.

Casa Olympe

48 rue St-Georges, 9th; tel: 01 42 85 26 01; www.casaolympe.com; €€/€€€; Mon–Fri noon–2pm, 8–11pm, closed one week in May, first three weeks in Aug and one week at Christmas; metro: St-Georges; map p.152 B3

Olympe Versini is one of Paris's best-known female chefs and in this, her latest restaurant, an intimate space served by the tiniest of kitchens, she offers a limited but strong menu to a smart and formal clientele. The food is Corsican and includes calf's brain, lamb roasted in thyme and a delicious Corsican-style lasagne.

Chez Jean

8 rue St-Lazare, 9th; tel: 01 48 78 62 73; www.restaurantjean.fr; €€€; Mon–Fri noon–2.30pm, 7.30–10.30pm, closed Aug; metro: Notre-Dame-de-Lorette; map p.152 B3

This popular brasserie has a lovely, high-ceilinged dining room, a high staff-to-diners ratio and a set menu that's excellent value. The slow-

> Bread is served free of charge with any meal, and you are entitled to as much as you can eat, so do not be afraid to ask for more.

Above: a rare vegetarian restaurant, in Montmartre.

cooked farmhouse pork with apricot chutney is outstanding, as are the cherries soaked in eau de vie come dessert time.

Chez Michel

10 rue de Belzunce, 10th; tel: 01 44 53 06 20; €€€; Mon 7–11pm, Tue–Fri noon–2pm, 7–11pm; metro: Poissonnière; map p.153 C3

One of the flag bearers of the wave of small, excellent regional restaurants that has been spreading across Paris since the late 1990s. Chef-proprietor Thierry Breton (from Brittany, of course) does fine, hearty food such as marinated salmon with purple potatoes. Blackboard specials, at extra cost, follow the seasons.

Chez Toinette

20 rue Germain-Pilon, 18th; tel: 01 42 54 44 36; €€; Tue–Sat 7.30–11.30pm, closed Aug; metro: Abbesses, Pigalle; map p.152 B4

Where many places in this part of town shamelessly fob off the unwitting tourist with overpriced fare, this amiable bistro has a good, well-priced blackboard menu that might run to steaks, wild-boar terrine, a lovely warm goat's cheese salad and prunes soaked in Armagnac.

Above: laid-back dining by the Canal St-Martin.

Le Velly

52 rue Lamartine, 9th; tel: 01 48 78 60 05; €€/€€€; Mon–Fri noon–2pm, 7.30–10.45pm, closed for three weeks in Aug; metro: Notre-Dame-de-Lorette; map p.152 B3

This 1930s-style neighbourhood bistro is a firm favourite among Parisians. The modest two-floored interior is the backdrop for some precise and imaginative cooking by chef Alain Brigant. The blackboard menu is improvised daily, depending on market finds. Choose from beef with herbs, grilled cod with mash, or a melon minestrone with fromage frais. Desserts are delicious, and the bread is home-made.

La Villette to Bercy

Café Noir

15 rue St-Blaise, 20th; tel: 01 40 09 75 80; €€; daily 7–11pm; metro: Porte de Bagnolet; map p.156 C1

A short walk from the metro down a pretty cobbled street is this bistro where the trendy 30-somethings of the neighbourhood come to graze. Whether you choose to sit inside among the proprietor's collection of hats, coffee pots and film posters or outside on the terasse, the atmosphere is fun and relaxed. The food, such as duck cooked with lavender, thyme and honey, is not always the most precisely executed; puddings are good.

Chai 33
33 cour St Emilion, 12th; tel: 01 53 44 01 01; €€€; www.chai33. com; daily noon–2pm, 7–11pm; metro: Cour St-Emilion

Innovative restaurant set in a light, airy former wine warehouse in the revitalised area of Bercy. Choose your wine according to six styles, from light with a bite to rich and silky, with refreshing fusion food to match. Unpretentious sommeliers are on hand to help with wine choices.

Chez Prune
71 quai de Valmy, 10th; tel: 01 42 41 30 47; €; daily noon–3pm, 7–11pm; metro: République; map p.153 D2

A cornerstone of the trendy Canal St-Martin area and a good place to watch the world go by. Good food is served at lunch time; tapas-style snacks at night.

L'Encrier
55 rue Traversière, 12th; tel:

Approximate prices for an average three-course dinner per person, including half a bottle of house wine, service and tax:
€ under €25
€€ €25–40
€€€ €40–60
€€€€ over €60

---

01 44 68 08 16; €/€€; Mon–Fri noon–2pm, 7.30–11pm, Sat 7.30–11pm; metro: Ledru-Rollin; map p.155 E2

This is one of those restaurants that you dream of stumbling across: amazing value, traditional decor, an open kitchen, bubbly local crowd, cheerful staff and decent bistro food: fried rabbit kidneys on salad dressed with raspberry vinegar, say, or homemade terrine, or goose *magret* (breast) with honey. End with profiteroles.

Ma Pomme
107 rue du Ménilmontant, 20th; tel: 01 40 33 10 40; €/€€; daily noon–2pm, 7–11pm, closed for two weeks in Aug; metro: Gambetta

Named after the Maurice Chevalier song, this relaxed

---

and unpretentious neighbourhood bistro offers a warm atmosphere and good value for money. Popular with the young bohemian crowd.

Le Square Trousseau
1 rue Antoine-Vollon, 12th; tel: 01 43 43 06 00; €€/€€€; Tue–Sat noon–2.30pm, 8–11.30pm, closed first three weeks in Aug, one week at Christmas and two weeks in Feb; metro: Ledru-Rollin; map p.155 E2

It is no surprise that this bistro has been used for film sets: the spacious interior has Art Deco lamps, colourful tiles and burgundy velvet. In summer, diners squeeze on to the terrace facing a leafy square. Gazpacho, tuna tartare, rosemary lamb and spring vegetables, a superlative steak tartare, and raspberry gratin are among the delights available.

Train Bleu
Gare de Lyon, 12th, tel: 01 43 43 09 06; www.le-train-bleu.com; €€€; daily 11.30am–3pm, 7–11pm; metro: Gare de Lyon; map p.155 E1

In the midst of the Gare de Lyon, the terminus for trains

Below: convivial atmosphere and excellent food at Le Square Trousseau.

Above: Le Train Bleu, for a romantic meal in a nostalgic setting.

from the Mediterranean, this huge, impressive brasserie was built for the 1900 World Fair. With its frescoed ceilings depicting destinations served by the trains from the station, mosaics and gilt detailing it is Second Empire style at its grandest. Classic French dishes are served quickly and efficiently. Excellent-value set menus; expensive wines.

The Latin Quarter and St-Germain

L'Alcazar
62 rue Mazarine, 6th; tel: 01 53 10 19 99; www.alcazar.fr; €€€; daily noon–3pm, 7pm–12.30am; metro: Odéon; map p.154 B3
Sir Terence Conran's contribution to the Paris restaurant scene was to transform this former musical hall into a designer brasserie. It's been a hit, thanks to the easy-going atmosphere and competitively priced menu, which includes an upscale interpretation of British-style fish and chips.

Allard
41 rue St-André des Arts, 6th, tel: 01 43 26 48 23; €€/€€€; Mon–Sat noon–2.30pm, 7–11.30pm, closed for three weeks in Aug; metro: St-Michel; map p.154 B2
The dark Art Nouveau decoration makes this one of the loveliest bistros in Paris, with two small but intimate and atmospheric rooms evocative of Left Bank life. The food is traditional: duck with olives, roast lamb, Lyonnaise sausage, for example, and very good.

Le Balzar
49 rue des Ecoles, 5th; tel: 01 43 54 13 67; www.brasserie balzar.com; €€; daily noon–11.45pm; metro: Cluny-La Sorbonne; map p.154 B2
If a brasserie could sum up the atmosphere of an entire city, then Balzar would be high on the Paris list. The classic menu and the comforting 1920s interior, with mirrors judiciously placed for discreet people watching, all make for a quintessentially Parisian experience.

Brasserie Lipp
151 boulevard St-Germain, 6th; tel: 01 45 48 53 91; www. brasserielipp.com; €€/€€€; daily noon–1am; metro: St-Germain-des-Prés; map p.154 A2
Everyone who's anyone in St-Germain-des-Prés has a table here: it is reportedly actress Emmanuelle Béart's favourite for a bite to eat. It's a good place to spot neighbourhood eccentrics too. The food is standard brasserie fare.

Le Comptoir
9 carrefour de l'Odéon, 6th; tel: 01 43 29 12 05; €€€; daily nonstop; metro: Odéon; map p.154 B2
One of the biggest stories in the restaurant world these past couple of years, Yves Camdeborde's recently acquired bistro serves a no-choice €40 meal in the evening that is so good

Approximate prices for an average three-course dinner per person, including half a bottle of house wine, service and tax:	
€	under €25
€€	€25–40
€€€	€40–60
€€€€	over €60

The *toque blanche* (literally, 'white hat') is the name for the tall, round, pleated, starched hat worn by chefs across the world since the days of kitchen legend George Auguste Escoffier (1845–1935). Its many folds are supposed to signify the multiple ways that an egg can be cooked (some have exactly 100 pleats).

you have to book months in advance. The brasserie dishes served at lunch time are pretty good too: iced cream of chicken soup, or rolled saddle of lamb are typical.

Polidor
41 rue Monsieur-le-Prince, 6th; tel: 01 43 26 95 34; www. polidor.com; €; Mon–Sat noon–2.30pm, 7.30–12.30am, Sun noon–2.30pm, 7–11pm; metro: Odéon; map p.154 B2

This bohemian restaurant, with its rickety furniture, dusty mirrors, and nicotine-stained walls, is a perennial favourite of students and budget diners. The plats du jour have been constant for around 150 years and arrive in hearty helpings. Blood sausage with mash, and rice pudding are just the kind of hearty dishes to expect. Excellent value for money.

Le Réminet
3 rue des Grands-Degrés, 5th; tel: 01 44 07 04 24; www.le reminet.com; €€€; Thur–Mon noon–2.30pm, 7.30–11pm, closed for three weeks in Aug; metro: Maubert Mutualité, St-Michel; map p.154 C2

The position just beside Notre-Dame could hardly be better for this delightfully run bistro, where Hugues Gournay's cooking is both inventive and tasty. It is also one of the few bistros in Paris open on Sunday, which doubles the appeal of the narrow din-

ing room. The mouthwatering dishes include snails, whiting on aubergine caviar, guinea fowl in cream sauce, chestnut cake and a delicious passion-fruit sorbet.

La Tour d'Argent
15–17 quai de la Tournelle, 5th; tel: 01 43 54 23 31; www.tour dargent.com; €€€€; Wed–Sun noon–1.30pm, 7.30–9pm, Tue 7.30–9pm; metro: Pont Marie; map p.155 C2

Famed Parisian restaurant owner, Claude Terrail, former boss here, has now retired, but this has not deterred the glitzy clientele who bask in the top-floor views over Notre-Dame.

The 7th and 15th

L'Arpège
84 rue de Varenne, 7th; tel: 01 45 51 47 33; www.alain-passard.com; €€€€; Mon–Fri noon–2.30pm, 8–10.30pm, closed for three weeks in Aug; metro: Varenne; map p.157 D4

Chef Alain Passard (also an accomplished musician) designed his restaurant to be an acoustically discreet model of contemporary elegance. His menus are imaginative: his signature dessert, for example, is tomato confite with 12 flavours (he has been known to lay down the challenge that if you can name all the seasonings, the

Below: exquisite presentation and smart interior at L'Alcazar.

Below: market-fresh fruit and vegetables.

House wine can usually be ordered in carafes or *pichets* (earthenware jugs) in bistros, brasseries and cafés, though often not in formal restaurants. Quantities are normally 25cl *(un quart)*, 50cl *(un demi)*, or sometimes 46cl *(un pot lyonnais)*.

dish is free). Good prix-fixe lunch menu.

L'Atelier de Joël Robuchon
5 rue de Montalembert, 7th; tel: 01 56 28 16 16; www.joel-robuchon.com; €€€; daily noon–2.30pm, 7pm–midnight; metro: Rue du Bac, St-Germain-des-Prés; map p.154 A3

Even jaded Parisians queue up in all weathers to sample the warm foie gras brochettes or tapenade with fresh tuna conjured by one of France's most revered chefs. The restaurant is built around an open kitchen, so you can watch the masters at work, and the atmosphere is slick, like that of a bar. Reservations are accepted for the first seatings only (11.30am and 6.30pm).

Au Bon Accueil
14 rue de Monttessuy, 7th; tel: 01 47 05 46 11; €€; Mon–Fri noon–2.30pm, 7.30–10.30pm; metro: Pont de l'Alma; map p.156 C4

What was once a Provençal bistro has been given a total makeover. The decor is now sleek contemporary and elegant, and the menu of classics has been modernised as well. The prix-fixe dinner menu (around €30 at time of printing) is viewed by many locals as one of the best deals in the neighbourhood, and the wine list is excellent. Seats on the terrace have views of the Eiffel Tower. Excellent, friendly service. A real find.

Le Jules Verne
2nd level, Eiffel Tower, 7th, tel: 01 45 55 61 44; €€€€; daily 12.15–1.30pm, 7.15–9.30pm; metro: Bir-Hakeim, RER: Champ de Mars; map p.156 B4

Location-wise, this restaurant on the second level of the Eiffel Tower is perfect for a celebration or romantic dinner, though the cooking is not quite as spectacular as the view (although that, admittedly, is hard to beat). Going up the special lift, reserved exclusively for diners, adds to the occasion, too. Specialities include a *tartare duo* (beef and langoustine), *noix de St-Jacques* (scallops) and delicious crêpes with Grand Marnier. Reserve well in advance, especially for dinner.

SEE ALSO MONUMENTS, P.86

L'Os à Moelle
3 rue Vasco-de-Gama, 15th; tel: 01 45 57 27 27; €€€; Tue–Sat noon–2pm, 7–11.30pm, closed three weeks in Aug; metro: Lourmel

For high-quality food at a very reasonable price, this unpretentious corner bistro is a worthwhile destination. Chef Thierry Faucher prepares a different six-course, prixe-fixe menu (€38) every night, with two choices for each course. The menue might be limited but it's all very good and offers fabulous value for money.

Le Voltaire
27 quai Voltaire, 7th; tel: 01 42 61 17 49; €€€€; Tue–Sat 12.30–2.30pm, 7.30–10.15pm; metro:

Approximate prices for an average three-course dinner per person, including half a bottle of house wine, service and tax:

€	under €25
€€	€25–40
€€€	€40–60
€€€€	over €60

Rue du Bac; map p.154 A3
Not the least of this vintage bistro's attractions is its river-side setting; others include the polished service and the food, which runs the gamut from elegant salads and rustic dishes, notably sautéed rabbit, to luxury dishes such as lobster omelette. A succesful marriage of cosy and chic.

Montpartnasse and Beyond

La Closerie des Lilas
171 boulevard du Montparnasse, 6th; tel: 01 40 51 34 50; www.closeriedeslilas.fr; €€€; daily noon–1am; metro: Port-Royal
This iconic brasserie still has a lot of charm and richly satisfying fare, though it lives off its reputation as a watering hole in the 1920s: tables are inscribed with the names of clients including Lenin, Modigliani and André Breton. Unsurprisingly, Ernest Hemingway's plaque rests on the bar. A pianist plays in the evening. Skip the overpriced restaurant annexe.

La Coupole
102 boulevard du Montparnasse, 14th; tel: 01 43 20 14 20; www.flobrasseries.com; €€€; Mon–Sat 8.30am–1am; metro: Vavin; map p.157 E2
This vast, legendary Art Deco brasserie (the largest in Paris) opened its doors in 1927 and is still going strong. Now run by the Flo Brasserie group, it

Above: the unbeatable L'Atelier de Joël Robuchon.

has a convivial atmosphere, and its popularity remains intact. The classic brasserie fare includes huge platters of shellfish, choucroute and Alsatian sausages, and steaks and hearty stews.

L'Entrepôt
7 rue Francis-de-Pressensé, 14th; tel: 01 45 40 60 70; €€–€€€; daily nonstop; metro: Pernety
This place used to be a paper warehouse, but is now a three-in-one: bar, restaurant and art-house cinema. The dining side of the operation serves fairly standard brasserie fare such as magret de canard (duck breast), beef tartare or fillet of salmon, with options including crème brûlée for dessert. Live music at weekends.

Hélène Darroze
4 rue d'Assas, 6th; tel: 01 42 22 00 11; www.helenedarroze.com; €€€€; Tue 7.30– 10.15pm, Wed–Sat 12.30–2.30, 7.30– 10.15pm, closed Aug; metro: Sèvres-Babylone; map p.154 A2
One of the city's top female chefs, originally from the Landes, Hélène Darroze has brought the best of the

southwest to town with a light, whimsical hand. The ground floor is reserved for tapas; for more formal dining head upstairs and sample wood-grilled foie gras with caramelised fruits, or lamb with couscous, chickpeas and mint. Colourful and stylish contemporary setting.

La Régalade
49 avenue Jean-Moulin, 14th; tel: 01 45 45 68 58; €€; Mon 7–11pm, Tue–Fri noon– 2.30pm, 7–11pm, closed Aug; metro: Alésia
A destination bistro for epicures across Paris for over 10 years, La Régalade is now under different ownership. New chef Bruno Doucet has injected with life, while retaining much of what was good about it before, especially the very reasonable pricing. Start with the complementary pâté de campagne with 'rustic' bread, then proceed with a cream of walnut soup poured over a flan of foie gras, duck hearts with oyster mushrooms, and Grand Marnier soufflé to finish. Prixe-fixe menu is €30. Reserve well ahead.

A service charge of 12 to 15 per cent is, by law, included in the price given at restaurants, bars and cafés, so you don't have to tip. However, it is polite when paying for drinks to round up the total, and to leave one to five euros after a meal, depending on the quality of the service and the restaurant concerned.

139

Shopping

How better to appreciate the city than to explore its historic department stores, its characterful covered arcades, its quirky boutiques and its bustling street markets? Paris has a wonderful variety of shops and retains a strong tradition of small specialist retailers. This chapter gives a general introduction, with listings of one-stop stores and our pick of shops and markets that are unique to the city. Note that shops for fashion, beauty products, books, CDs and food and wine are covered respectively under *'Fashion', 'Pampering', 'Literature and Theatre', 'Music',* and *'Food and Drink'.*

Right: trendy shopping in the Marais.

Small and Sweet

When shopping seems to be becoming increasingly uniform, with the same international groups and luxury labels in every major city around the world, Paris still retains its tradition of small specialist shops and individual boutiques, with chain stores and *centres commerciaux* (shopping malls) far less prevalent than in most other European capitals.

The Shopping Map

The city's different *quartiers* each have their own mood and atmosphere, and their shops often reflect their history and the type of people who live there. Expect to find shops selling classic and expensive items (antiques and up-market interior design as well as fashion labels, for example) in the wealthy, conservative **7th** and **16th** *arrondissements*, and boho designers and independent gift shops and boutiques on the hilly streets

of **Montmartre**, around the fashionable **Bastille** and **Marais** and along the banks of the **Canal St-Martin**. High-street chains abound around the **Forum des Halles**, the main shopping mall in the city centre; this area, which is currently drab and unappealing, is undergoing regeneration, due for completion in 2012.

The once-staid **rue St-Honoré** has become the focus for a more *avant-garde* fashion set, thanks to the establishment here of Colette, the original lifestyle store. Even the ultra-exclusive **avenue Montaigne** has

tempered its bourgeois image with the arrival of hip young labels Paul & Joe and Zadig & Voltaire; all this has had the knock-on effect of attracting other cool interiors boutiques and gift shops to the area.

Emblematic of glamour in the early 20th century, the **Champs-Elysées** nose-dived to tourist dross in the 1980s. Its return to favour at the end of the 1990s was confirmed by the arrival here of *pâtissier extraordinaire*, Ladurée, and in the last couple of years the avenue has been boosted by a rash of swish 'concept' stores.

Left: the wonderful gilt and stained glass of Lafayette.

Dating from 1826 and perhaps the finest of the passages, with wood-and-brass shop fronts and carved Corinthian capitals. Highlights include antique dolls at Rober Capia, leather goods at Il Bisonte and bespoke make-up by Terry.

Passage du Grand Cerf
10 rue Dussoubs–145 rue St-Denis, 2nd; www.passage dugrandcerf.com; Mon–Sat 8.30am–8pm; metro: Étienne Marcel; map: map p.154 C4
Probably the coolest of the arcades, this Sentier *passage* is something of a creative headquarters. Come here for cutting-edge graphic designers, milliners, jewellers and lighting shops.

Passage des Panoramas
10 rue St-Marc–11 boulevard Montmartre, 2nd; metro: Bourse; map p.152 B2
One of the earliest of the arcades, opened in 1800, and above all a focus for philatelists, with half a dozen specialist stamp dealers. Also of note is Stern Graveur, which has been engraving headed notepaper and wedding invitations since 1840.

Emile Zola's novel *Thérèse Raquin* starts with a less than favourable description of the Arcade du Pont Neuf, where his eponymous heroine works in the fabrics shop owned by her mother-in-law. The family live in a tiny apartment above the shop, and Thérèse's sense of entrapment is wonderfully evoked in Zola's atmospheric prose.

In the past decade designer stores have migrated to **St-Germain**, much to the chagrin of those who bemoan the loss of its literary cachet and favourite bookshops.

Some areas reflect the changing population of Paris. In the **13th** *arrondissement*, **Chinatown**, with its large Southeast Asian population, has Chinese food shops among the high-rises.

Not that every area is in the throes of regeneration. The aristocratic past of boulevards **Bonne Nouvelle** and Montmartre is sadly a distant memory blurred by the ranks of discount stores and fast-food chains there.

Galleries and Passages

In the 1840s Paris had over 100 *passages*, or covered arcades, built with shops below and living quarters above. They were places for Parisians to discover novelties and the latest fashions, while protected from the elements. Nowadays there are only around 20 left, mostly near the Palais Royal. The passages usually open from around 7am to 9 or 10pm, and are locked at night and on Sunday. Here is just a selection:

Galerie Vivienne
6 rue Vivienne, 2nd; metro: Bourse; map p.152 B1
The best-preserved gallery with a beautiful mosaic floor and gorgeous iron-and-glass roof. This fashionable spot is home to the *ateliers-boutiques* of Jean-Paul Gaultier and Nathalie Garçon, art galleries and the genteel A Priori tearoom.

Galérie Véro-Dodat
19 rue Jean-Jacques Rousseau–2 rue du Bouloi, 1st; metro: Palais-Royal Musée du Louvre, Louvre Rivoli; map p.154 B4

Below: inside the elegant Galerie Vivienne.

141

Markets

In addition to its many food markets, covered under 'Food and Drink', Paris is known for its flea markets (*marchés aux puces*), of which a selection is described below. These markets developed in the 19th century, as scrap-metal merchants and rag-and-bone men camped in the unbuilt zone outside the Thiers fortifications, thus avoiding the duties within the city walls.

SEE ALSO FOOD AND DRINK, P.64

Marché d'Aligre

Place d'Aligre, 12th; Tue–Sun 7.30am–1.30pm; metro: Ledru-Rollin; map p.155 E2

The city's oldest flea market, located on the square next to the rue d'Aligre food market. Expect to find a handful of stalls selling antiques, books and general junk.

Marché de Montreuil

Avenue de la Porte de Montreuil, 20th; Sat, Sun, Mon 7am–7.30pm; metro: Porte de Montreuil

Tatty and anarchic, Montreuil sells car parts, tools, bric-a-brac and second-hand clothes and jewellery.

Above: a famous and again super-glam name in Parisian retailing.

Marché de St-Ouen de Clignancourt

Rue Binet–the Périphérique; Sat–Mon 7am–7.30pm metro: Porte de Clignancourt

Reputedly the largest flea market in Europe, with over 2,500 dealers spread over a dozen markets and arcades. Be prepared to bargain.

Marché de Vanves

Avenues Marc-Sangnier, de la Porte de Vanves, 14th; Sun 7am–7.30pm; metro: Porte de Vanves

A relaxed flea market, selling mostly second-hand clothes.

One-stop Shops

Bazar de l'Hotel de Ville (BHV)

14 rue du Temple, 4th; tel: 01 42 74 90 00; www.bhv.fr; Mon–Sat 9.30am–7.30pm, Wed until 9pm; metro: Hôtel de Ville; map p.155 C3

A surprisingly practical oasis in the Marais, this sizable department store caters for all things domestic, with a strong emphasis on DIY. The men's store is at nearby 36 rue de la Verrerie, 4th.

Le Bon Marché

24 rue de Sèvres, 7th; tel: 01 44 39 80 00; www.lebonmarche.fr; Mon–Fri 10am–7.30pm, Thur until 9pm, Sat 9.30am–8pm; metro: Sèvres Babylone; map p.157 E3

Paris' first department store, whose name means 'good bargain', opened in 1848. Highlights nowadays include the ground-floor **Theatre of Beauty**, devoted to the hottest make-up artist brands; the men's section **Balthazar**, with its polished wood floors and designer boutiques; and the cutest Parisian fashion labels on the first floor. Next door is the **Grande Epicerie**, Bon Marché's fabulous food store.

Colette

213 rue St-Honoré, 8th; tel: 01 55 35 33 90; www.colette.fr; Mon–Sat 11am–7pm; metro: Pyramides, Tuileries; map p.152 A1

The pioneering concept store surged onto the Paris scene in 1997, not with the department store ideal of colossal choice but with the Colette vision of picking the best of what is stylish and innovative. So far, it has managed to stay ahead of its flock of imitators with a mix of famous names and, as yet, unknowns in the

Below: flea market chairs stacked up.

On most purchases the price includes VAT (TVA in French). Foreign visitors can claim this back, but only if you spend more than 640 euros (300 euros for EU citizens) in one shop. The store should give you a *bordereau* (export sales invoice), which you'll need to fill in and show, with the goods, to customs officials. You then send the form back to the retailer, who will refund the VAT.

world of art and design. Books, music, electronics, toiletries and homeware are covered on the ground floor; fashion is upstairs. The painfully hip Water Bar in the basement offers light meals and a range of mineral waters.

Drugstore Publicis
133 avenue des Champs-Elysées, 8th; tel: 01 44 43 79 00; www.publicisdrugstore.com; Mon–Fri 8am–2am, Sat–Sun 10am–2am; metro: Charles de Gaulle, Etoile; map p.150 B3
Renovated in 2004, this complex (hence its inclusion in this section) includes a hip café, a pharmacy, newsagent, bookshop and delicatessen, with design and lifestyle covered in the basement.

Galeries Lafayette
40 boulevard Haussmann, 9th; tel: 01 42 82 34 56; www.galerieslafayette.com; Mon–Sat 9.30am–7.30pm, Thur until 9pm; metro: Auber, Havre Caumartin; map p.152 A2
Along with Printemps, this is the grandest of the Parisian department stores. The magnificent stained-glass Art Nouveau dome has been renovated, and the fashion floors revamped to try and regain the image of glamour and abundance it had in the early 20th century when it first opened. The fashion choice

is colossal, and there is even a separate building for menswear, the adjoining **Lafayette Homme**. Upmarket supermarket **Lafayette Gourmet** stocks a wide choice of regional and exotic foods, rare *grands crus*, and plenty of opportunities to snack. Fabulous beauty department.

Monoprix
52 Champs-Elysées; 8th; tel: 01 53 77 65 65; www.monoprix.fr; Mon–Sat 9am–midnight; metro: Franklin D. Roosevelt; map p.151 C3
France's answer to the now defunct British bargain chain Woolworths has a shop on every high street. The Champs-Elysées store is not the biggest or the best but it carries all the Monoprix staples: low-price fashions, cosmetics and food.

Le Printemps
64 boulevard Haussmann, 9th; tel: 01 42 82 57 87; http://departmentstoreparis.printemps.com; Mon–Sat 9.35am–7pm, Thur until 10pm; metro: Auber, Havre Caumartin; map p.151 A2
The eternal rival of Galeries Lafayette has gone seriously upmarket of late. Whereas

the Printemps of old seemed to be full of clutter, the revamped version stocks an impressive array of designer fashion and footwear, and even incorporates a **'luxe'** floor, with individually styled mini shops of Gucci, Yves Saint Laurent, Van Cleef & Arpels, etc. In the adjoining **Printemps de la Maison**, amid classic porcelain and household linen, a new floor takes a lifestyle look at household objects.

Tati
4 boulevard Rochechouart, 18th; tel: 01 55 29 50 00; www.tati.fr; Mon–Sat 10am–7pm; metro: Barbès Rochechouart; map p.152 C4
As much a Paris institution at the budget end of the market as Printemps and Galeries Lafayette are at the top, Tati has to be experienced to be believed. The store, which sprawls along the boulevard, resembles a seige as women rummage through the boxes for tights, T-shirts or even a polyester wedding dress, at remarkably low prices. They also have menswear, table linen, beauty products, lingerie and related shops for sweets and jewellery.

Below: Tati by name and tatty by nature, bargains galore at the lowest price.

143

Sport

Paris caters fairly well for the sports enthusiast, with major events including the Six Nations rugby tournament in February/March, the marathon in April and the French Tennis Open in May/June at the Stade Roland-Garros. For those keen on horseracing, the fashionable Grand Prix de l'Arc de Triomphe is held in the Bois de Boulogne, in October. Below is a select listing of venues for a variety of spectator and participant sports. You can also find information on sporting events in *Le Figaro* each Wednesday or, for details (in French only) of sports facilities, call Allô-Sports, tel: 08 20 00 75 75.

Boules

Arènes de Lutèce
47 rue Monge, 5th; no tel; free; metro: Cardinal Lemoine, Jussieu, Place Monge; map p.155 C1
Locals play friendly games in the Roman arena. The 'clubhouse' is a bar over the road.

Jardin du Luxembourg
Place Edmond Rostand; 6th; free; summer: daily 8am–9pm, rest of year: daily 8am–sunset; RER: Luxembourg; map p.154 B1
At the eastern end of the park, locals meet for relaxed-looking games of *pétanque*.

Cycling

On an informal level, there is good cycling in the Bois de Boulogne and Bois de Vincennes, and along the quais de Seine and the Canal St-Martin. For clubs, *see below*.

Fédération Française de Cyclotourisme
12 rue Louis Bertrand, Ivry-sur-Seine; tel: 01 44 16 88 88; www.ffct.org; metro: Pierre Curie
The national cycling federation should be able to put you in contact with a local cycling club in Paris.

Above: a man holds his boules.

Fitness Centres

Club Med Gym
17 rue du Débarcadère, 17th; tel: 01 45 74 14 04; www.clubmedgym.fr; entrance charge; metro: Porte Maillot; map p.150 A4
One of a chain of health clubs that offer step classes, weights, martial arts and sauna. Some clubs have a pool.

Club Quartier Latin
19 rue Pontoise, 5th; tel: 01 55 42 77 88; www.clubquartier latin.com; entrance charge; metro: Cardinal Lemoine; map p.155 C2
Large health club in a 1930s building with squash courts

and a pool. The gym has plenty of machines and offers a variety of exercise classes.

Football

Palais Omnisports de Paris-Bercy
8 boulevard de Bercy, 12th; tel: 08 92 39 01 00; www.popb.fr; charge; metro: Bercy
This huge stadium offers a vast range of events, including football, ice sports, motor sports and horse riding.

Parc des Princes
24 rue du Commandant-Guibaud, 16th; tel: 01 47 43 71 71; www.psg.fr; metro: Porte de St-Cloud
Home to the city's premier division football team, Paris St-Germain.

Stade de France
Rue Francis de Pressensé, St-Denis; tel: 01 55 93 00 00; www.stadefrance.fr; entrance charge; daily 10am–6pm except during events; metro: Porte de Paris, RER: La Plaine–Stade de France, Stade de France–St-Denis
Football fans should pay homage at the massive Stade de France, designed by architects Zubléna, Macary, Regembal and Constantini

Left: show of skills on a pedestal.

retractable glass roof floats on the Seine.
SEE ALSO CHILDREN, P.42–3

Piscine Suzanne-Berlioux
Forum des Halles, 10 place de la Rotonde, 1st; tel: 01 42 36 98 44; Mon–Tue 11.30am–10pm, Wed 10am–10pm, Thur–Fri 11am–10pm, Sat–Sun 9am–7pm; entrance charge; metro: Les Halles; map p.154 C4
Pool and tropical greenhouse.

Tennis

Jardin du Luxembourg
Rue de Vaugirard; 6th; tel: 01 43 25 79 18; entrance charge; summer: daily 8am–9pm, winter: 8am–sunset; metro: Mabillon; map p.154 B1
Six tennis courts situated in central Paris; an excellent inexpensive option.
SEE ALSO PARKS AND GARDENS, P.121–2

Stade Roland Garros
2 avenue Gordon-Bennett, 16th; tel: 01 47 43 48 00; www.fft.fr/rolandgarros; metro: Porte d'Auteuil
The highlight of the year is the **Grand Slam French Open** played on clay courts (late May–early June; tel: 01 47 43 52 52; www.frenchopen.org).

Below: bowling is also popular with children, *see p.42*.

Every Friday, weather-permitting, around 15,000 Parisians pull on their in-line skates and take to the streets en masse. The route starts at the Tour Montparnasse at 10pm (arrive 30 mins early) and always takes a different route (published on the Thursday before, see www.pari-roller.com for details), although it always takes around three hours. It is quite a spectacle to watch.

and built in 1997 for the 1998 World Cup. The stadium, seating around 100,000 spectators, is also used for rock concerts and other major sports events, such as the 2007 Rugby World Cup.

Horseracing

Hippodrome d'Auteuil
Route des Lacs, 16th; tel: 01 40 71 47 47; metro: Porte d'Auteuil
One of two racecourses in the Bois de Boulogne, used for steeplechasing.
SEE ALSO PARKS AND GARDENS, P.120

Hippodrome de Longchamp
Route des Tribunes, 16th;

tel: 01 44 30 75 00; metro: Porte d'Auteuil followed by free shuttle bus
The Bois de Boulogne's flat-racing course, hosting the chi-chi **Prix de l'Arc de Triomphe Lucien Barrière**, France's biggest horse race (early Oct; tel: 01 49 10 20 30; www.france-galop.com; entrance charge).
SEE ALSO PARKS AND GARDENS, P.120

Swimming

Piscine Georges-Vallery
148 avenue Gambetta, 20th; tel: 01 40 31 15 20; entrance charge; metro: Porte des Lilas
Built for the 1924 Olympic Games, at which Johnny Weissmuller (Tarzan in the films of old) won the gold. The pool, with a retractable roof, has been renovated.

Piscine Joséphine Baker
Quai François-Mauriac, 13th; tel: 01 56 61 96 50; www.sport. paris.fr; entrance charge; Mon, Wed, Fri 7–8.30am, 1–9pm; Tue, Thur 1–11pm, Sat 11am–8pm, Sun 10am–8pm; metro: Bibliothèque F. Mitterrand
Opened in 2006, this complex with a 25m pool and

Transport

This chapter gives you the lowdown on how to get to Paris, whether by train, air, sea or land, plus details of how to travel around once you're there. The city has an excellent public-transport system, which is both efficient and relatively inexpensive, and this section explains how to purchase tickets and navigate the network. As driving in the capital is famously nerve-wracking, visitors are best advised to stick to public transport or to take a taxi instead. However, if driving is a necessity, details are given here on how to hire a car and a summary of the rules of the road.

Arrival

BY RAIL
The **Eurostar** has fast, frequent rail services from London (St Pancras) or Ashford station to Paris (Gare du Nord). The service runs about 12 times a day and takes just over two hours (two hours from Ashford). For reservations, contact Eurostar on tel: 0990 134909 (UK) or 08 92 35 35 39 (France) or visit www.eurostar.com. There are reduced fares for children aged 4–11; those under 3 travel free but are not guaranteed a seat.

BY SEA
Ferries from the UK, Ireland and Channel Islands to the northern ports of France have reduced their prices since the Channel Tunnel opened.

Catamarans offer the fastest service but are subject to cancellation if the sea is very rough. There are motorway links from Boulogne, Calais and Le Havre to Paris.

BY AIR
Air France is the main agent for flights to France from the US and within Europe and also handles bookings for some of the smaller operators, such as Brit Air. For British travellers, operators such as the low-cost airlines Ryanair, easyJet, Flybe and British Midland offer flights to Paris from London and other British cities.

BY CAR
For those coming from the UK by car, **Eurotunnel** takes cars and passengers from Folkestone to Calais on a drive-on, drive-off service, known as **Le Shuttle**. It takes 35 minutes from platform to platform and about one hour from motorway to motorway. Payment is made at toll booths, which accept cash, cheques or credit cards. The price applies to the car,

> Paris has two main airports: Roissy-Charles-de-Gaulle, 30km (19 miles) northeast of the city centre, and Orly, 18km (11 miles) to the south. Both have good transport links.

regardless of the number of passengers or car size.

You can book in advance with Eurotunnel on tel: 0990 353535 (UK) or 03 21 00 61 00 (France) or at www.euro tunnel.com. You can also just turn up and take the next available service. Le Shuttle runs 24 hours a day, all year, and there are between two and five an hour, depending on the season and time of day.

BY BUS
National Express Eurolines runs services from London's Victoria Coach Station to Paris daily, providing one of the cheaper ways to get to the French capital. Discounts are available for young people and senior citizens, and the ticket includes the ferry crossing (via Dover). For more information contact National Express Eurolines at

Left: the greenest and most convenient way to arrive.

4 Cardiff Road, Luton, Bedfordshire, LU1 1PP, tel: 08705 143219, www.national express.com, or Eurolines France, at the Gare Routière-Coach Station Galliéni, 28 avenue du Général de Gaulle, Bagnolet (Métro Galliéni), tel: 08 36 69 52 52, or visit www.eurolines.fr.

Airports

Roissy-Charles-de-Gaulle
The quickest way of getting to central Paris from Roissy-Charles-de-Gaulle is by **RER** train. These leave every 15 minutes between 5am and 11.45pm from terminal 2 (take the connecting shuttle bus if you arrive at terminal 1) and run to the metro stops at Gare du Nord or Châtelet. The journey takes about 45 minutes.

The **Roissy bus** runs between the airport and rue Scribe (near the Palais-Garnier) from terminals 1 gate 30, 2A gate 10 and 2D gate 12. It runs every 15 minutes from 6am to 11pm and takes 45–60 minutes. Alternatively, the **Air France bus** (to metro Porte de Maillot or Charles-

de-Gaulle Etoile) leaves from terminals 2A and 2B or terminal 1, arrival level gate 34. The bus runs every 12 minutes from 5.40am to 11pm.

By taxi, the journey from Charles de Gaulle can take anything from around 30 mins to over an hour, depending on the traffic. The charge is metered, with supplements payable for each large piece of luggage.

Orly

To get to central Paris from Orly, take the **shuttle** from

gate H at Orly Sud or arrivals gate F at Orly Ouest to Orly railway station. The **RER** stops at Austerlitz, Pont St-Michel and the Quai d'Orsay. It runs every 15 minutes from 5.50am to 10.50pm and takes around 30 minutes to Austerlitz.

Alternatively, the **Orlybus** (to place Denfert-Rochereau) leaves from Orly Sud gate F or Orly Ouest arrivals gate D. It runs around every 10 minutes from 6am to 11.30pm. The more expensive **Orlyval** automatic train is a shuttle to Antony (the nearest RER to Orly). It runs every 5–8 minutes, Mon–Sat 6.30am–9.15pm, Sun 7am–10.55pm, and takes 30 minutes.

Air France buses (to Invalides and Gare Montparnasse) leave from Orly Sud gate J, or Orly Ouest arrivals gate E. They run every 20 minutes from 6am to 11pm and take 30 minutes. Tickets are available from the Air France terminus. See also www.airfrance.fr.

By taxi, the journey from Orly to the city centre takes 20–40 mins, depending on the traffic.

Below: flying was more fun, and glamorous, in the past.

Transport within Paris

BUS (AUTOBUS)

Bus transport around Paris is efficient, though not always fast. Stops are marked by green and blue signs or shelters, with the bus numbers clearly posted, and you'll find bus timetables displayed under bus shelters. You can obtain a general bus route plan from metro station ticket offices.

Most buses run 7am–8.30pm, some until 12.30am. Service is reduced on Sundays and public holidays. A special bus for night owls, the **Noctambus**, runs along 10 main routes serving the capital, from 1.30am–5.30am every hour, with Châtelet as the hub.

Bus journeys take one ticket. You can buy a ticket as you board, but it's cheaper to buy a book of tickets *(carnet)* from any metro station or tobacconist. Bus and metro tickets are interchangeable. Punch your ticket in the validating machine when you get on. You can also buy special one-, three- or five-day tourist passes or the weekly ticket and *Carte Orange (see below)*. Show these special tickets to the driver as you get on, rather than putting them in the punching machine. The fine for being caught without a ticket is €120.

MÉTRO

The **Paris Métropolitain** ('*Métro*' for short) is one of

Above: the slick and efficient modern line 14 of the Paris metro.

the fastest, most efficient underground railway systems in the world. It's also one of the least expensive. You get 10 journeys for the price of seven by investing in a *carnet* (book) of tickets, also valid for the bus network and for the RER, provided that you stay within Paris and don't go to outer suburbs.

Express lines (**RER**, *Réseau Express Régional*) get you into the centre of Paris from the distant suburbs in about 15 minutes, with a few stops in between.

A special ticket called **Paris Visite**, valid for one, three or five days, allows unlimited travel on the bus or metro, and reductions to various entrance fees to various attractions. A day ticket, **Forfait 1 Jour Mobilis**, is valid for the metro, RER, buses, suburban trains and some airport buses.

For longer stays, the best buy is a **Carte Orange** (orange card), valid for unlimited rides inside Paris on the metro and bus, either weekly *(hebdomadaire)* Mon–Sun, or monthly *(mensuel)* from the

first of the month. Ask for a *pochette* (wallet) to go with it and have a passport photo ready.

Metro stations have big, easy-to-read maps. Services start at 5.30am and finish around 1am (last trains leave end stations at 12.30am). The **RATP** (metro organisation) has an information office at 54 quai de la Rapée, 12th. You can call them 24 hours a day on tel: 08 92 68 41 14 or visit www.ratp.fr.

TRAIN

The **SNCF** (French Railways Authority) runs fast, comfortable trains on an efficient network. The high-speed service (**TGV** – *train à grande vitesse*) operating on selected routes is excellent, but more expensive than the average train. Seat reservation is obligatory on TGVs. See www.sncf.com or www.voyages-sncf.com.

The main stations in Paris are: **Gare du Nord** (Eurostar to London, and for Belgium and the Netherlands); **Gare de l'Est** (eastern France and Germany); **Gare St-Lazare** (Normandy); **Gare d'Austerlitz**

> Validate your train ticket before boarding by inserting it in one of the orange machines (called a *machine à composter* or *composteur*) on the way to the platform. If your ticket is not clipped and dated, the inspector is entitled to fine you on the train.

Above: cycling around the quiet and pretty Ile St-Louis is very pleasant.

Driving

Driving in Paris requires confidence and concentration. If you do intend to drive, here are a few guidelines.

Seat belts are obligatory in both the front and back of the car, and the speed limit in town is 50kph. Do not drive in bus lanes at any time, and give priority to vehicles approaching from the right. This applies to some roundabouts, where cars on the roundabout stop for those coming on to it. Helmets are compulsory for motorbike riders and passengers.

Parking

Street parking is very difficult to find; spaces are usually metered Mon–Sat 9am–7pm (paid for with a *Paris Carte*, currently €10 or €30 and purchased from a local *tabac*). The maximum stay is two hours; most car parks are underground (see www.parkingsdeparis.fr). Illegally parked cars may be towed away. Do not leave any possessions on show, as theft from cars is unfortunately fairly common.

Petrol (Gas)

This can be hard to find in the city centre, so if your tank is almost empty head for a *porte* (exit) on the Périphérique (the multi-lane ring road), where there are stations open 24 hours a day.

(southwestern France and Spain); **Gare Montparnasse** (TGV to western and southwestern France); and **Gare de Lyon** (Provence, Switzerland and Italy). The TGV station at Charles-de-Gaulle Airport serves Disneyland.

TAXI

Taxis are generally reasonably priced, though there are extra charges for putting luggage in the boot (trunk) and for pick-up at a station or airport. Taxi drivers can refuse to carry more than three passengers. The fourth, if admitted, pays a supplement.

You'll find taxis cruising around or at stands all over the city. You can recognise an unoccupied cab by an illuminated sign on its roof. Fares differ according to the zones covered or the time of the day (you'll be charged more between 7pm and 7am and on Sunday).

An average fare between Roissy-Charles-de-Gaulle Airport and central Paris might be €140 by day, €150 at night. If you have any problems with a driver, you

can register a complaint with the **Service des Taxis**, 36 rue des Morillons, 12th; tel: 01 53 71 53 71.

The following taxi companies take phone bookings 24 hours a day:
Alpha: 01 45 85 85 85
Artaxi: 08 91 70 25 50
G7: 01 47 39 47 39
Taxis Bleus: 08 25 16 10 10

CAR RENTAL (LOCATION DE VOITURES)

To hire a car you will need to show your driving licence (held for at least a year) and passport. You will also need a major credit card, or a large deposit. The minimum age for renting cars is 23, or 21 if you are paying by credit card. Third-party insurance is compulsory, and full cover is recommended.

The international car-hire firms operating in Paris include:
Avis, tel: 08 20 05 05 05; www.avis.fr
Europcar/National/InterRent, tel: 08 25 35 83 58; www.europcar.fr
Hertz, tel: 01 39 38 38 38; www.hertz.fr

Bicycle Rental *(Location de bicyclettes)*
You can rent bikes by the day or week from the following two companies: Paris-Vélo, 2 rue du Fer à Moulin, 5th; tel: 01 43 37 59 22; www.paris-velo-rent-a-bike.fr; Paris à Vélo C'est Sympa, 37 boulevard Bourdon; tel: 01 48 87 60 01; www.parisvelosympa.com.

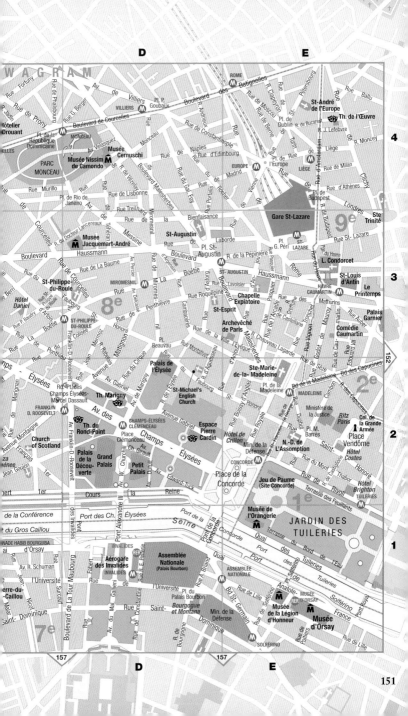

CIMETIÈRE DE MONTMARTRE

MONTMARTRE

LA FOURCHE

Moulin de la Galette

Moulin du Radet

Espace Montmartre S.Dali

Musée de Montmartre

PARC DE LA TURLURE

18e

CHÂTEAU ROUGE

St-Pierre Pl. du Tertre

Basilique du Sacré-Cœur

Funiculaire

Halle St-Pierre

ABBESSES

Moulin Rouge

St-Jean Montmartre

ANVERS Rochechouart

BARBÈS ROCHECHOUART

PIGALLE

Boulevard

Rue du Delta

St-André de l'Europe

Musée de la Vie Romantique

8e

Th. de l'Œuvre

Pl. Pigalle

Hôtel Amour

Dt. Evang. Christuskirche

Th. de Paris

Casino de Paris

Musée Gustave-Moreau

St-GEORGES

St-Constantin/ Ste-Hélène

9e

Gare St-Lazare

Ste-Trinité

TRINITÉ

N.-D. de Lorette

POISSON

ST-LAZARE

L. Condorcet

N.-D. DE LORETTE

Châteaudun

CADET

St-Louis d'Antin

LE PELETIER

Folies Bergère

Le Printemps

Galeries Lafayette

CHAUSSÉE D'ANTIN

HAVRE CAUMARTIN

AUBER

Palais Garnier

Haussmann

Hôtel Chopin

Grévin

Comédie Caumartin

Musée du Parfum

OPÉRA

Pl. de l'Opéra

RICHELIEU DROUOT

Bd Montmartre   Bd Poissonnière

GRANDS BOULEVARDS

BONNE NOUVELLE

Bd de la Madeleine

4 SEPTEMBRE

Quatre   Septembre

BOURSE

Palais Brongniart

2e

SENTIER

Ritz Paris

Place Vendôme

N.-D. de L'Assomption

Cour des Comptes

1e

BIBLIOTHÈQUE

Bibliothèque Nationale-Richelieu

Basilique N.-D. des Victoires

Hôtel Edouard VII

PYRAMIDES

JARDIN DU PALAIS ROYAL

Banque de France

Hôtel des Postes

St-Roch

TUILERIES

Terrasse des Feuillants

RIQUET

0 100 200 300 400 500 m

0 100 200 300 400 500 yds

Cube
Rooms

St-Bernard
la Chapelle
Polo...eau

Goutte d'Or

de la Charbonnière

LA CHAPELLE

STALINGRAD

Pl. de
Stalingrad

Boulevard de la Chapelle

Boulevard

Rotonde de
la Villette

4

Ambroise Paré

Hôpital
Fernand-
Widal

LOUIS
BLANC

St-Joseph
Artisan

Pl. de
Roubaix

Gare du Nord

GARE DU
NORD

Hôtel Apôllo

JAURÈS

19e

BOLIVAR

Vincent
Paul

des Petits Hôtels

CHÂTEAU
LANDON

Gare de l'Est

Pl. du
11 Nov. 1918.

10e

Pl. du
Colonel
Fabien

COLONEL
FABIEN

3

Chabrol

Hôpital
St-Lazare

GARE DE L'EST

Musée des
Cristalleries de
Baccarat

St-Laurent

JARDIN
VILLEMIN

B E L L E V I L L E

CHÂTEAU
D'EAU

Écuries

Hôpital
St-Louis

BELLEVILLE

2

JACQUES
BONSERGENT

STRASBOURG
ST-DENIS

Bd St-Denis

Boulevard St-Martin

RÉPUBLIQUE

Palais des
Glaces

St-Joseph

GONCOURT

1

3e

Pl. de la
République

Conservatoire
des Arts et
Métiers

Musée des
Arts et Métiers

Ste-Élisabeth

TEMPLE

Hôtel
General

11e

MUR
STOPOL

ARTS ET
MÉTIERS

St-Nicolas
des-Champs

OBERKAMPF

p150	p151
p156	p157

p152	p153
p154	p155

155

155

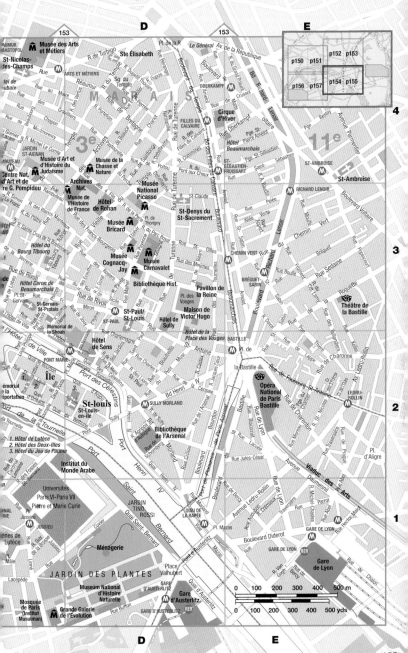

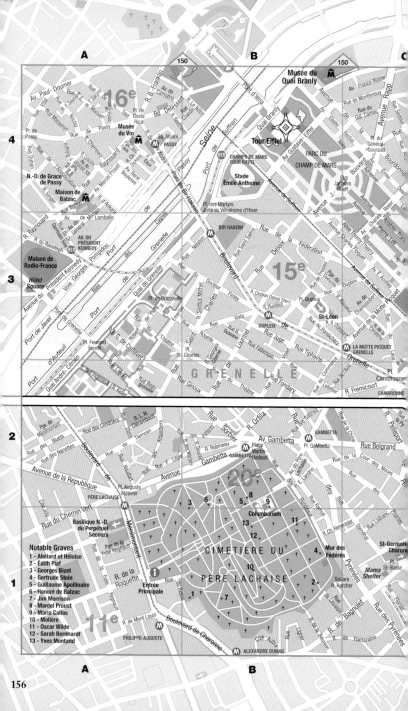

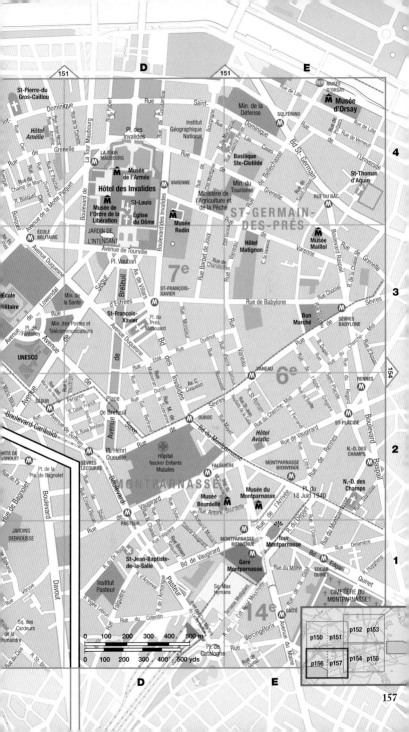

Atlas Index

Index

Insight Smart Guide: Paris
Cartography: James Macdonald
Compiled by: Michael Macaroon
Photography by: Apa: Kevin Cummins, Pete Bennett, Jerry Dennis, Annabel Elston, Britta Jaschinski, Maria Lord, Ilpo Musto; 4Corners 76; Akg-images London 83b; Alamy 73br, 74, 75tr&cr, 113br; Art Archive 5cl, 30c; Bridgeman Art Library 68br; Le Bus Palladium 112; Concore Hotels 70–71, 70b; Corbis 17t, 69b, 110bl; Getty Images 56/57t, 69; Hotel Plaza Athenee 73, 74T; Image-Works/TopFoto 20t; Istock 17; Jay Tong 129; Mary Evans, 81; Musée Association les Amis d'Edith Piaf 97tr; Courtesy Paris Tourism 43t, 60c, 60/61t, 77,

119b; Clare Peel 114/115t; TopFoto 52/53t

Picture Manager: Steven Lawrence
Series Editor: Jason Mitchell
Proofread by: Penny Phenix
First Edition 2008, revised 2010.
© 2010 Apa Publications GmbH & Co. Verlag KG Singapore Branch, Singapore.
Worldwide distribution enquiries:
Apa Publications GmbH & Co. Verlag KG (Singapore Branch); tel: (65) 6865 1600
Distributed in the UK and Ireland by:
GeoCenter International Ltd; tel: (44 1256) 817 987
Distributed in the United States by:
Langenscheidt Publishers, Inc.; tel: (1 718) 784 0055

Contacting the Editors
We would appreciate it if readers would alert us to errors information by writing to:
Apa Publications, PO Box 7910, London SE1 1WE, UK; insight@apaguide.co.uk
No part of this book may be reproduced, stored in a retrieval system or transmitted in any form or by any means (electronic, mechanical, photocopying, recording or otherwise), without prior written permission of Apa Publications. Brief text quotations with use of photographs are exempted for book review purposes only. Information has been obtained from sources believed to be reliable, but its accuracy and completeness, and the opinions based thereon, are not guaranteed.

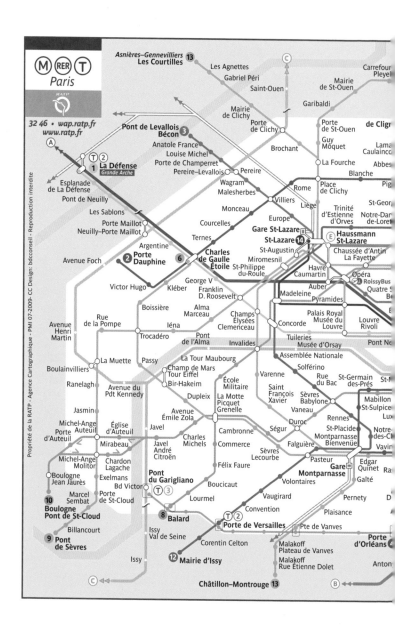